OWNING THE SUN

OWNING THE SUN

A PEOPLE'S HISTORY OF MONOPOLY MEDICINE
FROM ASPIRIN TO COVID-19 VACCINES

ALEXANDER ZAITCHIK

Counterpoint
Berkeley, California

ISBN: 978-1-64009-506-9

The Library of Congress Cataloging-in-Publication Data is available.

Jacket design by Brian Lemus
Book design by Wah-Ming Chang

COUNTERPOINT
2560 Ninth Street, Suite 318
Berkeley, CA 94710
www.counterpointpress.com

Printed in the United States of America

1 3 5 7 9 10 8 6 4 2

For Alba and Izzie

Inventions financed with public funds should inure to the benefit of the public, and should not become a purely private monopoly under which public-financed technology may be suppressed, used restrictively, or made the basis of an exaction from the public to serve private interests . . . Public control will assure free and equal availability of the inventions . . . [and] will avoid undue concentration of economic power in the hands of a few large corporations . . . Scientific and technological research conducted or financed by the United States represents a vast national resource, rivalling in actual and potential value the public domain opened to settlement in the last century . . . The soundest disposition of Government-financed technology is as a general rule to open it freely to the public . . . and spread the benefits of the scientific advances as widely as possible.

—Final Report of the Attorney General to the President on Government Patent Practices and Policies, 1947

CONTENTS

INTRODUCTION

I N THE BEGINNING, THERE WAS ALCHEMY, A FUSION OF METAL-lurgy and magic. The alchemist probed nature in pursuit of the unnatural, of eternal life and the power to make silver from lead and turn copper into gold. The alchemic grail known as the philosopher's stone was never found. But the foundations of modern chemistry and pharmacy were laid in those discoveries made in failure, and upon them grew an industry that over the last century finally achieved the elusive sorcery of turning base elements into precious gold.

Consider this. Between 2000 and 2018, the thirty-five largest drug companies reported cumulative gross profits of almost $9 trillion. During that same period, the value of the world's total gold reserves crested at just over $7 trillion. The magic behind this feat has nothing to do with synthesizing common molecules into more valuable ones. The industry's Merlins aren't its scientists and technicians but its patent lawyers and lobbyists. The products these companies sell have value, but not so much as to surpass all the gold that's ever been mined. The science, once released, can be copied, in most cases very easily. The kind of wealth amassed by the pharmaceutical industry can be created only by the political magic of monopoly. If the state ceases to grant, enforce, and extend exclusive rights to the production and sale of drugs and medicines, the power to spin private gold from public investment and human illness combusts and disappears, like the purified bone dust phosphorus of alchemy legend.

This is not a book about how to hasten the combustion of monopoly medicine, or about the many fine alternatives that could take its place to humanity's benefit. It is the story of how monopoly medicine came to be, from the earliest debates over the morality and practical value of granting monopolies on life-saving inventions, to the globalization of this right by Washington on a basis of forced consent. It is the long prequel to our current age of crowdsourced online medical fundraisers; of hedge funds and Martin Shkreli getting a say in who lives and for how long; of the minting of biotech billionaires during a pandemic while vaccine factories sit idle; and of the lobbying, propaganda, and marketing machines that protect the system from the steaming volcano of a public that understands it to be fundamentally corrupt and unjust.

The drug companies spend heavily on telling and retelling their version of this story. That's actually their in-house trade name for it—"the drug story." According to the industry narrative, monopolies and the outsized profits they generate can alone incentivize and deliver innovation. The system is working just fine; any interference will cost humanity dearly. The following account is told from the perspective of the dissenters, critics, and antagonists who see this as a dishonest and dangerous fiction. These figures have shadowed and challenged the development of medical monopoly at every step, issuing democratic echoes of the English king Henry IV, who in 1404 decreed it a felony to "multiply gold or silver, or use the craft of multiplication" by alchemic means. The Act Against Multipliers wasn't about shutting down pagan rituals or taking a stand against supernatural criminality—it was a preemptive strike against private wealth becoming private power strong enough to challenge the authority of the Crown. Centuries later, the same fear inspired spirited republican opposition to monopoly in the North American colonies. This hostility survived the founding and continues to make cyclical appearances of varying intensity. Since World War II, the pharmaceutical industry has provided a sitting target for the country's deep if suppressed democratic instinct to favor broad public interests over narrow private ones.

Over the last seven decades, the industry has become a target so fat and unmissable that taking a swing at it unblindfolded almost feels unfair. But its grotesque girth is the very thing that has allowed it to become so devilishly elusive. As Henry IV, Thomas Jefferson, and Louis Brandeis understood, if you allow the unnatural multiplication of private wealth, eventually its power will slip all social constraints. You will wake up one day to find Merlin wearing the crown.

Franklin Delano Roosevelt's famous speech to the 1936 Democratic convention was a warning against this scenario coming to pass. Though Roosevelt declared war against unnamed "economic royalists," the New Dealers understood the real targets to be the invisible sources of their awesome power—the weak regulations, bad laws, and corrupted statutes that enabled monopolies to dominate the economy and threaten the country's experiment in self-government. Patents were a major concern of the late New Deal, but not drug patents specifically, not quite yet. In the 1930s, the pharmaceutical industry was in the final throes of a painful molting process. It was shedding the last vestiges of its own anti-monopoly tradition and assuming the mindset and characteristics of those "new economic dynasties, thirsting for power" fingered in Roosevelt's speech. Anyone listening to that speech from the worlds of academic research, drug manufacture, corner druggery, or organized medicine must have heard echoes of the sulfurous anti-monopoly sermons that had filled the broad canopy of American medicine for as long as anybody could remember.

The drug industry had mostly severed its connection to this tradition by the end of World War II, when the U.S. government began to nest the biggest bounty of scientific research the world had ever seen. The contest between public and private interests vying for guardianship of this science runs throughout the following pages. That storyline is charged by the inherent tension created by granting medical knowledge, or any knowledge, the same property status as a clarinet or a tractor. We've become dulled to the strangeness of it, but the concept of "intellectual property" remains profoundly counterintuitive, if not paradoxical. If you possess a milking cow, and your neighbor steals that cow, you have lost your cow. Consult any culture—East or West, ancient or modern—and some form of revenge or legal remedy would be prescribed. If, however, you discovered a process for making cow's milk healthier or safer to drink, and your neighbor imitated the method to make his cow's milk healthier or safer, the balance of opinion would swing against the judgment that a "theft," or any other punishable crime, had occurred. This is because your neighbor's possession of your idea does not reduce your store of it. In fact, the opposite is true: scientific knowledge, especially related to food and medicine, is a public good whose benefits— say, maximizing vaccine production at the lowest cost during a pandemic— increase the more broadly the knowledge is diffused. Economists call such goods "non-rivalrous." In Thomas Jefferson's formulation, "He who receives an idea from me, receives instruction himself without lessening mine; as he who lights his taper at mine, receives light without darkening me."

It is often observed that our current social and economic system imbues oppressive feelings of inevitability and permanence. A shrinking historical horizon doesn't help. If you believe something has always been some way, it is difficult to imagine changing it. This is apparent in the current debate over the waiving of intellectual property rules enforced by the World Trade Organization. Speak to someone born in 1980 and there is a good chance they think the WTO has always been there, a Taj Mahal of global trade. But they and everyone else born in 1980 were alive at a time when U.S. drug monopolies were not only widely condemned but also ignored, and the intellectual property regime imposed through the WTO was considered the twisted fantasy of a few Pfizer executives. If you were born in 1975, you inhabited a world where Switzerland, a pharmaceutical powerhouse, still did not issue drug patents. That changed in 1977. In Italy and Sweden, in 1978. In Spain, not until 1992.

Long before medicines entered the monopoly debate, many countries were hesitant to accept the general Anglo-American concept of "owning ideas." A debate over the legitimacy and value of monopolies as awards for invention was a tempest across Europe throughout the nineteenth century and into the twentieth. The Netherlands proudly maintained what it called a "free trade in inventions" until 1912. During this long argument, the fiercest denunciations of intellectual property were found not in left-wing journals but in the pages of *The Economist*, whose editors advocated for the abolishment of the English patent system. The magazine asserted in 1850 that for inventors to "establish a right of property in their inventions," they first would have "to give up all the knowledge and assistance they have derived from the knowledge and inventions of others ... That is impossible, and the impossibility shows that their minds and their inventions are, in fact, parts of the great mental whole of society, and that they have no right of property in their inventions."

The free traders and liberals lost the argument, and in the early twentieth century, patent monopolies were normalized across the industrialized world as a reward for every kind of invention and discovery. With one major exception.

✦

If people know one thing about the history of medical patents, it's that Jonas Salk's polio vaccine was nobody's monopoly. They know this because of a line Salk delivered on live network television on the day his vaccine was announced a success, one of the biggest news days of the 1950s. In five words, Salk took a nascent postwar debate over drug patents and stripped it down to its naked core with a rhetorical question for all time—"Could you patent the sun?"

The details surrounding this famous quip are worth recalling. After the placement of all the scientific and technical knowledge associated with the vaccine into the public domain, the U.S. government signed manufacturing deals with several drug companies and put a hard cap on the price per dose at three times the cost of production. When the companies requested reimbursement for building out production infrastructure, the government said no. They were being paid to do a job, were turning a profit, and that was enough. When the nationwide vaccine field trial was declared a success, Dwight Eisenhower delivered a speech announcing that "full details of its manufacture, and the technique of injecting it, would be given to every country that welcomed the knowledge, including the Soviet Union."

Compare this to the Strangelovean comedy of corporate vaccine nationalism. Operation Warp Speed, the federal program announced in May 2020 to accelerate pandemic-related research, extended the $42 billion annual subsidy currently enjoyed by the industry, let the companies maintain controlling patent rights without any corresponding obligation on pricing or technology transfer to the rest of the world, and treated the resulting vaccine monopolies as national security secrets in a medical-themed *Spy vs. Spy* cartoon. The first and most effective COVID-19 vaccines are based on mRNA technology developed largely by the National Institutes of Health (NIH). Though the government owns and has stakes in many of the patents, it has assumed the now-familiar role of obsequious junior partner to its commercial contractor, Moderna. When a group of House Democrats attempted in early March 2020 to legislate a few modest conditions on the first $8 billion tranche of coronavirus research subsidies, they were flung aside like so many Lilliputians by the pharmaceutical and biotech lobby machines. Pharma's man in Washington, Stephen Ubl, warned legislators that the industry would take its ball and go home "if collaboration with the government even in a limited way results in a loss of intellectual property or the government setting the price."

The pharmaceutical industry makes ultimatums like this all the time—indeed, it is an industry built on threats—but in the context of the pandemic, it is easier to see the backwardness of the industry threatening the government that funds its work and protects its business model. In the private sector, it is standard policy for titles on inventions to revert to the company paying the bills. That the U.S. government does not enforce a similar arrangement on NIH-funded research is a hydra-headed betrayal explored in the following pages.

The industry's defense, now decades worn, is that monopoly riches are the only possible incentive for scientific progress and medical innovation. That this is simply false is easily demonstrated with a cursory review of history and the breakthroughs routinely made by the world's public research sectors, including our own. Humanity was developing medicines long before the first company ran up the price of a drug because it could. Ever since cowpox put the *vacca* in the word *vaccine*, governments have demonstrated the possibility of contracting with the private sector from a position of self-respect and authority. Equally wrong is the industry's claim that curtailing its monopoly grip on public science would constitute an attack on free market principles. There is no free market in pharmaceuticals. The industry is based on a double protection racket of artificial monopolies granted and enforced by the state. This arrangement is frosted with a continuous public research subsidy that underwrites nearly all of the industry's products. When Donald Trump submitted a budget proposing cuts to this subsidy in 2018, the free-marketeer drug companies howled in pained protest. The cuts were reversed.

The industry's last refuge is a dark warning intended to frighten: get anywhere near our monopolies, they say, and there will be nothing holding humanity back from a long sliding return to the days of the four humors, of leeching and cutting, of death by childbirth and common infection. Without the dangling enticements of monopoly to lure science forward, life will again become brutish and short, passed in pain while subsisting on diets of pounded roots and herbs. This is rich coming from the same companies that built money printers in the 1950s from a long run of patented antibiotics that they systematically mis- and over-prescribed, hastening the current crisis of antibiotic resistance. When regulators curtailed the practice in the U.S. market, the companies moved the game to the developing world, where they pushed branded antibiotics with bogus indications, but showed little interest in researching so-called diseases of the poor—tuberculosis, Chagas, dengue, dozens of others—that affect a billion people in the global south.

Twenty years ago, the legitimacy of this system was challenged and shaken for its miserable response to the African AIDS crisis. It now faces another test over the right to make vaccines and medicines during the first pandemic of the twenty-first century. As I write this in the summer of 2021, the G7 countries are on track to be fully vaccinated by the end of the year. Low-income countries are on pace to be fully vaccinated in 2078. And yet, to hear the drug and biotech trade associations and their political allies tell it, it's meddling with the intellectual property regime known as Trade-Related Aspects of Intellectual Property Rights (TRIPS) that constitutes, in the words of U.S. trade representative Katherine Tai, an "extraordinary measure." In truth, there is nothing extraordinary about disregarding TRIPS, because there is nothing extraordinary about TRIPS. Its backstory is almost impossibly shallow and grubby; its founding documents are younger than Justin Bieber. TRIPS is not the expression of a universal post–Cold War consensus, in the way the UN Universal Declaration of Human Rights gave voice to human aspirations after World War II. It was born as a brute and profoundly undemocratic expression of concentrated corporate power—the work of "less than fifty individuals," according to a U.S. official present at the creation. One of that official's reluctant Indian counterparts, Prabhat Patnaik, has described the road to TRIPS as "a parody of the wildest conspiracy theory."

The negotiations that resulted in the globalization of U.S.-style medical monopoly were not so much held over a table as conducted on a rack. It was the only way to enforce a concept as peculiar and universally rejected as rent-seeking from medicines. This is the story of how one of history's worst ideas took root against centuries of tradition and came to dominate the world.

OWNING THE SUN

One

ORIGINS

Rise of the Great American Patent

MANKIND'S FIRST ATTEMPTS AT A RUDIMENTARY SCIENTIFIC process date to the Late Stone Age. Roughly ten thousand years ago, villages along the Fertile Crescent began using observation, trial, and error to cultivate flax, wheat, and barley. Their Asian counterparts were doing the same and innovating new labor-saving uses for yak and oxen. From there, technology, science, and art developed at a rapid clip, often exponentially, from the Mesopotamian delta to the inland empires of Mesoamerica. The production, diffusion, and application of knowledge—what we today call progress—took place on every front. Timekeeping, metallurgy, astronomy. The Maya discovered the mathematical concept of zero. Egyptians began to measure fractions. Indians produced the first scales. A Cretan king thought to make condoms from a goat's bladder. Progress.

The first medicines appear early in the timeline of invention. Around 4000 B.C., ancient Sumer is thought to have pioneered the concept of the hypothesis. It was soon applied to the development of medical and surgical products and techniques. Sumerian religion associated these with the god Ninazu, whose symbol was a serpent-entwined rod, representing health and sickness, life and death. This symbol passed through ancient Greece and Rome into our own time, where it adorns the trademarked logos of U.S. hospital chains and insurance companies.

Sumer was not alone in making new therapeutic concoctions. The global trade roads of antiquity that we remember for caravans carrying silks and spices also hosted a heavy traffic in herbal medicines. Around one hundred of these remain in use today: balm of Gilead, cannabis, opium, oleander.

Let us imagine that one of those ancient traders fell from his pack animal, bonked his head, and, like the hero of a nineteenth-century literary timeslip, awoke in the present century. What would he find most mystifying? Certainly not the use of powders, plants, and serums to reduce pain, clear rashes, and treat illness. He might also recognize inequality in access to medical treatment, as medicine in many ancient societies was reserved for the elite, with most people dependent on religious rites, superstition, and nights slept in the temples of healing gods.

What would baffle our ancient trader, and which baffles most of humanity still, is our belief in an invisible power that surrounds our modern tinctures, powders, and serums, a force that restricts their manufacture and trade, even though their ingredients are cheap and plentiful, and the knowledge to make them widespread. Given the entwinement of religion and medicine in the ancient world, the trader would no doubt assume this force represented the wishes of some malevolent god, or was perhaps a god unto itself, one demanding routine human sacrifice in the form of the untreated ill.

This wouldn't be wrong.

The invisible force limiting the application of knowledge was a child of mercantile Europe. In late Renaissance Italy, princes began to ritualize the announcement of royal grants of privilege conferring the right to control the production and trade of certain goods and even entire classes of goods. With pomp and ceremony, the terms of the privilege were announced by the reading of an open public letter—a *litterae patentes*—bearing the sovereign's seal. From the very beginning of the practice, these letters were designed around a florid acknowledgment of the frictional contradiction at their center: the granting of a private, exclusive claim on knowledge that would otherwise be practicable by all. The princes who first formalized limited monopolies anticipated the resentment and dissent they would cause and thus presented them not as a property claim of the sort that might cover a house or a fleet of ships, but as a temporary and beneficial three-way social arrangement uniting the interests of the sovereign, the patentee, and the realm at large. Patent privileges would benefit the recipient of the privilege in the short term, but were presented as a cause for celebration by all—a spur for spreading new knowledge that in the long term would benefit prince and pauper alike.

This triangular social contract was further developed in England during the sixteenth and early seventeenth centuries. It was there that the modern patent took form in the crucible of a struggle over the limits of royal prerogative to decide the shape and duration of ownership over knowledge, practices, and markets. The questions that framed this struggle remain unresolved five centuries later: *Do intellectual property claims really spur the diffusion of knowledge and its benefits for broad public gain? Or are they fig leaves for immoral enclosures of the commons, sources of private gain that slow the spread of the very progress they promise to advance?*

The first political skirmish over this question was waged during the reign of Queen Elizabeth I. The political context was the set of economic pressures created by the fifteenth-century enclosure of the English countryside. Previous to the long process of enclosure, peasants had access to the land and the resources of the forest, which they managed collectively. Denial of that access effectively removed the physical basis of subsistence for agrarian communities across England. An army of dispossessed farmers were forced into neo-feudal tenant arrangements and the emergent system of wage labor. This in turn put pressure on the Crown to expand new industries as a social safety valve. Many of the earliest English patents were used to lure foreigners in possession of specialized knowledge to help develop the economy. The foreigners' knowledge, it was reasoned, would allow new industries to flourish—first on a temporary monopoly basis, and then, after the patent term, by a general diffusion that would bring down prices and increase domestic supply of the product or trade in question.

However, the Queen's patent policy was erratic. As often as Elizabeth recruited inventors, she rewarded favored courtiers with privileges that brought no apparent benefit to anyone but themselves and the House of Tudor. Parliamentary critics alleged that the social contract fanfare written into royal grants of privilege served as a cloak for a crude and arbitrary patronage system that kept prices artificially high, blocked and slowed the adoption of new technologies and trades, and, when applied to the new industry of printing, served as an effective tool for royal censorship. Infringers on these royal monopolies had little recourse and became targets for private patent police who were hated and feared in equal measure.

The depth of public resentment engendered by early English patents was proportional to their breadth. Some patents were time-limited and covered specific inventions or novel manufacturing processes; others bequeathed what amounted to permanent control over entire industries and trades. A third category of patent granted rights to profit from the enforcement of the first two categories by levying fines and other penalties on infringers. Patent police performed many of the functions now associated with the regulatory state. While making rounds to monitor manufacturing standards, they served as instruments of social control. This was especially true of the loathed "book police" established by the Stationers' Company publishing monopoly. Its agents used the power of search and seizure to torture and imprison unauthorized publishers, including those making underground Bibles. Similar grants of power fired anti-royal sentiment on the other side of the English Channel. In France, the book police supplied the Bastille with close to half of its prisoners in the years leading up to the Revolution.

Even if the reality said otherwise, the language of Elizabethan patents always bowed to the conceit of public benefit. In their letter, royal grants of monopoly remained conditional on serving early modern notions of the public good. By touting stipulations regarding price controls and access, they anticipated the "reasonable terms" clauses found in modern laws governing the dispensation of patent rights resulting from state-funded research. These public-interest provisions were integral to the bugle-and-scroll court readings that announced new patent grants. The historian Oren Bracha notes that Elizabethan patent ceremonies began with detailed recitals of their various benefits to the commonweal. Many of these will sound familiar today, such as promises that the limited monopoly will create jobs and relieve "decayed towns."

If a grantee abused their coveted monopoly privilege, or failed to realize their royally underwritten promise, the sovereign could, in theory, revoke the patent and call the holder to account. In practice, this was rare. Well-connected court patrons routinely abused patent privileges to entrench their power and wealth while forgetting about the other side of the bargain. As the abuses grew more flagrant—with price-gouging monopolies dominating common products like vinegar and raisins—simmering discontent had turned to boil by the latter years of Elizabeth's reign. A leading parliamentarian, Sir John Culpeper, described the growing population of royal patent holders as "a Nest of Wasps or swarm of Vermin which have over-crept the Land . . . These are the Leaches that have sucked the Common-Wealth so hard, that it is almost become hectical."

Rising Puritan opposition to her patent power spooked the aging Queen. In 1597, she sought to mollify her critics by thanking them for bringing the subject to her attention and asking for their patience and trust. She promised to model her future patent decisions on the stricter letter of English common law. In a message delivered to Parliament through the Lord Keeper of the Privy Seal, the Queen described her patent prerogative as "the chiefest flower of her garden and the principal and head pearl of her crown and diadem."

In 1603, James I inherited the problem upon the passing of the heirless Elizabeth. Future generations would remember James for the eponymous Bible translation he commissioned, but contemporaries were focused on the patent dispute—"the ongoing 'grievance' that gave structure to the developing relationship between the Commons and the Crown," in the words of historian Chris Dent.

The breaking point came in 1624, shortly before James's death, when the king conceded an Act of Parliament known as the Statute of Monopolies. The law effectively banned monopolies as "contrary to the lawes of the Realme," but followed an older Venetian law in allowing one significant carve-out. "The true and first Inventor" of new modes of manufacture were eligible to receive a limited and exclusive grant to use and profit from their invention. The privilege expired after fourteen years, estimated to be the time required to train two sets of apprentices in a new art or trade. This was the knowledge's incubation period. At the fifteenth year, it would be diffused, the invention made available to all.

As before the statute, patents on compounds or discoveries with alleged healing properties could be granted if deemed "novel compositions of matter." But such patents were rarely issued. One of the first exceptions to prove the rule was a patent granted in 1693 to the English plant anatomist Nehemiah Grew, a prize for the formula he called "The Salt of the Purging Water," better known as Epsom salts.

Six decades before the Bill of Rights 1688 enshrined "English rights and liberties," the Statute of Monopolies ended a powerful system of royal patronage by hacking down the legal scope of patent monopolies. Nearly five centuries later, patent law retains the basic shape of the 1624 statute that sanctioned monopolies in the form of inventor's rights. The socially minded common-law stipulations attached to these rights were also codified. Temporary exclusive rights were denied (and if granted in error, voidable) in the case of monopolies judged to be "mischeavious to the State, by raising Prices of Commodities at home, or Hurt of Trade, or generally inconvenient." For the first time, the public could contest such "inconvenient" patents and claim injury in a civil forum; the patent holder, meanwhile, was stripped of immunity. Here we have the enshrinement of the modern limited-term patent on inventions and its public-interest justification and requirements. Both endure.

This reflected the rising power of Parliament and a new mercantilist class that saw royal control of the economy as a threat not only to its interests, but to social stability. The years preceding the statute were marked by growing unemployment and widespread poverty, with repeated bad harvests compounding the social and economic dislocations caused by enclosure. The reformers in the House of Commons weren't just anti-royal Puritans, but included investors in new trading companies and joint-stock ventures, backed by financiers and increasingly powerful creditors in the City of London. They saw monopolies as stifling the growth of new industries, employment, and investment opportunities. Rather than diffusing new technologies and trades, monopolies were seen as defensive walls around vested interests that benefited from restrictions on trade—they were "the bottlenecks of business," as an influential American critic of patent monopolies would put it three hundred years later. Because of the Crown's deepening credit entanglements with the City of London, it was not in the strongest position to argue these points. Here, too, 1624 set the tone for the next five centuries: not for the last time, a major paradigm shift in intellectual property was driven by powerful private and internationally minded actors focused on investment opportunities and balance of trade.

While politically less explosive, the post-1624 patent remained a paradox. A valuable privilege that could bring enormous private gain, it was justified as a trade-off promising social benefits that could be enjoyed by all. It allowed a private stake in the commons on the promise that the social debt would be repaid, in multiples, at some point in the near future. Then as now, this trade-off was contested and debated.

The patent system codified by the Statute of Monopolies served as a model for the American colonies. The first colonial patent system, enacted in Massachusetts in 1641, adopted the English statute ban on all monopolies "but of such new inventions that are profitable to the Country, and that for a short time." As in the English example, the government in Boston retained the right to cancel a patent if the holder charged an "unreasonable" price, and reserved the right to set that price at the time of the patent's issue.

The general patent skepticism of the Enlightenment also took root in the colonies. When the time came to establish the embryonic nation's law, tepid enthusiasm for a patent system based on the English model had to contend with profound doubts about the legitimacy and benefits of knowledge monopolies, no matter how temporary or severed from Crown power they may be.

Patents appeared at the constitutional debate in Philadelphia near the close of business. It was toward the end of the convention's third and final month, the famously sweltering August 1787, when the subject was introduced by two southerners, James Madison of Virginia and Charles Pinckney of South Carolina. The general reception was understandably cool. The delegates had recently fought a war of independence against a monarch who wielded control of the colonies through strategic monopolies. Their views were informed by this experience as well as the views of influential patent skeptics like John Locke, Adam Smith, and the convention's own Benjamin Franklin. Pinckney and Madison were the loud exceptions, taking the floor to champion the adoption of a federal patent office in the English mold. The delegates were already familiar with Madison's case, as he had devoted much of *Federalist Paper 43* to a defense of copyright and patents on utilitarian and natural-rights grounds. Writing as "Publius," Madison concluded, "The public good fully coincides in both cases [copyright and patents on invention] with the claims of individuals."

This was far from obvious to many of those in the convention hall, but Madison was persuasive, and benefited not a little from the quiet support of his fellow Virginian and federalist George Washington. On September 5, following a short debate, a single sentence was unanimously approved for Article I, Section 8 of the new Constitution. Long known as the Progress Clause, and more recently as the "intellectual property clause," the sentence empowers Congress to "promote the progress of science and useful arts by securing for limited times to Authors and Inventors the exclusive rights to their respective writings and discoverings." It joined the Commerce and Contract Clauses as the only enumerated Constitutional powers related to the promotion of trade and economic development.[1]

Here it is worth pausing to note that Madison's enthusiasm was the restrained emotion of the Enlightenment. Even he, the biggest booster at the convention, was alert to the dangers of patent monopolies and sympathetic to the arguments of those who remained wary of their constitutional embrace. Prominent patent critics included Thomas Jefferson, who monitored the convention's progress through correspondence while in Paris. In a 1788 letter to Madison, Jefferson expressed unease over the idea of a U.S. Patent Office dispersing exclusive intellectual property rights. The benefits of these rights, he wrote, were "too doubtful to be opposed to that of their general

---

1. In the spirit of experimentation, some founders were inclined to continue considering alternatives to the English forms of exclusive rights following the Philadelphia convention. In a report to Congress submitted in 1791, Alexander Hamilton followed Adam Smith in musing on the benefits of a system of "pecuniary rewards"—basically an award or bonus system—to incentivize invention alongside a stingier allocation of patents. Such a system would reduce the number of monopolies, but the idea could not overcome concern that it would invite favoritism and shift risk onto the government.

suppression." Jefferson maintained these misgivings throughout his years as the country's first patent administrator and until his death in 1826.

Jefferson shared Adam Smith's doubts that patents functioned as promised and suspected they may hinder progress as much or more than they promoted it. "Generally speaking, other nations have thought that these monopolies produce more embarrassment than advantage to society; and it may be observed that the nations which refuse monopolies of invention, are as fruitful as England in new and useful devices," he wrote to a Pennsylvania miller named Isaac McPherson in 1813.

As a slave owner, Jefferson was a rank hypocrite on the theme of human liberty. On the question of intellectual property, he lived his words. After inventing a tool that reduced the labor required to process hemp stalks, Jefferson did not seek a patent on the device, but published the specifications of his invention anonymously, "in order to forestall the prevention of its use by some interloping patentee."

Benjamin Franklin will forever be the icon of republican patent skepticism. At eighty-one, Franklin attended the constitutional convention in his home city as a global celebrity, at once the most famous American and the age's most famous living scientist-inventor. No record survives of Franklin's comments during the deliberations over Article I, Section 8; according to lore, he kept his silence. Whatever he may have said, or declined to say, no delegate possessed a crisper record on the subject. Over the course of an era-defining life, Franklin never sought a patent on any of his ideas, discoveries, or inventions. When those opportunities presented themselves, he took the opposite tack, often going out of his way to proselytize against the very concept of a "lone inventor" with a credible claim of "ownership." In his autobiography, Franklin explains his position through the story of an English ironmonger who made "a little fortune" by patenting Franklin's published blueprints for a novel stove design. "I declined [the patent] from a principle that has weighed with me on such occasions," wrote Franklin, "viz., *that as we enjoy great advantages from the inventions of others, we should be glad of an opportunity to serve others by any invention of ours, and this we should do freely and generously.*" The italics are in the original, giving the advice the weight of maxim in his manual for right living.

The idea that every discovery is built on previous discoveries, and that every generation merely contributes to a great flow of knowledge that can be no more owned than it can be controlled or stopped, was a major theme of the era's patent debate. In a 1781 speech to the American Philosophical Society, Owen Biddle, a Pennsylvania astronomer and associate of Franklin, waxed at length on what might be called the republican position on knowledge. His subject was printing, not patents per se, but the implied position on intellectual property is clear, and provides a defense of the practices that made America notorious in Europe as a center of publishing "piracy."

> The facility with which copies are multiplied by the press, and books distributed amongst all ranks of people, has made every invention of art, or improvement of science, as universal as the influence of the sun. In short, this art [printing] is of a perfect republican nature; without respect of persons, it diffuses its benefits alike to all.

In Biddle's view, the knowledge contained in the booming black market in scientific journals only backed up Franklin's thoughts on the fallacy of "sole" invention and any subsequent ownership claims on knowledge related to that invention. "All our valuable attainments depend upon facts ... which are painfully and laboriously acquired," wrote Biddle. "Discoveries have succeeded each other, by a slow and gradual advancement, and that one invention is linked in with and leads to many others which are remote and unforeseen."

The post-Revolutionary period was fertile soil for a native anti-patent movement. In the republican ethos that swept the country, every special legal status and privilege was considered suspect, a remnant of Crown power to be sniffed, poked, and interrogated to determine its threat to the American experiment. This included patent monopolies and corporate charters that were seen as two sides of the same undemocratic coin. In popular debates over the issuing of state grants and immunities, corporate charters were denounced as "mercantile monopolies" that had no place in a republic. "Such franchises and privileged grants may have made sense in monarchies as devices serving 'to circumscribe and limit absolute power,'" observes Gordon Wood in his classic study, *The Radicalism of the American Revolution*. "But now that only the people ruled, these grants of corporate privileges seemed pernicious."

Early Americans may have hated all traces of the old regime, but they never followed Franklin and Jefferson's lead when it came to patent monopolies. They used the Patent Office in such numbers that Jefferson was forced to concede the system's role in, if not unleashing, at least bringing order to "a spring to invention beyond my comprehension." By the turn of the century, thousands of citizen-inventors were appearing every year at the Philadelphia patent office with sketches of innovative machines and methods. Most involved the processing of plants, crops, and crude chemicals. The first U.S. patent, signed by George Washington in July 1790, secured for Samuel Hopkins of Philadelphia fourteen years of exclusive rights to a new method of producing pot-ash for fertilizer, the forerunner of industrial potassium. Four years later, U.S. Patent 74 gave a Connecticut schoolmaster named Eli Whitney control of the market for a fateful machine that sped up the process of deseeding raw cotton.

Keeping pace with this steady overall rise in the number of patents was a boomlet in patents issued for recipes said to hold curative powers. Usually these were little more than bitter-tasting placebos whose proprietors promised miracles but offered no refunds. Ailing people of the time had good reason to distrust doctors still enamored with bleeding and the four humors, and nineteenth-century Americans bought branded concoctions by the millions, giving rise to a cottage industry in so-called patent medicines. The term was coined and used in derision, and its meaning soon grew to denote dubious nostrums of all kinds, both under patent and not. What united them was the scorn heaped upon them by the gatekeepers of orthodox medicine in Philadelphia. Drawing from the same republican and Enlightenment traditions as Franklin, Jefferson, and Biddle, "ethical" doctors and druggists rejected the intermixing of medicine, commercialism, and monopoly, tarring "patent medicines" with implications of charlatanism and quackery that would last well into the twentieth century.

The house of medicine was a lonely holdout in its opposition to patents. Elsewhere in the bustling, fast-growing country, the old republican patent skepticism had all but faded by the election of Andrew Jackson in 1828. As the Virginia and Boston dynasties of the founding generation disappeared from politics, and then from living memory, so did their understanding of patents, the Commonwealth, and the inherent social value of open science and the broad diffusion of knowledge for knowledge's sake as a humanistic first principle. The void was filled with the grubbier values and patent philosophy that defined the Age of Jackson.

Jackson and his fellow Democrats had little use for the founders' vision of the patent as a two-way social contract. Beginning with an administrative overhaul of the patent system in 1836, they stripped intellectual property of its republican clothing and reintroduced patents and copyright as plain property rights—shorn of the old commitment to shared progress and unburdened by the founders' fancy Enlightenment ideas about a common transhistorical store of human knowledge.

This shift was institutionalized with Jackson's signing of the 1836 Patent Act, a law that transformed the previously understaffed and chaotic Patent Office into an orderly agency overseen by bureaucrats who understood their charge as democratizing patent rights. As part of Jackson's reforms, the Patent Office moved to what is now the National Portrait Gallery, where it oversaw a period of exponential growth. Of the 650,000 U.S. patents issued between 1790 and 1900, those issued pre-Jackson amounted to a trickle compared to the torrent unleashed by the Patent Act of 1836. This surge was not reflected in England, where the patent system that provided the colonies their blueprint remained wed to the old Puritan skepticism. The difference was noted in 1839 by Supreme Court justice Joseph Story, who contrasted the United States' "liberal and expanded view" of patents with the English understanding that patents "were in the nature of monopolies, and, therefore, to be narrowly watched."

Jackson's key ally in remaking the American patent was a Democratic senator from Maine, John Ruggles, known as the father of the patent office. In the Jackson-Ruggles view, the rights conferred by patents constituted a concrete currency comparable to the rights attached to physical property.

Like the owners of any plot of land or piece of machinery, patentees could choose to till their staked intellectual soil or let it lie fallow as they saw fit. Whatever they chose, it was none of the government's damn business. "The decision to make productive use of the [patented] innovation," writes Herbert Hovenkamp, "became purely private, emulating the law of real property." Concerns about economic development, meanwhile, were "increasingly relegated to boilerplate."

A satirical ode to this Jacksonian conception of the patent comes early in Mark Twain's 1889 novel of time travel, *A Connecticut Yankee in King Arthur's Court*. When a Hartford factory engineer named Hank Morgan awakes from a crack to the head in sixth-century England, he quickly begins remaking the Court of Camelot in America's nineteenth-century image. "The very first official thing I did, in my administration—and it was on the very first day of it, too—was to start a patent office," Morgan explains to the reader, "for I knew that a country without a patent office and good patent laws was just a crab, and couldn't travel any way but sideways or backways."

As Twain understood, Hank Morgan's unwavering folk-faith in patents was rooted in a past that bore an increasingly tenuous relationship to the reality of post–Civil War America. By the middle and late decades of the century, backwoods inventors and workshop gadgeteers had been largely displaced by modern corporate research laboratories such as the one Thomas Edison established in Menlo Park, New Jersey, in 1876. Companies were not only coming to dominate entire fields of invention; they were using patents in ways anticipated by the Jacksonian redefinition of patents as simple property rights. Patents were valued—and increasingly hoarded—not to advance technological progress as per English common law and the U.S. Constitution, but to actively and strategically *block* it. Rather than spurring the creation of new industries, they were used as moats to protect established ones and defend them from competition.

The fight to bring patent law into alignment with new realities was part of the antitrust movement that emerged during the corporatizing, industrializing era that Twain christened the Gilded Age. Hank Morgan may have faced little opposition in imposing his patent policy on sixth-century England, but back in his own time, an agrarian-populist uprising challenged corporate knowledge monopolies on everything from sewing machines to locomotive parts. For the first time since the writing of the Progress Clause, "patent exceptionalism"—the belief that patents represented a benign form of monopoly—was placed under scrutiny by Congress and the courts.

The first bubbles of a populist patent backlash were seen in the smallholder farms of the South and Southwest. This was the feeding ground for a new species of predator enabled by the Jacksonian turn. As federal courts established precedent for enforcing intellectual property rights as simple property rights, entrepreneurs arose to capitalize on the freshly opened opportunities for chicanery and mischief. Historians Steven W. Usselman and Richard R. John describe how these "patent sharks" executed scams by threatening infringement suits against farmers who used common rural technologies such as swing gates and gravity-fed wells:

> To the outrage of thousands of farmers and ranchers in the arid Southwest, patent agents had swarmed into the region warning gate and well users that, if they wished to avoid paying fifty-dollar license fees, they must travel to St. Louis to defend themselves in court. The [farmers'] outrage at the patent agents' audacity was compounded when it became known that the patent office had originally assigned the well patent to a Union army officer who claimed to have invented it while on active duty during the Civil War. Even staunch Unionists wondered why they should have to pay for the rights to an invention that had been devised in wartime by a federal employee.[2]

---

2. Note this last detail of the farmers' angry disbelief at being asked to pay for use of a technology invented by a government employee on the government clock. This point of resentment presages a fight over the private acquisition of public science that would run for three decades in the next century.

The country's seething farmers came together under the banner of a proto-populist national farmers' association called the National Grange of the Order of Patrons of Husbandry. Before they were superseded by the larger and more radical Farmers' Alliance, the Grange organized campaigns around patents and pushed them to the center of the broader antitrust movement taking form, driven by deepening rural resentment toward monopolies they saw as responsible for driving up prices on everything from basic equipment to rail shipping fees. The politics of patents intensified in 1872, when Congress and the Supreme Court extended an about-to-expire patent held by the Singer Sewing Machine Company, in effect forestalling the arrival of cheaper models on the market.

The Grange found an unlikely ally in the railroad barons. The fast-paced turnover in thousands of interlocking parts required to maintain railroads opened the rail companies to numerous accusations of patent infringement; like the farmers, the barons sought reforms that kneecapped patent sharks and reduced the scope for sympathetic judges to order massive payouts for patent violations. To this end, the industry helped write a bill imposing strict limits on infringement suits and penalties. The barons then withdrew into the shadows and allowed the populist farmers to become the sympathetic public face of the bill.

The Grange waged a potent campaign to keep the patent issue front-and-center in the run-up to the 1874 midterms. For two years, the farmers rained hellfire on any legislator who opposed the bill or publicly supported the Singer patent extension. The campaign succeeded in electing enough Democrats to flip the House and usher the bill into the Senate. There it died, likely at the hands of a teetotaling New York Republican named Roscoe Conkling, one of the drafters of the Fourteenth Amendment and a former patent lawyer who specialized in infringement cases.

Aside from this one-off alliance of convenience with the rail barons, the populists' fight against patent abuse was a lonely one. They did, however, have a friend on the Supreme Court. In 1883, Justice Joseph Bradley wrote a landmark decision dismissing the infringement claim of a Boston shipbuilder. Bradley took a more jaundiced eye to the post-Jackson patent than any of his colleagues, and he used the opportunity of the unanimous decision to unload on a patent system he believed had lost its constitutional moorings. Instead of advancing science and the useful arts as called for in Article I, Section 8, he wrote, the patent system had degenerated to the point of creating and favoring "a class of speculative schemers, who make it their business to watch the advancing wave of improvement and gather from its foam in the form of patented monopolies, which enable them to lay a heavy tax upon the industry of the country . . . It embarrasses the honest pursuit of business with fears and apprehensions of concealed liens and unknown liabilities to law suits and vexatious accountings for profits made in good faith."

Bradley's was an isolated expression of support for the populist-led crusade to roll back the power of corporations, trusts, and opportunists to use patents as weapons against the public interest. At nearly every turn, they were otherwise stymied by Congress and the courts. Of the two landmark bills passed in response to rising antitrust sentiment—the Interstate Commerce Act of 1887 and the Sherman Act of 1890—both remained mute on the subject of patents. The Supreme Court, meanwhile, issued a series of decisions that reaffirmed the Jacksonian view of patents as property rights, broad and absolute, that can be wielded however their owner sees fit. These decisions included several related to the first banes of the Grange: swing gates and well designs.

While the patent sharks plied the infringement racket, the public benefit logic of Article I, Section 8 was threatened from the other side by the rise of the corporate laboratory. As technology grew more complicated and dependent on specialized knowledge, the independent inventor was replaced by teams of financiers, executives, and the professional scientists in their employ. Those lone inventors that did survive soon ran up against the reality of "patent thickets"—huge numbers of patents that covered every conceivable (or patentable) aspect of knowledge related to an invention or object of research. The scope for independent research of the sort conducted by Benjamin Franklin was being choked off with great fistfuls of corporate patents.

This development was captured in a 1941 report published by Franklin Roosevelt's Temporary National Economic Committee, a New Deal study group tasked with interrogating concentrations of power in the economy, including the role of patents. The rise of the corporate research lab, the author wrote, had displaced the solo inventor of yore with "the research technician" who is little more than

> a hired specialist creating monopolistic credits which after corporate endorsement are put into circulation . . . This shift lifts the patent out of the province in which it is supposed to operate, separates it from the objectives it is supposed to serve, . . . [and] sets the grant down in a universe of business [where it is a tool] in the acquisition game and subjects it to the discipline of money-making. A radical change in its character attends the journey of the instrument to a new habitat [where it is] enlisted in the pursuit of gain, whether used, held in reserve, or laid away in moth balls was no longer dependent on its merits; instead its employment was to wait upon the exigencies of corporate policy.

The nineteenth-century names most associated with the legend of the individual genius—Edison, Morse, Goodyear, Westinghouse, Ford—were in fact its most prominent gravediggers. They built research castles and pulled the drawbridge, forcing those who might wish to follow them to overcome rising financial and legal barriers maintained by teams of in-house corporate patent lawyers. The representative figure of this shift is Alexander Graham Bell. Hailed during his life as a lone American genius in the Franklin mold, Bell understood the mythic power of the image of the heroic inventor, and he cultivated it with care. He did so while dispensing with the now-inconvenient republican ideas that once came with it—especially the understanding of knowledge as a fundamentally cumulative commons, maintained and added to, a little by each, passed down from age to age. The larger Bell's research empire grew atop its patent thickets, and the more he invited and reveled in comparisons to Franklin, the louder the Sage of Philadelphia must have groaned in his grave.

In 1888, the Supreme Court upheld Bell's telephone patents and handed him a monopolistic head start in a new industry. The decision had critics on all sides. Some said Bell's patents were based on principles of nature that were fundamentally unclaimable. Others maintained Bell and his team had merely reverse engineered the results of a competitor named Daniel Drawbaugh. Whatever the merits of the claims, the decision announced a new era for the secure corporate enclosure of scientific knowledge. It midwifed one of the country's most enduring monopolies and set the stage for the government sanction of the generational patent-based lightbulb cartel managed by General Electric and Westinghouse. The last of several *Bell* decisions in 1897 testified to the distance that now separated U.S. law from the social contract that had defined the grand patent bargain for a thousand years. "The inventor is one who has discovered something of value," wrote the majority in *United States v. American Bell Telephone Co.* "It is his absolute property. He may withhold the knowledge of it from the public."

In American law schools, the *Bell* decisions are taught alongside a less famous case involving the more primitive technology of the paper bag. In 1908, the Supreme Court ruled that the Eastern Paper Bag Company could not use a manufacturing method patented by its competitor, the Continental Paper Bag Company, even though Continental admitted it had no intention of using the technology covered by the patent. The meaning of the precedent was clear: the court had removed any remaining doubts about the rights of patent holders to strategically block the diffusion of a new technology, no matter the uses to which it might otherwise be put.

That decision entered history, aptly, as *Paper Bag*. Had any of the founders present at Philadelphia lived to see it, they might have placed the product in question over their heads, rather than be identified as the authors of a clause so debased as Article I, Section 8.

The conquest of this corporatized intellectual property regime wasn't yet complete, however. Within the research-based industrial economy of fin de siècle America, there remained holdouts to the new order. Within the worlds of medicine, research, and pharmacy, more than anywhere else in the economy, the old line against monopoly still held. In 1908, the year of *Paper Bag*, the founding meeting of a new scientific organization called the American

Society for Pharmacology and Experimental Therapeutics adopted a strict ethical code that reflected the longstanding rejection of patents and monopoly by physicians, researchers, and drug makers. The society's bylaws included a ban on its members working in the fast-growing pharmaceutical industry, where the distant cannon shots in a very different kind of patent war were just starting to be heard.

Two

ETHICAL MEDICINE IN THE REPUBLIC OF SCIENCE

FOR MOST OF HUMAN HISTORY, PEOPLE WHO MIXED AND APPLIED medicines were held apart. Even in cultures where everything was in some sense sacred, healers and their tools were nearest the gods, possessors of the most powerful magic. In Amazonian cultures, shamanic medicine men by custom have lived in remote isolation. Their counterparts in pagan and early Christian Europe—such as the Druids and medieval women who were keepers of medical plant knowledge, magic, and lore, later denounced and terminated as practitioners of witchcraft—lived in or on the edges of forests and were said to commune with spirits. The oldest records of a connection between medicine, magic, and religion are clay tablets dating to 3000 B.C. They illustrate the reverence shown in ancient Sumer to the healing goddess Gula, the Great Physician, user of herbs and powerful incantations. This overlap persisted well after the "birth of reason" in ancient Greece. The culture that produced Aristotle and the Hippocratic Oath also worshipped Asclepius, god of medicine and healing. For centuries after the Roman physician Galen began to systematically disentangle the scientific from the supernatural, the cult of Asclepius flourished throughout the empire and Near Asia. Adherents suffering illness would sleep in his temples in hopes that he would appear in their dreams carrying a staff wrapped by a single coiled serpent, a symbol of health and sickness inherited from the Sumerians.[3]

As a healer of last resort for the poor, the cult of Asclepius was so popular it threatened to undermine the recruitment efforts of the early Christians, who considered the popular Greek god to be the most serious rival to Jesus Christ. The eventual substitution of Asclepius by Jesus owes less to the promise of eternal salvation than the tireless promotion of the latter's superior healing power. The close association between Christianity and healing colored the development of Christian teachings on the duty to attend to the suffering of all those made in God's image. Red Sea miracles that cured blindness were followed by cloister-clinics for the poor and afflicted administered by monks and later nuns. Out of these emerged the first hospitals.

Medicine's base in religious institutions shaped the conception of knowledge described in the previous chapter. Medical and scientific knowledge especially were considered gifts from the mind of God, free to all and belonging to no earthly power. Any expression or use of this knowledge, including "novel" and potentially profitable ones, remained God's gift. "To traffic in its fruits was a sin of simony," writes the historian and critic Lewis Hyde. This spirit is captured in the often-quoted line of Martin Luther, later echoed by Benjamin Franklin: "Freely have I received, freely have I given, and I desire nothing in return."

---

3. Hermes, the god of commerce, was represented by a similar rod entwined with *two* snakes, rather than one. These snakes often had wings that in Roman telling represented speed, with Hermes appearing as Mercury, the messenger god. The rod of Asclepius did not have wings because speed was thought to be antithetical to healing, and the rod was associated with the administration of opium, a frequently used medicine. Which symbol is used—one or two snakes, flanked or not flanked by wings—is important because, for both the Greeks and the Romans, medicine was an art of the temple, not the bazaar. In the temple, a place set apart, avoidance of harm is paramount. The agora, by contrast, is a place of risk, haggling, and aggrandizement. That the modern health industry sometimes confuses the two ancient symbols is a poetic and revealing error.

✦

When the Enlightenment created space between religion and science, it secularized the medieval belief in the sacredness of knowledge. Medical science occupied a hallowed place in an Age of Reason defined by rapid advances in the physical and natural sciences. Many Enlightenment figures were physicians, naturalists, or some combination of the two. They believed the application of reason would unlock the secrets of human health, now seen as the natural state of man. Illness was not the physical manifestation of sin, or the work of demon spirits, as had previously been taught; it was a problem to be studied and solved. Those doing the studying and the solving were citizens of a borderless republic of science, deploying reason to vanquish disease and suffering in service to all mankind.

Reason's potential appeared limitless, promising the eventual conquest of death itself. "It is possible to imagine," Ben Franklin wrote to the eminent British scientist Joseph Priestley in 1780, "All Diseases may by sure means be prevented or cured, not excepting even that of Old Age, and our Lives lengthened at pleasure even beyond the antediluvian Standard."

While pondering the prospect of physical immortality, it is unlikely that Franklin imagined the wondrous medicines of distant centuries being strictly controlled in a futuristic version of royal monopoly privilege. The idea would have seemed far-fetched and pessimistic in an optimistic age. But it was Franklin who told the waiting Philadelphia crowd that they had a republic "if you can keep it." He understood that while scientific knowledge and progress were irrepressible, the republican values enjoyed no such guarantee.

In the English patent tradition, medicine's sacred origins informed a compromise: *techniques* used to manufacture medicines were legitimate subjects for patent consideration, but not the medicines themselves. As European states began to adopt patent systems in the nineteenth century, they followed the English lead in drawing a hard distinction between medical process and product patents. If a European drug maker wished to claim a monopoly on a new drug, they had to make the transatlantic crossing to the United States.

In permitting the patenting of medical products, the United States remained an outlier well into the twentieth century. For most of this time, it was a global oddity with the added quirk of having a split personality. The dual U.S. drug economy contained one market for so-called patent medicines, the herbal mixtures and potions that promised to cure every possible ailment and formed one of the busiest, most colorful, and most profitable trades in nineteenth-century America. The opposing drug economy was self-consciously sober and staid in comparison, less profitable by design, and limited to the official pharmacopeia maintained by a class of elite medical gatekeepers. This so-called ethical wing of medicine dismissed the peddlers of patent cures with disdain.[4] The self-appointed keepers of the Enlightenment flame considered themselves dual citizens of the United States and an international, transhistorical republic of science. One of the fastest ways to lose this second passport was to break the hard taboo against all forms of profiteering and secrecy in medicine, symbolized by the patent monopoly. The "ethical" medical and pharmaceutical guilds were allied in a "profound belief in their own supposed benevolence and dedication to the advancement of scientific knowledge," writes Joseph M. Gabriel, the preeminent historian of nineteenth-century American medical ethics and mores. "For most physicians, there was little difference between patenting and secrecy when it came to drugs. Both were considered unethical forms of selfish monopoly. Indeed, it was generally assumed that patented remedies and quack nostrums were the same thing."

The capital of "ethical" medicine was Philadelphia. The University of Pennsylvania Medical School and College of Pharmacy, together with a

---

4. The quotations around "ethical" should be read with two meanings in mind. While trumpeting the humanistic ideals of open publication and the knowledge commons, the gatekeepers of "ethical medicine" also condoned medical experimentation on slaves, colonial subjects, prisoners, and the mentally handicapped. This parallel history continued into the middle of the twentieth century. During its national conferences of the 1930s, the American Medical Association would spend the morning debating the morality of patenting medicines, then celebrate the architects of the Tuskegee Syphilis Study in the afternoon.

number of influential professional and trade associations, closely monitored their professions for rogue attempts to "grow fat on human misery," as one nineteenth-century gatekeeper described profiting from medicines. At its founding convention in Philadelphia in 1847, the forerunner of the American Medical Association adopted a code of ethics declaring patents "incompatible with the duty and obligation enjoined upon physicians to advance the knowledge of curing diseases." Describing patents as "derogatory to professional character," the association forbade members from seeking patents or prescribing patented medicines.

The code was modeled closely on a statement of principles published by the Medical Society of New York in 1823. Both reflected a view of medical science as an island of virtue and reason in a sea of avarice and flimflam.

Where orthodox medicine led, pharmacists and drug companies followed. In 1852, the newly formed American Pharmaceutical Association adopted a strict anti-patent policy. At its founding convention, also in Philadelphia, the drug makers cited an ethical duty to ensure medical discoveries and related science are widely disseminated for the nation's and the species' benefit. The druggists adopted the doctors' broad philosophical approach to the patent taboo, couching the prohibition in a rejection of the myth of the lone genius. Given the cumulative nature of scientific discovery, in which increment is added to increment over the span of time, claims of being "sole inventor" were deemed fraudulent.

Succumbing to the temptations of medical monopoly guaranteed exile from the republic of science and excoriating public censure. The Philadelphia doctor who patented a novel twist on curative leeching in 1805 found his claim roundly ignored, infringed, and denounced as "unjust and illiberal . . . a knavish piece of monopoly." This was the standard treatment of any physician, scientist, or druggist who sought riches by controlling access to medical discoveries. "If a medicine was patented, it was reasoned, other physicians could not investigate it freely or prescribe it to their patients as they saw fit," writes Gabriel in his history of early American medical ethics, *Medical Monopoly*. "Secrecy was also understood as a form of monopoly that undermined the progress of medical science and threatened the public."

On the other side of the ethical divide was a busy continental traffic in cure-all potions and nostrums, noisy with jostling entrepreneurs and hustlers mostly untrained in medicine and pharmacy. There was no such thing as "honest haberdashery" or "moral masonry" because those professions were not divided into camps with wildly divergent values, styles, and missions.

Name-brand patent medicines were ubiquitous and tremendously profitable. The bestselling medicine of the nineteenth century was Brandreth's Vegetable Pills, a "blood-purifying" purgative used by an estimated 150 million Americans at its mid-century peak. Its promise to "build up a new and sound body in place of one feeble or diseased" may have been bogus, but it did build a new and sound fortune for the patent-medicine magnate Benjamin Brandreth, whose factories occupied a New York City block by the late 1830s.[5]

Among the hustles of a young P. T. Barnum on the make was writing copy for patent-medicine labels and advertisements. Later in his life, as a famous impresario, his Barnum-branded patent medicines were known by a brash marketing campaign that symbolized everything "ethical" pharmacy defined itself against. A campaign for Barnum's proprietary castor oils featured the image of his biggest circus star, Jumbo, a giant African bush elephant he purchased in 1882 from London's Royal Zoological Gardens.

Barnum-style hustlers and cure-all-selling con men were common characters and tropes in the literature of the time. The title charlatan of Herman Melville's 1857 novel *The Confidence-Man* is an herb doctor who sells bottles to profit in the name of a fraudulent charity. Mark Twain immortalized patent-medicine quackery in *The Adventures of Tom Sawyer*, and then again in the characters of Duke and the King in *The Adventures of Huckleberry Finn*. The

---

5. The national market for patented purgatives was so busy it was a cliché of the age to say that the way to open a man's purse was "to open his bowels."

Twain novel that gave an era its name, *The Gilded Age*, follows the adventures of Colonel Beriah Sellers, peddler of a product known as the Infallible Imperial Oriental Optic Liniment and Salvation for Sore Eyes, consisting of nine-tenths water and one-tenth whatever ingredients "don't cost more than a dollar a barrel."

In 1905, Twain received a solicitation from the San Francisco proprietor of a new patent medicine called T. Duffy's Solution, described by its maker, J. H. Todd, as "the Elixir of Life. Blood Purifier, Antiseptic, Disease Destroyer [and] Giver of Life Everlasting." Twain called in his secretary and dictated a response that was never mailed. "A few moments from now my resentment will have faded and passed and I shall probably even be praying for you," it reads. "But while there is yet time I hasten to wish that you may take a dose of your own poison by mistake, and enter swiftly into the damnation which you and all other patent medicine assassins have so remorselessly earned and do so richly deserve."[6]

In fairness, there was good reason to seek out nostrums and settle for their questionable effects, including the as-yet-unnamed placebo effect. Until the advent of "scientific" medicine toward the end of the nineteenth century, the options available to physicians were rudimentary, meager, and full of pain. The foremost physician in early America, Benjamin Rush was a fanatical advocate of bleeding to treat just about any illness. The esteemed former surgeon general of the Continental Army advanced the view that all disease resulted from an excess in "capillary tension" and should be managed by heavy bleeding and purging. It was muttered that Rush "shed more blood than any general in history," drawing the vital fluid from his patients "till they were as pale as Jersey Veal."

---

6. According to K. Patrick Ober, author of *Mark Twain and Medicine*, the writer privately admitted in a letter to a friend that the only thing that helped his hemorrhoids was a nostrum he described as "a rather deadly quack medicine."

The miserable limitations of pre-scientific medicine also worked to reinforce the patent taboo. With so few effective solutions to suffering and disease, what could possibly justify monopoly claims on the few tools that actually alleviated pain and cured disease? This was the question hurled in outrage at a Boston dentist named William Morton in 1846 following his discovery that sulfuric ether could safely suppress consciousness during surgery. Had Morton simply published his findings, his name would have been celebrated for ending one of humanity's longest-running horrors. For thousands of years, surgery had been performed on conscious patients held down by the force of men; the only palliatives available were wine, opium, and, with any luck, blackout. But Morton was a dentist, not a doctor steeped in the ethical code of the guild, and he successfully sought a patent on his discovery. This triggered a wrathful response from organized medicine aimed not at the U.S. Patent Office, but at Morton for using its services. This response could sound indistinguishable from genuine incomprehension. As one doctor told a Boston medical journal, "Why must I now purchase the right to use [ether] as a patent medicine? It would seem to me like *patent sun-light.*"

The first attempt to answer this question within the framework of ethical medicine was made by a New York City physician and pharmacist named Francis E. Stewart. After earning degrees from the Philadelphia College of Pharmacy and Jefferson Medical College, Stewart established a New York City medical practice with a side career in drug research. His life took a dramatic turn early in his career when he discovered an effective treatment for wasting disease.

The ethical code of the time called for Stewart to publish the substance of his discovery in the medical journals, then allow others to follow up his work and determine its value. Instead, he crossed a bright red line by accepting a partnership with George Davis of the Detroit-based Parke-Davis drug company. Parke-Davis was itself known for pushing at the edges of "ethical" manufacturing by advertising its products with illustrations and dramatic flourishes that, it seemed to some, veered closer to Barnum than the sober text-only ads of most approved medicines.[7] When Stewart partnered with Parke-Davis, the usual insults ensued, including calls for his professional excommunication. His crime was not in patenting his treatment for wasting disease, but in helping the company promote it for use before its inclusion in the list of approved medicines featured in the *Pharmacopeia*, a tome updated only once every ten years.

The system Stewart devised with Parke-Davis for bypassing the *Pharmacopeia* involved compiling reports of the results in each hospital using the new treatment. When twenty-five of these "working bulletins" came back, they were presented to the journals for summary publication. The original 1881 version of Stewart's "working bulletin" system did not push against the patent taboo. Although he and Parke-Davis were beginning to have quiet doubts about that stricture, too, they understood that monopoly control of the drug in question would cast doubt on the bulletins by increasing the incentive (or the perception of such an incentive) to bury or ignore negative bulletins, which were essentially human field trials.

Another decade would pass before Parke-Davis began to edge closer to the ethical third rail of medical patents. When a competing firm used its bulletin reports to scoop Parke-Davis's market for a new plant-based laxative, George Davis judged the episode "an apt illustration of the unpractical working of our ethical policy in the present condition of affairs." In 1894, his company set a major precedent by receiving a process patent on the production of an enzyme found to aid digestion.

With Davis's support, Stewart took these controversial ideas into the belly of the beast. Offering himself as proof that it was possible to work with industry without betraying the ideals of the old ethical code, he lectured to skeptical medical and scientific audiences around the country on the need for reform. For three decades, Stewart walked this line in public view, seeding

---

7. In 1877, the American Medical Association passed bylaws banning testimonials and endorsements in the advertisements for products listed in its approved pharmacopeia.

his "working bulletin" model as one of the first medical men to offer unapologetic, full-service consulting to the drug industry.

Thus did Stewart emerge as the standard-bearer for the novel concept of ethical drug patenting. In Joseph Gabriel's estimation, he became "perhaps the best-known expert on patent law and its relationship to pharmacy in the medical and pharmaceutical communities, publishing widely." In dozens of articles, including a series in the *Journal of the American Medical Association*, he argued that patents aligned with the ethical dictate to circulate medical knowledge because "a thing patented was a thing divulged." Moreover, he argued, patents could help fund the expensive modern laboratories required in the dawning age of scientific medicine. In the middle of the twentieth century, drug companies would make a public relations art and industry out of this justification for patents first articulated by Stewart, refining it for deployment against any and all criticism of its power, profits, and prices.[8]

The taboo against medical monopolies weakened in the century following the cracks inflicted by Stewart. The next generation of Parke-Davis executives would live to see the making and selling of medicines dominated by corporations that openly wielded intellectual property claims in brazen pursuit of profit and market control. They would do so in alliance with their old associates in ethical medicine, the medical establishment, whose role flipped from senior partner and guardian of an ancient code to handmaiden and accomplice tasked with using its social esteem to erase that code's legacy.

This was still a fantastical prospect when Stewart planted a heretical flag for ethical patenting inside the house of medicine around the turn of the

---

8. Stewart's liberality did not extend to the use of trademarks and brand names, the use of which he believed could be used to turn a temporary monopoly into a permanent one by cementing the association between a brand and the medicine for all time. On this issue, Davis and Stewart joined their conservative brethren to keep newly arrived trademarked German drugs out of the pharmacopeia.

century. It would continue to seem so during the jagged and multi-decade erosion process whose most important players were not Parke-Davis or any other U.S. drug company. While the most respected native firms conferred with the deans in Philadelphia and measured the moral consequences of loosening the patent taboo, no sentimental attachments slowed down the chemical-pharmaceutical combines of Wilhelmine Germany that stormed the U.S. drug market in the 1880s.

German scientists did much of the work that brought medicine into the modern age. The paradigm-smashing breakthroughs of the kaiser's lavishly funded research centers rivaled the Pasteur Institute in developing the fields of bacteriology and immunology. The German chemical industry, meanwhile, oversaw leaps in organic chemistry that enabled the production of synthetic dyes and drugs based on coal tar. These firms' biggest market was the United States, where they were a major presence in the new industrial economy. In Washington, D.C., their U.S. lawyers were regular visitors to the U.S. Patent Office, amassing hundreds of patents on increasingly essential chemical products and processes. In New York, German drug companies established subsidiaries and hired law firms to extend and protect their patent monopolies. Many favored the services of H. A. Metz and Company, run by a thirty-three-year-old dynamo named Herman Metz, a chemist-turned-businessman who divided his time importing chemicals, overseeing their manufacture, and enforcing patents on behalf of German clients like the chemical and drugs firm Farbwerke Hoechst Aktiengesellschaft.

The arrival of the German companies transformed the U.S. drug economy, the research landscape, and the legal and cultural mores around them. Until then, the use of patent barricades to obstruct the study and sale of medicines was, as the foreign newcomers to the industry might say, *verboten*. It was known in other industries, but not pharmaceuticals. With rare exceptions, patents were still associated with the mass-market stuff peddled by P. T. Barnum and other fraudsters of bright plumage and no scientific training. The German firms pioneered the patent as an instrument for building and protecting exclusive markets around drugs that otherwise appeared "ethical." Aside from the use of trademarks, the products were marketed to doctors in the sober fashion expected of ethical drug companies. More important, they were real contributions to medicine that could not be ignored. This presented a thorny dilemma for the house of medicine and U.S. drug makers. In their bylaws and codes of conduct, the American Medical and Pharmaceutical Associations barred the prescribing of patented and trademarked drugs on principle, believing that any trusted drug should be available to all and subject to research and price competition. At the same time, how could the establishment justify blocking the approval of new breakthrough drugs of incontrovertible benefit?

The German patent strategy went beyond the establishment of market monopolies. The firms conducted "a carefully devised strategy of patenting every chemical in the course of the research effort, effectively patenting around the final, marketable drug," writes the industry historian Jonathan Liebenau. "This technique was successful in discouraging competition because there was little incentive to work through a development phase when patents were already held on every conceivable related product."

The chemical and drug firm Farbenfabriken vormals Friedrich Bayer gained notoriety for deploying these strategies around a string of breakthrough drugs that they were barred from patenting elsewhere, including the kaiser's Germany. Throughout the 1880s and 1890s, the firm's U.S. subsidiary, the Bayer Company, took out patents on three synthetic wonder drugs. The first was a powerful sedative released in 1887 called Sulfonal; it was followed a year later by a fever-reducing pill called Phenacetine. Both drugs were popular, but also the source of much grumbling. An ounce of Phenacetine cost six cents in Germany, fifteen cents in England, Canada, and Europe, and one dollar in the United States, where Bayer enjoyed its only monopoly.

The Phenacetine patent was followed in 1899 by a third that broke the dam of public and professional anger. That year, Bayer debuted a new anti-inflammatory and anti-pain medicine under the brand name of Aspirin. Acetylsalicylic acid, its scientific name, had been synthesized by Felix Hoffmann two years earlier, in August 1897, the same month Hoffmann created a powerful synthetic opiate the company marketed as Heroin. A synthetic derivation of willow leaf tea, Bayer sold Aspirin as a white powder in glass bottles that took on a Janus-faced symbolism. Immediately and widely adopted as a standard treatment for headaches and rheumatism, it was a true wonder drug of its time. It was also a hated symbol of un-American medical monopoly.

By the standards of "ethical" medicine, the patenting of the first non-addictive pain reliever was the crudest German obscenity of them all. Yet Aspirin's unquestionable utility and scientific origin left the country's medical gatekeepers with an impossible choice. They could take a stand for the anti-monopoly code and deny Aspirin medical legitimacy, or they could accept yet another Bayer monopoly as the changing price of progress in an age of corporatized scientific medicine. The price wasn't only a metaphor for principles. Bayer's markups on Aspirin in the United States rivaled those of Phenacetine.

The medical associations and the major drug manufacturers temporized. Not so the nation's neighborhood and corner druggists. For them, the stakes went beyond their profession's code of ethics. The prepackaged and branded Bayer products also represented an attack on guild interests by threatening the tradition of mixing and preparing generic drugs in-house. In a future shaped by the branded Bayer model, their skills would be obsolete. In response to the introduction of trademarked Phenacetine, the druggists worked with smugglers to bring in black market Bayer products and resell them at costs similar to those available in Canada. When the first Aspirin monopoly prices were announced in 1899, they expanded the smuggling network and began pouring resources into an organized public campaign against the German patents. The agitation and infringement campaign continued in one form or another until the United States entered the European war in 1917. Waged through criminal networks, speaking tours, the press, congressional proxies, and personal visits to the White House, the druggists' war on Bayer put a spotlight on the newly relevant matter of the legal and moral right to control the price and market of an important new medicine.

The Aspirin war's main front was one of the most extensive and systematic smuggling operations in the nation's history. Within a year of Aspirin's arrival in the U.S. market, black marketeers in cahoots with the nation's druggists were supplying much of the country with wholesale shipments of staggering size—both packaged drugs and their bulk ingredients—brought across U.S. land borders and into its ports. Thomas M. Reimer described the network in an unpublished history dissertation:

> Many [smugglers] worked from the Canadian border, out of reach of Bayer, for they broke no Canadian law. To avoid being chased by Treasury secret agents for smuggling, the more astute paid duty, and worked through peddlers to avoid charges of mail fraud. As long as they only infringed Bayer's patent rights, they committed a tort and not a felony, and Bayer was on its own until it could obtain and serve an injunction, after which smugglers who persisted were in contempt of court . . . Many retail druggists hailed them as freedom fighters.

Few druggists could claim they were just on the sidelines of this operation. As the smuggling network expanded, so did the number of bootleggers and Aspirin mules in police custody. In plea deals, they revealed an operation of continental scope, naming enough names for Bayer to threaten suit against seven thousand retail druggists, or roughly one out of every five pharmacists in the country. Unable to bring suit against them all, Bayer's U.S. lawyers selected targets for maximum impact. By 1906, the company had pressed charges against eight hundred community pharmacies.

The country's local pharmacists believed they had justice and national custom on their side, regardless of the legal status of the Bayer patents. When Bayer's lawyers began working with local and federal police to dismantle the Aspirin black market, the druggists dug in. Knowing they had the public's sympathy, they used Bayer's lawsuits as rallying points and press opportunities. One early inflection point came in November 1896, three years before the Aspirin patent, following the arrest of a Denver drug distributor named Hugh Tinling on charges of illegally importing 125 pounds of Bayer Phenacetine. When the company's lawyers demanded Tinling pay a heavy fine and publicly recognize the validity of Bayer's patent, he refused. Tinling instead denounced Bayer's greed in exploiting his country's peculiar and immoral tolerance of medicine monopolies. The Circuit Court of Appeals judge overseeing the case disagreed. He rebuked Tinling for dragging "immaterial" antitrust issues into the case and upheld Bayer's injunction.

The case added fuel to what had become a druggist-led prairie fire of anti-monopoly activity. Behind the radical leadership (by druggist standards) of the Chicago Retail Druggist Association, regional groups of druggists filed a flurry of suits challenging Bayer's patent claim of "novelty." Their efforts mirrored a campaign in England, the only country other than the United States to briefly grant Bayer an Aspirin patent. In 1905, an English high court judge voided Bayer's Aspirin patent as unoriginal, leading to changes that tightened that nation's laws around drug patents and sharpened the contrast between the United States and the rest of the world. As in the United States, the German firms' ingenious use of elaborate patenting strategies was poorly received in England. "Big [German] syndicates have one very effective way of destroying British industry," observed Lloyd George, England's minister of trade, at the time. "They first of all apply for patents on a very considerable scale [that] suggest every possible combination . . . which human ingenuity can possibly think of [but] are not in operation . . . so as to cover any possible invention that may be discovered afterwards in this country."

Bayer and America's druggists entered the twentieth century like two entangled fighters. The druggists continued to land punches in the press, extending their starting advantage in public sympathies, and stepped up lobbying efforts through the National Association of Retail Druggists (NARD), founded in 1898. Bayer rolled with NARD's punches and continued to find satisfaction in the courts. Frustration over Bayer's strong legal position was palpable at the 1901 meeting of the American Pharmaceutical Association, convened shortly after a federal judge dismissed a patent challenge by the Pennsylvania Pharmaceutical Association. During the rowdy proceedings, a western Pennsylvania druggist lambasted the timidity of the medical establishment, the pharmacists' traditional ally, and implored the house of medicine to join their fight to "knock the grasp of this devil fish" that is "leaving no method allowed to them, within legal bounds, unused to rob the sick and suffering of the United States." Joseph Helfman, the editor of *Bulletin of Pharmacy*, spoke on "Abuses of Proprietary Rights in Pharmacy" and called

for scorched-earth resistance to foreign drug companies that priced products in the United States at significant markups over prices in Canada and
Europe.

The druggists and their allies had grounds for optimism as the twentieth
century opened. The early progressives injected life into the country's anti-
monopoly tradition and called for the tighter regulation of industry. Opposition to foreign monopoly power seemed to be growing stronger by the
year. By 1900, more than 90 percent of U.S. patents on chemical processes
and products were issued to foreign firms and conglomerates. The Spanish-
American War of 1898 had unleashed a jingoism that dovetailed with these
concerns, as did a flourishing new form of journalism known as muckraking
that focused on the depredations of the modern corporation.

The spirited public mood was reflected in a 1902 article by Wilhelm
Bodemann, chair of the Illinois State Board of Pharmacy. Widely distributed by NARD, the piece detailed the multiple insults inflicted by Bayer
on the United States. The Bayer patents, Bodemann argued, were immoral
because they blocked related research by American scientists, exploited the
U.S. legal system to pick the country's pockets, and forced upon its people
the final humiliation of knowing monopoly prices paid in dollars were pad-
ding the foreign currency vaults of "that effete monarchy" in Berlin.

In October 1903, NARD gathered for its first national convention in
Washington, D.C. During the proceedings, the group sent a delegation to
the White House, where Theodore Roosevelt listened to their complaint that
Bayer was fleecing Americans in a way no other country would allow. The
delegation left the meeting in high spirits, believing that Roosevelt was on
their side. What they didn't know was that the president was being pressured
from the other side by the U.S. patent commissioner, Frederick I. Allen,
who believed the druggists petty and thought the Aspirin patent should be
protected until its natural expiration in 1916. Allen counseled Roosevelt to
adhere to the nation's obligations as a signatory to the 1883 Paris Convention, which mandated that nations grant foreign firms the same intellectual
property protections as domestic firms. The fact that U.S. drug companies
generally did not seek these protections was irrelevant.

When Allen's counsel to Roosevelt was leaked, *The Western Druggist* called for the commissioner's immediate firing. "The promptings of avarice and the rule of might as against right," the paper said, "shall not be part of our national or international policy."

The thriving underground trade in generic and smuggled Bayer Aspirin and Phenacetine had a fatal flaw: quality control. While many professional druggists dealt only in Bayer-produced pills and active ingredients smuggled directly from Europe and Canada, others bought their headache powders from bootleggers and middlemen who replaced one of the Bayer ingredients, acetophenetidin, with a mixture of talcum and acetanilide, a dangerous heart suppressant that cost a third as much.

Reports of deaths and illness caused by acetanilide received national exposure in *Collier's* magazine in the fall of 1905. The revelation was made as part of an investigative series about the patent medicine industry by Samuel Hopkins Adams, entitled "The Great American Fraud." In turning the public's attention to questions of drug regulation and safety, the articles had the effect of recasting the politics of the Bayer patent war. Now the story was less black and white; greed was evident on both sides. Citing the series, Bayer's representatives positioned the firm as the protector of standards and public safety. It was an effective strategy, both with the public and with a medical establishment that was already nervous about accusations it was allying with criminals engaged in potentially harmful adulteration. When leading medical journals started distancing themselves from the druggists' crusade, Bayer's U.S. lawyers sent copies of the editorials to seventy-five thousand doctors around the country. The druggists countered with mailers of their own. An editorial in *The Druggists Circular* argued that the Germans were ultimately to blame for any harm resulting from adulteration: an ethical U.S. drug firm, after all, would not have engaged in the monopoly pricing that led to the smuggling and powder cutting in the first place. But the larger ethical firms were unusually quiet on the issue. Like the doctors, they feared association with criminality as well as Bayer's lawyers. Some of them—covetous of Bayer's monopoly profits and success in the courts—were also beginning the process of embracing Stewart's once-heretical ideas about "ethical patenting."

The sudden and unexpected turn in the Bayer patent war caused by the *Collier's* series proved decisive in shaping and passing the Pure Food and Drug Act of 1906. Usually understood as the child of Upton Sinclair's depiction of the Chicago meatpacking industry in *The Jungle*, the 1906 law was just as much a child of Adams's *Collier's* series and other contemporaneous reports of deaths from black market Aspirin. The law made the selling of fake drugs a federal offense and required mandatory labeling for drugs containing a number of ingredients, including acetanilide.

What the law did not do, to Bayer's chagrin, was end or even much reduce the American black market in Aspirin. In 1909, with seven years left on Bayer's patent, it was estimated that 75 percent of all Aspirin sold in the United States was smuggled in from Canada and Europe after being purchased at much lower, non-monopoly prices abroad.

There were plenty of ways to die young in the overcrowded slums of the 1890s, but few were as dreaded as the death caused by respiratory diphtheria. The fearsome bacteria preyed on small children five or younger, with infection spread through sneezes and coughs. A sore throat and raspy voice were the first signs, followed by a thick mucous membrane that took root in the back of the throat. As the membrane grew, breathing became difficult, then excruciating; in about a quarter of cases, the afflicted slowly suffocated to death in their beds. Medical efforts to save diphtheria's young victims resulted in the first primitive attempts at medical intubation using rubber tubes. In the immigrant tenements where the disease was most prevalent, the airborne germ was known as the strangling angel.

Great hope greeted reports in 1888 that researches at the Pasteur Institute in Paris had produced a moderately effective diphtheria antiserum from infected animal plasma. The antiserum was effective for only two weeks, but it could blunt outbreaks, and it was better than nothing. In Germany, a rival group of researchers began work to refine the process, led by a scientist and entrepreneur named Emil von Behring then in the employ of Hoechst, a Frankfurt-based drug company. In 1895, Behring quietly applied for a U.S. patent on a method for harvesting the antiserum from horse plasma. But the claim of novelty was so weak, and the audacity of the claim so far off the known scale of shame, that reports of Behring's application were not taken seriously. "The medical world at first refused to credit a rumor which pointed to a line of action so contrary to the first principles of scientific ethics and morality," wrote the editors of *The Lancet*. In any event, the method was already being used by New York City's municipal health department, and leading U.S. drug companies Parke-Davis and H. K. Mulford were planning to begin commercial production.

When the U.S. Patent Office approved Behring's claim on his horse plasma method, in 1898, the transcontinental medical and pharmaceutical establishments reacted with a different kind of incredulity. They subjected Behring to waves of withering scorn. *The Medical Age* described Behring's pursuit of personal gain as evidence of "a high degree of moral perversity." *The Lancet* took a slightly wider approach to its condemnation, rejecting the notion that anybody was "entitled to be regarded as the sole discoverer of a method which was the outcome of slow and prolonged scientific investigation and reasoning pursued in all directions." The implications of the Behring-Hoechst precedent troubled the editors as much as the specific monopoly grant in question. "No one desires to see pharmacology entangled in a maze of monopolies or therapeutics dominated by patent medicines," they wrote.

The editors of *The American Medico-Surgical Bulletin* argued that the effect of approving Behring's claim was to "violate every principle of justice and negate the whole utility of patent law" and to "steal from society its just heritage and give it to an individual." The diphtheria patent, they continued,

> stands in the way of all work in the same field and hinders progress. It can never in any manner encourage future discovery. It has its menacing hand up against seekers of new serums. It invades a department of research where work was going on with vigor and where the results would have gone to the public without money, patents or price. If other medical men follow in the wake of Behring where shall we find ourselves? This starting of the closing of the doors of knowledge will prove a serious affair if not quickly arrested by the frowns of the profession.

As we will see, the frowns of the profession proved incapable of arresting this closing of the doors. They creaked slowly at first, then shut with a slam. If this future was just becoming imaginable at the turn of the century, it still seemed distant and preventable. Behring's patent was first denounced in the United States, then roundly ignored. So deeply was the patent loathed, Hoechst's lawyers didn't bother to sue the companies that continued manufacturing the serum using Behring's method without interruption. When Behring was awarded the Nobel Prize in 1901, the AMA *Journal* editorialized that his attempt to "reap the benefit" of the diphtheria vaccine should "preclude him from award for humanitarian advances."

A member of the old upper class, Behring did not need the money anyway, and he died a wealthy man in 1917. In the years after his death, Hoechst, the company he helped build, continued to grow, eventually merging with five other companies to form IG Farben, a keystone industrial cartel of the Nazi state and war machine. Behring's memory survived the consolidation, and his legend in Germany approached the level of Pasteur's in France. In 1940, the Nazi Party held a grand ceremony in his honor at Marburg University. In the book published to commemorate the event, the Nazi health minister, Leonardo Conti, describes Behring as "an immortal representative of German diligence, German science and German culture." Adolf Hitler himself contributed a statement to the volume, lauding the first great international villain of monopoly medicine as a credit to the Reich.

Living up to its reputation as the bad boy of ethical drug makers, Parke-Davis followed the Germans' example in pushing against the boundaries of the patent taboo in the early 1900s. The most controversial episode involved the company's patents on a purified form of the hormone adrenaline that drastically reduced bleeding during minor surgeries. Made from the glands of animals, Adrenalin (as Parke-Davis branded it) was first made in the New York City laboratory of a Japanese expatriate chemist named Jokichi Takamine. The U.S. Patent Office's Division of Chemistry rejected Takamine's first three patent applications on the grounds that they covered "a product of nature, merely isolated by the applicant." It was only with help from a team of patent lawyers that Takamine was finally granted a number of product and process patents in 1903. He promptly sold them to Parke-Davis, which the following year sold $200,000 worth of Adrenalin behind the claim, "As cocaine is to painless surgery, so Adrenalin [is] to bloodless surgery."

The company's attempt to corner the market on a medically important discovery did not sit well with its competitors, a number of whom entered the market in violation of the Parke-Davis patents. Led by Eli Lilly and the H. K. Mulford Company, the competition cut the market for patented Adrenalin by roughly half in 1905. Before Parke-Davis had posted that year's disappointing sales numbers, it filed an infringement suit against H. K. Mulford in the U.S. Circuit Court for the Southern District of New York. Mulford welcomed the opportunity to take on the company and stop the Germanification of the U.S. pharmaceutical industry. In court, Parke-Davis was represented by a team that included a number of lawyers last seen defending Bayer during the Aspirin wars. Mulford, representing the ethical old guard, hired the leading patent firm in Philadelphia, Howson & Howson, and entered the courtroom continuing "to trumpet its high-minded stance against drug product patents," writes the legal historian Christopher Beauchamp.

For five years, lawyers for the two companies submitted thousands of pages of competing legal and scientific evidence. In 1911, the case landed before a thirty-nine-year-old judge named Billings Learned Hand. The Second District was the primary venue for patent cases, and Hand had adjudicated more than a dozen during his first two years on the bench. But none had prepared Hand for the bewildering scientific, technical, and legal complexities surrounding the inventing, processing, and patenting of Adrenalin. In the end, Hand upheld Parke-Davis's argument that Adrenalin was a "novel composition of matter" (patentable) and not a "product of nature" (unpatentable). In delivering a judgment, Hand admitted his struggles to master the technical and scientific issues involved and called for the creation of a specialized patent court supported by neutral technical advisers with expertise.[9]

---

9. This idea would be taken up and championed by drug companies in the 1950s as a way to circumvent liberal federal judges—especially those of a New Deal cast who populated the Southern District. The goal was finally achieved with the establishment of the patent-focused Court of Appeals for the Federal Circuit in December 1981.

✦

It was around the time of Hand's decision that Francis Stewart was winding down a long career spent at the contentious outer boundary of the ethical paradigm. Although Stewart had been the first to openly question the patent taboo in the 1880s, he had since changed his mind and returned to his youthful rejection of medical patents. After closely observing how the possession and pursuit of monopoly influenced the research and business of pharmaceuticals—as practiced by the German firms, and his own company of Parke-Davis—his swan song was a warning that patents did more harm than they could ever do good. In a report written during his final 1909 chairmanship of the American Pharmaceutical Association's Committee on Patents and Trademarks, he argued that patents blocked competition, suppressed innovation, and incentivized companies to delay publication and otherwise obstruct the free flow of information that is central to the scientific enterprise. Monopolies, Stewart concluded, "make the existence of *professional* pharmacy impossible."

However, it was too late. Stewart's earlier efforts on behalf of ethical patenting had set in motion an inertial shift already visible within the house of medicine. In 1909, the gatekeepers at the American Medical Association politely rejected Stewart's call for a ban on medical process and product patents, calling such a sweeping policy "impractical." Over the next five years, the AMA amended its bylaws to permit a greater array of medical patents. It justified the decision with a resolution allowing the Board of Trustees to hold patents on the inventor's behalf, provided "neither the American Medical Association nor the patentee shall receive remuneration from these patents." To accept a dollar from such a patent, the Board declared, was "unprofessional." The AMA would spend the remaining prewar years debating various proposals for the creation of a central agency responsible for the "ethical" management of the nation's medical intellectual property. None ever came to fruition, and the project was abandoned in 1916.

✦

As war with the Central Powers drew near, a final controversy drew attention to the German firms' sophisticated use of industrial patent strategies to protect drug monopolies. The episode involved the antisyphilitic drug Salvarsan, also known as the magic bullet, patented by Hoechst in 1910. The drug was in wide use in 1914 when the British naval blockade started to affect German shipping traffic. As the naval noose tightened, U-boats began arriving in New York Harbor with sporadic and dwindling shipments of German goods, including patented drugs.

The supply shock led to a sobering realization: American researchers had no idea how to manufacture Salvarsan. Beginning in 1915, researchers at Philadelphia's Dermatological Research Laboratories initiated a crash program to synthesize the drug based on information in the original Hoechst patent application. They found the task far more difficult than expected. Not only was the information intentionally vague and partial, it was embedded in a larger patent thicket, masterfully constructed by Hoechst's lawyers. In 1916, after the researchers succeeded in synthesizing a generic version of the drug, the director of the Philadelphia lab, Dr. Jay Frank Schamberg, approached Hoechst's New York representative about acquiring manufacturing rights. When Hoechst denied the request, Schamberg proceeded to manufacture off-label Salvarsan anyway.

By then, anti-German sentiment approached wartime levels of hysteria, and it took a special kind of confidence to defend the Salvarsan patent in this atmosphere. But H. A. Metz and Company, the New York firm retained by Bayer and Hoechst, had pugilistic instincts and confidence to spare. Its founding director, Herman August Metz, was famed for a zealous commitment to protecting drug patents—even on the cusp of war and at the expense of Americans suffering with syphilis.

Metz's contract to defend Hoechst's patents was short-lived. The matter was settled, together with every other German patent dispute, by America's entry into the European war on April 6, 1917. Within days Woodrow Wilson established the Office of Alien Property and ordered its director, A. Mitchell Palmer, to confiscate all German corporate investments, including intellectual property. Palmer's haul included thousands of patents and trademarks held by German chemical and pharmaceutical interests. The

U.S. government wasted no time in licensing them far and wide to American firms of every size. Many licenses were attached to federal contracts that put two hundred previously imported drugs into domestic mass production. But Washington's generosity with formerly German patents was not the model adopted by a rapidly expanding industry. Following the Armistice of 1918, it would become apparent that America's "ethical" drug companies had absorbed more from their German counterparts than the branded product lines expropriated during the war.

Three

DEATH OF THE TABOO

Sunshine in a Bottle

THE GREAT WAR WAS A SHORT ONE FOR THE UNITED STATES. But in sixteen months of fighting alongside the Entente powers, 116,000 American soldiers were killed. Contemporaries grasped that a break had occurred, forming two distinct periods in the political and cultural life of the country. The defining novel of the prewar decade was Upton Sinclair's *The Jungle*, a work of social protest and journalism that captured the tone and preoccupations of the Progressive Era. Sinclair's depiction of the Chicago meatpacking industry will forever be paired with the Pure Food and Drug Act of 1906, signed by Teddy Roosevelt six months after the novel's publication. In the postwar decade, the shrunken public imagination and concerns of the Harding Era were indelibly recorded by the other Sinclair of American literature. Sinclair Lewis's 1922 novel *Babbitt* depicted America's stultifying embrace of the idea, expressed with pith by Calvin Coolidge in 1925, that the country's natural concern is not civic duty or social improvement, but the business of business.

The celebration of commerce and its values colored the drug patent debate when it resumed shortly after the war. But the main theater of this debate shifted from the drug companies to the American university, where a collision of science and commerce spurred development of institutions and mores to manage and rationalize the new business of "ethical" academic patenting. Together, the worlds of academic science, organized medicine, and drug companies initiated the process of revising and shaking off the honor codes that had long buffered them from the crass commercialism of other industries and their own worst natures.

The context for this shift was the maturation of scientific medicine. New research fields were extending the vistas of medical science in every direction, but conducting this research cost money and required expertise. This reality drew academic researchers, medical gatekeepers, and drug companies closer together by necessity. The only guidebooks on hand for ordering these new relationships, however, amounted to a long list of restrictions and negative commandments dating to Hippocrates. The process of formulating and establishing new rules and codes would occur in fits and starts during the interwar decades, eventually supplanting the "ethical" system that had provided medicine and drug making with identity and purpose since Benjamin Rush collected leeches in the swamps outside Philadelphia.

As drug companies took their place alongside other modern research-based industries, they turned cautiously to long-taboo arguments about the uses of intellectual property. On the academic side, scientists in search of funding streams wondered if patenting and licensing models might be devised that retained the old idealism and did not open the door to unscientific avarice. Both sides settled on a similar two-pronged justification for exploring "ethical" patenting: First, holding exclusive rights on inventions could help pay for more research and hire more scientists; second, by limiting production to trustworthy manufacturers, drug companies could wield patent monopolies in the name of public safety.

The ensuing battle over the legitimization of ethical patenting was wrapped in an irony. The academic hardliners most opposed to patenting and industry partnerships remained under the influence of a romantic vision of pure research associated with the great German universities. Yet it was the products of these same universities who arrived in America like visitors from the future to demonstrate how medical inventions could be harnessed to the pursuit of maximum profit and market power. The monopolies established by doctorates from Heidelberg and Munich during the late nineteenth century would shape the U.S. drug patent debate in life and death. By smashing the German intellectual property piñata and seeding U.S. companies with the contents, the government cleared entire research areas of ingeniously complex German patent thickets and facilitated the very industry-academic partnerships that proved to be the graveyards of the patent taboo. Following the licensing of the German patents, writes the historian Nicolas Rasmussen, industry "collaborations with university life scientists became more common [and] drug companies were forced to rely heavily upon their links with universities both for new drug discovery and for clinical trials."

What followed was a coevolution of institutional cultures, with modernizing drug companies leading an awkward dance of legitimacy with academic research partners. Once again it was Sinclair Lewis who processed this as art in real time. His 1925 novel *Arrowsmith* chronicles the disillusionment of a young academic scientist who rejects the hybridization of business and medical science and flees to pursue knowledge on his own terms in a laboratory shack, deep in the Vermont woods.

Flying a kite in the rain one night in 1752, Ben Franklin demonstrated that lightning could be directed. But despite the old saying that emerged from the famous experiment, he never captured anything in a bottle. It was a Wisconsin biochemist named Harry Steenbock who literalized the phrase by distilling and capping something as elemental as the thunderbolt: sunlight.

Steenbock's discovery occurred during a 1923 investigation into the causes of rickets, a bone disease associated with vitamin D deficiency. He observed that rats deprived of sunlight and the necessary vitamins routinely developed the condition, but rats similarly deprived in one particular cage in his lab never did. While attempting to isolate the cause, Steenbock tested a coating of sawdust in the cage of the healthy rats. It turned out to be rich in vitamin D; the rats had been eating it. He then traced the source of the vitamin D to light emanating from the laboratory's new quartz-vapor lamp: its ultraviolet rays had produced significant amounts of the "sunshine vitamin" crucial to human health.

The discovery secured Steenbock's place in medical history, but there is every reason to believe the young professor's mind was on other things: namely table butter and the challenge it faced from an upstart oleomargarine industry. His loyalty to butter and his determination to block the infusion of its artificial rivals with vitamin D would accelerate the emergence of a post-taboo world of academic-industry partnerships and university patenting.

Steenbock grew up on a family dairy farm in eastern Wisconsin and earned all of his degrees at the University of Wisconsin at Madison. In 1908, he was hired by the university's department of agricultural chemistry to tackle the problems of the state dairy industry that funded most of its work. Steenbock, ever the Wisconsin farm boy, saw himself as working for the industry that raised him and provided a living for nearly everyone he knew and loved. His discovery put him in a position to keep vitamin D out of the enemy hands of the oleomargarine industry. The new butter substitutes were cheaper than real butter, but they lacked vitamins, severely limiting their appeal. The weight of responsibility to keep it this way fell heavy on Steenbock. Several years earlier, he'd developed a method for producing a concentrated form of vitamin A. When he failed to secure a process patent, the margarine industry pounced and used its enhanced product, now rich with vitamin A, to cut into butter's nutritional and market dominance.

Vitamin D was the last line of defense, and Steenbock was determined not make the same mistake twice. Although the situation was urgent, Steenbock knew he could not patent his irradiation method himself. He believed in the ethical code that drew a clear line between research and private gain; anything that blurred that line also risked his reputation. To avoid the appearance of avarice, Steenbock convinced university officials to establish a corporation responsible for handling the legal and financial aspects of patenting and licensing. The resulting entity was named the Wisconsin Alumni Research Foundation (WARF). It remained distinct from the university while managing the patent on its behalf. This provided the thinnest of buffers separating the sacred and the profane.

The establishment of WARF in 1925 broke the ethical code of academic science, just as Stewart, Davis, and the Germans had each fractured the ethical frame around drug manufacture. Steenbock was sensitive to this, and devoted himself, like Stewart and Davis, to publicly defending his patent against criticism. In the pages of *Science*, he claimed it was necessary to "protect the interest of the public in the possible commercial use of these findings." To bolster his case, Steenbock cited the recent and equally controversial decision by the University of Toronto to partner with the Lilly company to produce a trademarked drug called Iletin, the first insulin product. The Toronto researchers likewise defended the patent on grounds first prepped by Stewart and Davis: it protected the public and funded future research. Like Steenbock, the Canadian researchers did not personally seek or accept any royalties from licensing deals.[10]

No matter how loudly or often Steenbock proclaimed his scientific virtue, everyone knew he held a butter knife behind his back.

Steenbock licensed out his discovery to companies that introduced a number of new vitamin D–infused food products—except one. He and WARF made sure the margarine industry was denied access to a publicly financed invention of obvious medical and public health value. As Steenbock knew, those most impacted by vitamin D deficiency were poor children whose parents bought margarine because it was cheaper. The WARF monopoly served to deprive them of an important nutritional supplement. This was considered especially scandalous in Britain, where vitamin D had first been isolated and its deficiency identified as the cause of rickets, and where winters in the smokestack north are long and dark. In response to Steenbock's vitamin D patent, the British Medical Association adopted a resolution condemning any researcher who used "discovery and invention for his personal advantage." Not to be outdone, Britain's Medical Research Council and the Royal Colleges of Physicians and Surgeons proposed an international treaty banning patents on medicines. The Steenbock patent hung over the proceedings where the proposal was announced, writes historian

---

10. By 1967, the year Steenbock died at age eighty-one, his irradiation patent had generated $9 million in royalties. WARF invested most of this money in the stock market, passing the interest back to the university to fund research.

Peter Neushul, as a yankee symbol of "a new way of managing science which would seem to threaten the process of science itself."

Controversy also festered in Wisconsin. The university faculty and administration were split over the ethics of the WARF model of "ethical" monopoly, as were the dairy farmers on whose behalf Steenbock claimed to be acting. The veteran editor of *Hoard's Dairyman*, A. J. Glover, penned an outraged letter to the university deans who approved the patent and the creation of WARF. "Why should the public devote money to discovering new truths only to permit them to be patented and their use determined by some corporations?" Glover demanded to know. "It seems to me that information discovered by the use of public money belongs to the public and it is difficult for me to understand how such discoveries can be patented and some private corporation determine how they shall be used."[11]

In the aftermath of the next world war, this critique would resound through the U.S. Senate during a national debate over the legitimacy of private claims on federally funded science. That it was uttered with clarity in a provincial trade publication is a testament to how Americans—even those outside the worlds of medicine and academic research—understood and intuited the implications and stakes of the debate around patents related to public health.

"The WARF was the inflection point," says Gerald Barnett, a former patent official at the University of Washington who writes on the history of university patent policy tech transfer. "It was an influential early adopter of patents before scientists became captivated with producing dollars and IP rather than serving their professions."

By the mid-1930s, a number of public and private research universities

---

11. Late in his life, Steenbock addressed these criticisms without apology. "In its broad humanitarian aspects, it must be granted that any process which can be used to improve our food and thus improve our health should not be encumbered by restrictions of any kind," he told an interviewer after his retirement. "But there is another aspect to this matter and that is the effect which such a laissez-faire policy would have upon the prosperity of that industry which has contributed most to our nutritional welfare, namely, the dairy industry."

across the country began patenting and experimenting with variations on the WARF model. In most cases, patents on medical inventions were approved in the name of "protection without profit," with the nitty-gritty of licensing and royalties kept at arm's length and under the discretion of the board of regents. Columbia, MIT, and Princeton together outsourced the management of faculty patents to the Research Corporation, a private firm that invested royalties in promising nonprofit research projects around the country.

Even as academic patenting became common, it did not cease to be a source of embarrassment. In announcing its contract with the Research Corporation, Columbia's regents felt obliged to emphasize that patenting "is not deemed within the sphere of the University's scholarly objectives." Those institutions with the deepest pedigrees as medical gatekeepers, notably the University of Pennsylvania and Harvard Medical Schools, made stands against the tide and banned faculty from patenting in 1934.

Even these principled rejections, however, were drafted with wiggle room. By the early 1930s, not a single major research university maintained a categorical opposition to the notion that medical monopolies could be benign, so long as the patent holder was committed to protecting knowledge only from those with ignoble designs. The quandary was fixing the new boundaries into place in a way that ensured ethical behavior and noble ends in substance and appearance. Many involved in this process were haunted by the question posed in 1894 by the stern medical gatekeeper Nathan Smith Davis. Yes, ethical patenting is progress, Davis orated during an AMA meeting in response to Stewart's controversial ideas, "but in what direction—that of science and honor, or that of mammon and dishonor?"

In 1933, the American Association for the Advancement of Science formed a committee to study the growing influence of industry and patenting on university research. The committee settled on a measured endorsement of Stewart's old arguments: handled correctly and transparently, patents could assure quality control, deter unscrupulous actors, and help fund research.

But the report also noted causes for concern. Most worrying was evidence that the expanding industry presence in universities was contributing "very unfortunate strictures on other men who subsequently do fundamental work in the same field." Under the pressure of private sector collaborators who were themselves edging away from the old ethical framework, academic researchers began to emulate the German practice of strategically patenting incremental advances, delaying publication, and otherwise impeding the flow of knowledge for commercial reasons.

Arguments over these shifting mores dominated medical and scientific conferences throughout the 1920s and 1930s. The speeches for and against were reprinted in medical journals, where responses and the counter-responses from physicians and medical school deans dominated the letters' pages. As the country moved deeper into the Depression, the spectrum of acceptable opinion expanded. Occasionally, one could even hear defenses of personal gain—the ultimate ethical no-no—as an acceptable aspect of patenting and industry sponsorship. "Bread, or even a little butter on the bread, for a man and his family is one of the prime requisites for research, although this nutritional requirement of productive scholarship is often overlooked," wrote a Yale physiologist named Yandell Henderson in a 1933 *Science* article. This allusion to monetary reward was harder to criticize during a time when actual bread lines trumped contracting research budgets as an issue. To some, the old ethical opposition to patents appeared as the rarefied obsession of another time.

The old ways did not disappear without a fight. Any attempt to justify patenting, ethical or otherwise, was sure to be met with the resistance of traditionalists at conferences and in the pages of leading journals. Ethical patenting and industry-academic partnerships, wrote New York physician Alan Gregg to *Science* in response to Henderson, "[are] proving dangerous. It tends to shut off unselfish exchange of ideas and information, it tends to kill a critical and impartial attitude, it tends to introduce quarrels and bitterness and to consume time and funds in lawsuits. Why should gifts intended for the general welfare play the role of capitalizing a business? And what becomes of the peculiar function of university research as contrasted with that of the shrewdly administered business enterprise?"

Serving a dual role as both participant and referee in this debate was Morris Fishbein, the imposing Chicago physician and longtime editor of the *Journal of the American Medical Association*. Fishbein was a reluctant reformer who accepted the rise of ethical patenting with more resignation than enthusiasm. Obligated to stand by the new bylaws of the AMA, he gave his approval to the group's theoretical defense of ethical patenting in the public interest. But he refused to sugarcoat his views on its practice. The WARF seemed "more interested in industry than in science," Fishbein noted in 1933, demonstrating "how remarkably remunerative a patent may be for a fund for a university. The word has gone around that the Wisconsin University has gone royalty crazy."

At the 1937 meeting of the Chemical Society in Rochester, New York, Fishbein took further measure of the dizzying changes of the postwar years. Republished in the AMA *Journal* under the title "Medical Patents," the speech is the era's definitive statement on the post-1918 upsurge in ethical patenting. If monopoly claims and industry partnerships were to be aligned with the principles of medical ethics, Fishbein believed, order was required. He called for the creation of a "disinterested body capable of viewing the matter objectively . . . wholly altruistic in character, capable of administering medical patents for the benefit of the public, and assuring a reasonable remuneration to the investigator, the devotion of much of the profit to research, and adequate return to manufacturers willing to develop quantity production and distribution in an ethical manner."

Medical products alone required this because they were different from all other categories of invention. Paraphrasing an argument made by the immunologist Hans Zinsser, Fishbein argued that the relief of human suffering and maintenance of public health demanded rules and mores distinct from those governing "the invention of improvement in the mechanism of automobiles or of a shoe buckle." To inhibit in any way the use or development of a discovery touching on public health was as "unjustified as cornering the wheat market." Fishbein observed that such a "cornering" mentality was being normalized by a surge in university patenting after the WARF model. Alert to the symbolism of Steenbock's grip on the production of vitamin D, the Chicago doctor deployed a time-honored rhetorical device to illustrate its grave implications for medical research and science itself.

"The sun in the sky should be freely available to all who wish to use it," said Fishbein. "Yet it has been hinted that there are some concerned with patents on vitamin D who would even inhibit investigators from experimenting with the sun."

The university patenting debate sometimes spilled beyond the professional journals. The April 1936 issue of *Harper's* featured an essay by the Scottish scientist G. W. Gray in defense of keeping industry and its values at a healthy distance from the scientific enterprise. "One of its greatest glories is its intellectual integrity and independence," wrote Gray. "But can this reputation continue unsullied in the clash of competitive sales campaigns of patented commodities, infringement suits, and other contentions of the marketplace in which the financial interest of the research institution is on one side of the dispute?" But popular articles like Gray's were few, and the patent question was rarely treated as a front-burner matter of national consequence for the economic, political, or physical health of the country. Since the receding of the Populists, patent politics were all but thrown to the courts and forgotten.

This ceased to be true, in dramatic fashion, just as "ethical" patenting completed its conquest of the American university in the late 1930s.

The transition from an intra-professional parlor debate to something much bigger is reflected in an essay by Fishbein published in the March 1941 issue of the *Journal*. Its subject was price-fixing among the companies licensed by the University of Toronto to produce insulin. In another era, the companies in question might have worried about the reputational scars a Fishbein editorial could inflict. But in 1941 they had bigger problems than being reprimanded by the official organ of the AMA. They would soon plead nolo contendere in a case prosecuted by Franklin Delano Roosevelt's Justice Department for violations of the Sherman Act. Fishbein did not title his essay "The Insulin Patent" or "The Insulin Controversy," as he might have done a decade earlier. He used a word that had recently stormed back into America's political vernacular, just as the umbilical cord was cut from a post-ethical pharmaceutical industry that had finally arrived, as Fishbein feared, kicking and screaming for more, more, more.

The article was titled "The Insulin Monopoly."

Four

THURMAN'S ARMY

The New Deal Against Monopoly

THE FIRST SIGNS OF EROSION IN THE DRUG PATENT TABOO appeared just as the Populist push for radical change gave way to a more genteel, top-down reformism. For Progressives in the Teddy Roosevelt mold, trusts and concentrations of power weren't inherently bad; they were to be opposed only to the extent they resisted management by technocrats like him. Whether Woodrow Wilson would have developed a more muscular approach to monopolies and cartels after the war is a matter of speculation. In October 1919, just months after his administration established an antitrust division within the Justice Department, his presidential agenda was dashed by a debilitating stroke that kept him out of public view until the day he was seen, gaunt and leaning on a cane, at Warren Harding's inauguration.

Harding had no interest in antitrust enforcement or patent reform. Nor did Calvin Coolidge or Herbert Hoover. The three Republican administrations of the 1920s were united by Andrew Mellon's eleven-year reign as treasury secretary. A financier and industrialist whose empire was based on strategic patenting, Mellon connected the age of robber barons to the Roaring Twenties, embodying the decade's politics with a meanness and open corruption that resisted caricature and left prewar Progressivism looking like a historical blip.

With Franklin Delano Roosevelt's election to the White House in 1932, the patent question appeared set to return as an object of political and economic contest. This would happen, but it took a while. The early New Deal was focused on rationalizing and centralizing economic management, not breaking up concentrations of corporate power. When the managerial approach failed, Roosevelt steered New Deal policies toward the goal of fostering competition, a course correction that required a reconsideration of the country's patent system, in theory and in practice. By 1936, central figures in the New Deal were questioning not only the social benefits of granting exclusive inventor's rights, but the very legitimacy of any claim to "invention."

A second and related development that pushed patents back into public view was the emergence of the U.S. government as the world's dominant funder of scientific research. Early in World War II, factions in Washington squared off over a looming billion-dollar question: Who would have access to the cornucopia of patentable products created in federally funded laboratories come peacetime? The New Dealers, backed by small business and labor, argued that publicly funded research should be kept under public control, with inventions and knowledge licensed widely for maximum public benefit. The position of the Republican opposition, backed by industry, was that private-sector contractors should be allowed to stake exclusive claims on these inventions and the underlying knowledge.

The Democratic platform of 1932 contained much that alarmed Republicans and the business community. On patents and the larger issue of antitrust, however, it wasn't clear they had much to fear. FDR's first New Deal brain trust held views similar to those of his distant cousin, Teddy Roosevelt. TR was known as a trustbuster for breaking up J. P. Morgan's railroad company and securing the first executive funds for antitrust enforcement in 1903. But the thrust of his first administration was to subordinate the trusts and make them junior partners in the centralized management of the economy—not bust them up. FDR likewise viewed leading industries, including ones based on patent kingdoms and cartels, as potential allies in the effort to pull the country out of the Depression. In a centrally planned economy, bigness and concentration could be advantages.

What FDR failed to account for was the deep hatred harbored for him by the men who ran these industries. In November 1934, leading figures in this disloyal opposition attempted a coup against the fledgling New Deal, as detailed in the memoirs of Marine Corps Major General Smedley Butler. There was also discontent within his own party. In 1935, the Supreme Court unanimously ruled the central agency in FDR's plan, the National Recovery Administration, unconstitutional.[12] The NRA's critics spanned the political spectrum and included FDR's longtime friend and supporter, the liberal justice Louis Brandeis, who believed it promoted cartelization. In private, Brandeis urged the president to drop centralization in favor of competition as the New Deal's guiding principle. Instead of trying to enlist the biggest companies, he should break them up. An economic philosophy favoring competition and small business was not only a superior growth strategy, argued Brandeis and others in FDR's inner circle, it was a prerequisite for a democratic society.

In a series of now-famous speeches beginning with the 1936 nominating convention, Roosevelt announced this pivot by calling for the "overthrow" of "economic royalists" whose boots pressed upon the necks of what New Dealers called the "little fellow." The recession of 1937 accelerated the formation of the new policy. Those closest to FDR, notably secretary of the interior Harold Ickes and secretary of state Cordell Hull, pushed him to put these words into policy. In this they followed the lead of John Maynard Keynes, who as early as 1932 urged Roosevelt to treat big business roughly and without apology—like an animal "badly brought up and not trained as you would wish," as the economist put it in a private letter.

FDR fleshed out his plans in a speech delivered before Congress on April 29, 1938. Not before or since has a U.S. president so pugnaciously articulated the Brandeisian position on inequality, concentrations of power, and the fate of democracy. Roosevelt fingered outsized agglomerations of corporate power as the cause of inequality and recession and assailed them as threats as serious as those posed by any foreign power. "The first truth is that the liberty of a democracy is not safe if the people tolerate the growth

---

12. The other major pillar built during FDR's first term, the Agricultural Adjustment Administration, not only survived but thrived. It is generally credited with being the most successful program of the New Deal.

of private power to a point where it becomes stronger than their democratic state itself," he said. "That, in its essence, is Fascism—ownership of Government by an individual, by a group, or by any other controlling private power."

This controlling private power was organized into what Roosevelt called private collectivisms. These clusters of power had become tumors on the free enterprise system; their propagandists mouthed familiar American homilies even as they built a "concealed cartel system after the European model." Roosevelt promised to revive and modernize the country's rusted-out antitrust laws, beginning with a $200,000 appropriation to expand the Department of Justice's antitrust division. It was a needed infusion for an office that had become a backwater in the two decades since Wilson opened it.

Roosevelt declared that patents should be studied with an eye to reforms that "prevent their use to suppress inventions, and to create industrial monopolies." While defending the right of inventors to royalties as a reward for their work, Roosevelt alluded to the benefits of patent pools and open-licensing models in which "future patents might be made available for use by any one upon payment of appropriate royalties." He went on to say, "The power of a few to manage the economic life of the nation must be diffused among the many or be transferred to the public and its democratically responsible government."

Diffused, transferred—this is the spirit and language of the patent's original social contract. It had not been heard for a long, long time.

When Roosevelt delivered his barnstormer to Congress in 1938, monopoly and patents weren't just matters of jump-starting the economy or renewing the republican promise of small-scale competitive free enterprise. American cartels presented a grave national security problem. In 1935, FDR's right-hand lawyer and future Supreme Court justice, Robert Jackson, had voiced concern over Andrew Mellon's interlocking industrial-financial control over the production of coal and aluminum. In the event of war, these vital strategic sectors would be dominated by a private monopoly surrounded by intricately constructed stockades of intellectual property. In his history of modern anti-monopoly politics, *Goliath*, Matt Stoller locates the seed of Jackson's

concerns in a trip to Berlin shortly after Hitler's rise to power, where the
New Dealer noted with alarm the role the German industrial cartels played
in the rise and maintenance of the Nazi state. If not constrained, Jackson
warned, Mellon and his fellow industrialists posed a "menace" on par with
Germany's steel magnates, in wartime and in peace. In 1937, FDR appointed
Jackson to lead the Justice Department's antitrust office. He immediately
launched an investigation to identify concentrations of power capable of
obstructing or slowing war production. His first target was Alcoa. Weeks
after Jackson's appointment, the Justice Department hit the company and its
subsidiaries with a raft of conspiracy and antitrust violations involving the
use and abuse of hundreds of patents amassed since the 1890s, an armory of
intellectual property claims that empowered Mellon to build out and protect
his empire while at the same time crushing or obstructing possible competitors. The ensuing trial provided a picture of Mellon's operation that justified
Jackson's worst fears: the company not only resembled its Nazi counterparts
in scope, it was actively conspiring with them in a number of market- and
patent-sharing arrangements.

For critics frustrated by America's singular tolerance for broad and
socially harmful intellectual property claims, the Alcoa case was overdue
vindication. Over the course of the seven-year suit, Jackson's team revealed
how the accumulation of patents—some the result of in-house invention,
some purchased, some poached from federally funded laboratories—had
allowed Mellon to achieve an economy-deforming stranglehold on multiple strategic industries. Jackson's warnings received further validation after
the United States entered the war in December 1941. That following spring,
Alcoa was unable to meet wartime production needs, causing shortages and
work stoppages in bomber factories. Only as the war was winding down,
in March 1945, did a federal appeals court finally rule Alcoa in violation of
the Sherman Antitrust Act of 1890. The company's patent vault was forced
open and its contents distributed among upstarts in aluminum and other
sectors, effectively diffusing a half century's worth of scientific-industrial
knowledge.

✦

Press accounts of the Alcoa case educated the public about how Mellon and his fellow titans of industry worked in tandem with their German counterparts, creating de facto alliances that continued throughout the war. In January 1942, the House Military Affairs subcommittee opened weeks of hearings on the role monopolies played in wartime shortages and price hikes. In the Senate, Missouri Democrat Harry Truman took up the issue of wartime corporate betrayal, symbolized by a Justice Department suit against Standard Oil that alleged a cartelistic relationship with the German industrial combine IG Farben. The government case detailed how the U.S. company shared important technologies with the enemy while dragging its feet on war-related efforts such as the program to develop synthetic rubber.

The iconic oil empire of John D. Rockefeller struggled to defend its image against evidence of corporate behavior described by Truman as "approaching treason." As in the ongoing Alcoa trial, the oil company's arrangements with Farben involved de facto patent pools.

Alcoa and Standard Oil were the biggest U.S. names accused of working with their Nazi counterparts, but they were far from alone. Investigations into more than a dozen major U.S. companies—including DuPont, General Electric, Dow, and Bausch & Lomb—revealed the rampant use of secret agreements and patent pooling to cement relationships with Nazi industry. Most of the suits, including the one against Standard Oil, ended with the confiscation of the company's patents, followed by their royalty-free dispersal to smaller firms.

Truman owed his brightening political prospects to his association with these wartime investigations. But his thinking on the issue of monopoly wasn't really his own. It leaned heavily on the words and ideas of an influential 1940 book called *The Bottlenecks of Business*, written by Robert Jackson's successor as assistant attorney general for antitrust, Thurman Arnold. The book documented the myriad ways that patents and monopolies constitute what Arnold called bottlenecks throughout the economy and catalogued the benefits to be gained from their removal. By Arnold's reckoning, there were a great many of these bottlenecks, the most dangerous of them being the 162 cartelistic arrangements he identified linking U.S. and Nazi industry.

Arnold's path to one of the most powerful positions of the late New Deal began as the mayor of Laramie, Wyoming. He decamped east for an academic law career at Yale punctuated by the 1937 publication of his most famous book, *The Folklore of American Capitalism*. As the title implies, the book attempts to separate the legends and realities of the U.S. economy 150 years after its founding. This was also the thrust of the "legal realism" movement with which Arnold was closely associated. The basic idea was that the myths of American individualism, self-reliance, and autonomy had become mismatched with the facts of modern industrial society, resulting in policies and outdated thinking that ranked among "the most unrealistic in the world." Among the ideas he considered fonts of magical thinking, bad policy, and undemocratic concentrations of power: corporate personhood and an outdated, idealistic attachment to the patent as a sensible reward for plucky "lone inventors."

Arnold's long preoccupation with the myths and modern realities of intellectual property prepared him to continue Jackson's project to liberate wartime production from the suffocating grips of corporate patent strategies. A scholar and connoisseur of economic bottlenecks, he was not surprised when the cause of a holdup in aircraft production was traced back to a screw fastener patent. Adept at using the media to his advantage, Arnold took seriously his obligation to educate the American public. In a nationally broadcast speech delivered to a business group in July 1942, he made a plainspoken case that "the most effective instrument of monopoly control and restriction of production has been the abuse of patent privilege."

In 1943, Arnold left the Justice Department for a judgeship on the First Circuit Court of Appeals. During his five years as the bane of U.S. industry, he grew the antitrust division from a bare-bones staff of eighteen to an army of five hundred. Arnold's antitrust office was a busy division—and a feared one. Rather than wait to be dragged before high-profile congressional hearings, executives were known to line up outside Arnold's office with plea deals and patent offerings in hand, eager to sign consent decrees before they were named in a suit, summoned to Washington, and thrown before New Deal bulldogs with camera bulbs flashing.

In his April 1938 address to Congress, Roosevelt did more than herald a new era of vigorous antitrust enforcement. He teased the launch of a related research project called the Temporary National Economic Committee, or TNEC. Launched that summer with a budget of $500,000, its investigators were tasked with undertaking a thorough study of concentrated power in the U.S. economy. It was overseen by a joint committee composed of two teams, one picked by the White House (including Thurman Arnold) and another bipartisan group drawn from the House and Senate. In the three years leading up to war, TNEC hearings gathered extended testimony from 552 figures in government, business, academia, and labor. In 1941, it began publishing its findings and recommendations in dozens of monographs. The thirty-first in the series was titled "Patents and Free Enterprise."

The patent monograph's lead writer was a Yale economist and law professor named Walton Hamilton. A former colleague of Thurman Arnold and prominent proponent of legal realism, Hamilton approached the subject with a fighting liberal spirit tempered by his well-known judiciousness as a historian, legal scholar, and economist. The modern patent did not function as a diffusion pump for scientific knowledge, he concluded, but suppressed innovation and provided cornerstones for anticompetitive monopolies that often outlasted the standard seventeen-year patent term. Hamilton illustrated this with dozens of detailed case studies. Several of the studies related to the urgent matter of war production, from chemical products to tanks and machine tools.

Hamilton concluded the TNEC report on a sweeping note that seemed addressed to history as much as to Roosevelt and Congress. "A crisis in the history of the Nation is upon us," Hamilton declared.

If the common good is to be served, an economics of scarcity must give way to one of abundance. The right of a man to his own exists within the commonwealth; he may do as he pleases with that which is his property. But liberty and property stop short at the line marked out by the general welfare. Long ago law joined policy to decree that no man is to exploit his wealth in such a way as to create a scarcity, make for a lower standard of life, or drive a barrier between a people and their resources. The great task of Government is to realize these ancient values in the conduct of the modern industrial republic; to this great task the productive genius of a people must be encouraged to contribute, unrestrained by private claims in the economy. The imprisonment of invention and production spells doom; the nation which discovers how to release to mankind the great storehouse of creative energy shall inherit the earth.

The idea that patents represented the "imprisonment of invention" was not a radical break from American tradition. The acceptance of intellectual property at Philadelphia in 1787 was at best hesitant, and the skeptical vein in the country's thinking on patents never died. This was partly due to the influence of Enlightenment ideas about knowledge and invention as a cumulative and incremental process. The cult of the lone genius, of the self-reliant inventor-entrepreneur, was a suckling by comparison. Hamilton agreed with Arnold that this character of the lone genius, never terribly convincing, had become a self-serving if not ridiculous bit of modern capitalist folklore. But as Arnold wrote in his 1937 book on the subject, folklore is powerful. Challenging the folklore of patents would require telling a new story about invention, genius, and progress in the industrial age. "Releas[ing] to mankind the great storehouse of creative energy," as Hamilton's TNEC report put it, required reestablishing mankind as the collective source as well as the natural beneficiary of this energy. This rendered a much smaller and more suspect role for patent monopolies as rewards for individual achievement. Building this alternative framework required returning to fundamentals, starting with the question: *What is an invention?*

✦

The year before the publication of Hamilton's TNEC report, an article appeared in the Autumn 1940 issue of *The American Economic Review*, titled "Deficiencies of American Patent Law." Its author was a previously unpublished graduate student in economics at Yale named Alfred Kahn.[13] In New Haven, Kahn had absorbed the legal realism of Arnold and Hamilton, and his essay on patents placed a legal realist lens over the foundational assumption of all patent systems—that inventions happen in the present and are the floating achievements of individual ingenuity and genius. If this is not true, then the scope for private individual claims on knowledge is drastically reduced, if not invalidated, and the more natural course for inventions is to have them "diffused among the many or be transferred to the public and its democratically responsible government."

Kahn accepted the New Deal critique that corporate research labs had disconnected the patent system from its constitutional mandate to spread new knowledge for broad social benefit. "From the business standpoint [the great research laboratories] are patent factories," he wrote. "Their product often is nothing but [a] basis for threatening infringement suit and scaring off competitors." What caught Thurman Arnold's attention was the way Kahn deepened the critique by questioning not just the use of the patents, but the underlying claims to invention. "The individualistic conception of the process of invention," wrote Kahn, was "a fallacious assumption."

"In order to look upon a single inventive contribution as patentable and exploitable, one must look upon each invention as an entity, self-contained and distinct from all others," he wrote. If the concept of self-contained invention was always something of a folkloric conceit, its persistence in a century of complex multidisciplinary research was a bald absurdity. The process of invention had become an openly organic and cooperative process, containing

---

13. Kahn would go on to a long career in government for which he is remembered as the "father of deregulation," beginning with the airline industry during the Carter administration.

"within itself the dynamic factors that make for constant cumulative move-ment," Kahn wrote. "The man who brought to a certain stage of fruition the efforts of myriad predecessors may have made a great contribution. But seen in its proper setting and perspective, that contribution is something less than cataclysmic . . . The individual does not construct new chains; he fills missing links."

The outdated and romantic cult of individual invention, he argued, was responsible for the slowing of technological progress enabled by entrenched monopoly power based on patents. The implications of this circular logic led back to the views that dominated the thinking of the founders, Madison included, who acknowledged that inventions "grow so much out of preced-ing ones that . . . the discovery might be expected in a short time from other hands." In closing, Kahn suggested Thurman Arnold take up this hybrid legal-scientific realism to drive "a cleavage between desirable essence and predatory excrescence" in patent law. The article was passed around the Jus-tice Department and absorbed into the thinking of Arnold's antitrust divi-sion, which hired Kahn straight out of graduate school in 1942.

One victim of the New Deal's stringent criteria for inventors' rights was the WARF's vitamin D monopoly. In 1944, an assistant attorney general named Wendell Berge published a wide-ranging investigation into cartels that fingered the WARF "as a screen behind which a group of monopolis-tic chemical, pharmaceutical, and food companies control Vitamin D." Not long after, a federal court invalidated Steenbock's patents in a ruling that described them as "unwarranted and against the public interest."

The New Deal crusade against patents and monopoly power did not survive the war. In 1943, Arnold accepted a federal judgeship, and soon his five-year run began to look like the cresting of a passing wave. Since 1938, Arnold had wielded a power unmatched by his successors—able to wring consent de-crees from powerful corporations and entire industries with the mere hint of a federal probe. He rebuilt his division on a philosophy described by the journalist Joseph Alsop as "hit hard, hit everyone, and hit them all at once." A former head of the American Patent Law Association in 1943 summarized

Arnold as a zealous prosecutor working on the presumption that anyone who "asserted and relied on patent protection walked with criminals."

Harry Truman owed his place on the 1944 Democratic ticket to Arnold's wartime crusade against patent power and profiteering, but he brought a cooler approach to the presidency. This reflected the Republican takeover of Congress in 1946, as well as a broad postwar shift in the focus of economic planning from solving "problems of production" to stimulating consumption. "If the goal of public policy was not to redistribute power but to enhance mass consumption, it was both easier and more efficient to pursue other strategies to achieve this goal [that avoided] the politically and bureaucratically difficult task of confronting capitalist institutions," writes the historian Alan Brinkley.

The Brandeisian critique of patents and monopoly did not vanish completely, however. Patent debates that began during the war gained new relevance amid the expansion and subsuming of wartime research programs into a vast peacetime federal science establishment. A robust national debate took place around a series of questions that the New Dealers believed had been answered in Hamilton's TNEC report. The most far-reaching concerned who would have access, and on what terms, to the fruits of the multibillion-dollar research programs being planned for after the war. There was little doubt that a peacetime science leviathan would produce what one Justice official in 1947 predicted would be "a golden stream of patentable inventions pouring from the scientific research and development conducted or financed by the Federal Government." Whether this stream flowed into public or private hands was the hundred-billion-dollar question up for grabs. The United States was on the verge of becoming the richest power in the history of nations, and its government the biggest funder of science the world had ever seen.

Five

HOMESTEADING THE ENDLESS FRONTIER

Patents, Penicillin, and Superpower Science

IN THE SPRING OF 1869, THE MAP OF THE UNITED STATES WAS still not complete. Twenty years after the state of California joined the Union, a large area to its east remained a geological mystery. Often depicted on maps as an enormous, undistinguished splotch, it stretched a thousand desert miles across Wyoming, Utah, and Arizona. The Green River traversed all of it, flowing south from Wyoming and converging, it was thought, with the Colorado, which then passed through a near-mythical gorge that would come to be known as the Grand Canyon. When John Wesley Powell announced a geological and mapping expedition down the length of the Colorado River, he was told it was a suicide mission; if the rapids didn't get him, they said, he'd be sucked into the middle of the earth by deep crevices of canyon lore and never be heard from again, as had been the fate of so many before him. But Powell was a physical scientist; he was certain that rivers cut paths, and he believed the unmapped territory was navigable. On May 24, 1869, he launched a four-boat, ten-man expedition to chart the continent's last piece of what he called the "Great Unknown."

Wesley at the time was an explorer and autodidact of minor fame. At twenty-two, he rowed the Mississippi from Minnesota to the Gulf; three years later, he became the youngest member of the Illinois Natural History Society. In 1869, however, though only thirty-five years old, he was an unlikely candidate for a thousand-mile run of treacherous whitewater. As a Union Army major at the Battle of Shiloh, a bullet shattered his right arm; it was amputated above the elbow. For the canyon expedition, Powell recruited nine hard frontiersmen, trappers, and veterans. They traveled in four specially designed wooden dories packed with rations for ten months. Fearing for their lives, three of the crew abandoned the mission, climbing the canyon walls to imagined safety on the other side of the rim. Historians are split on whether it was the native Paiutes or westward Mormons who killed them.

When the surviving seven emerged from no-man's-land in northern Arizona at the end of August, Powell's fame was secured as the country's last great explorer. Along with official accolades and commendations, he was celebrated in books and popular songs. As a folk hero, Powell was less Davy Crockett than Meriwether Lewis. His signature tool was not the Bowie knife but a sextant. He was an early advocate for Native American rights and culture and had no interest in "conquering the west" as most understood the words. The goal of his famous expedition, he said, was to "add a mite to the sum of human knowledge." His notebook observations of rock strata advanced the study of geologic structures whose sedimentary layers he viewed as metaphors for the progress of human understanding of the planet's long story—"as the stony pages of some great book," he wrote in his diary.

Powell believed it was the duty of government to help complete this book. Until his death in 1902, he used his fame to advocate for federal investments in science, exploration, and research. He considered this among the highest expressions of patriotism. Promoting science for the public good, after all, was the intended if forgotten purpose of the Constitution's Progress Clause. Powell was distressed to see Article I, Section 8 narrowed and degraded to the administrative matter of dispensing patents to trolls and corporations—a farce he doubted advanced science at all. The founders had deployed the clause with more ambition. Thomas Jefferson had cited its powers in disbursing $38,000 to fund Lewis and Clark's 1803 scientific expedition to the Pacific. During his 1869 exhibition, the only support Powell received from the government was a promise of rations at desert army outposts, should he survive long enough to find one.

Powell's public stature as an advocate for government science increased during the 1870s, first as the director of ethnology at the Smithsonian Institute, then as director of the U.S. Geological Survey, a position he held from 1881 to 1894. He developed a special interest and expertise in the west's water resources, and more generally in the field now called sustainable development. Christopher Ketcham, a chronicler of the region, writes that Powell emerged as "the premier expert—ethnologist, geographer, hydrologist, naturalist—to advise the federal government on how most efficiently to settle the arid lands of the West."

That the government had any budget at all for such matters was something new. In the decades before the Civil War, government science funding was sparse and collected around research into weapons design. This had some spillover effects—West Point emerged as a hub of engineering—but mostly the job of "promoting science and the useful arts" was left to the Patent Office. This changed in 1862 when Abraham Lincoln established the Department of Agriculture, a cabinet-level agency staffed by botanists and entomologists, and signed the Morrill Land Grant College Act, providing federal land to institutions to advance "the agricultural and mechanical arts." A year later, a group of scientists led by Ben Franklin's great-grandson received a federal grant to found the National Academy of Sciences.

Powell benefited personally from the revival of federal interest in science. Most of his work from the 1870s onward was funded by the government. Yet he observed developments with one wary eye on the west, and another on the U.S. Patent Office. The government had rediscovered the language of promoting science, knowledge, and progress, but it used this language to justify opening the great western commons to rapacious industry. This was done one presidential signature at a time: the Northwest Ordinances, the Desert Land Act, the Preemption Act, the Timber Culture Act, the Homestead Act. Each law seemed to parcel off more of the country to private interests in the name of public progress. Powell wasn't the only critic of this process, but his understanding of layered sandstone flats as pages in a great book of natural history made him uniquely attuned to what the western land grabs might portend for the intellectual commons.

Powell's first rhetorical pairing of the country's natural and intellectual commons occurred in 1886, during a congressional debate over western water policy. Probably confusing some in the audience, he delivered a philosophical defense of keeping knowledge generated by public investment forever in the public domain. "Possession of property is exclusive. Possession of knowledge is not exclusive," Powell said,

> for the knowledge which one man has may also be the possession of another . . . Discovering breeds discovery [and] knowledge is utilized and preserved by multiple ownership. It may be wrong to take another man's purse, but it is always right to take another man's knowledge, and it is the highest virtue to promote another man's investigation. The laws of political economy that relate to property do not belong to the economics of science and intellectual progress. When research is properly organized, every man's work is an aid to every other man's.

Powell's farsightedness was remarkable. Though others also objected to the parceling of the natural commons, he alone connected it to the revival of public science and the century's judicial embrace of an antisocial, Jacksonian view of patents as simple property rights. The fact that there was so little public science to protect during the Grover Cleveland administration made Powell's concern visionary, but not misplaced. At the time of Powell's speech, the first stirrings of a post-ethical pharmaceutical industry could be heard in the "ethical patenting" debates sparked by Stewart and George Davis. In less than a century, that industry would parcel and claim the nation's scientific commons as completely as railroad and ranching barons divided up and claimed the west for themselves. Just as Powell had foreseen.

In August 1878, a yellow fever epidemic ravaged the city of Memphis. Most fled. Ninety percent of those who stayed suffered "the yellow plague's" miserable combination of high fever, chills, and nausea. A year later, the mosquito-borne virus brought low communities across the Mississippi Delta region. Congress responded with a bill to fund infectious disease research under the direction of the newly formed National Board of Health. This investment—most of it funding a small navy research complex on Staten Island—made the United States a laggard by European standards. Beginning in the early 1870s, Germany and France had underwritten the early development of bacteriology in the laboratories of Robert Koch and Louis Pasteur.

Once again it was war that pushed the government into new territory. During the 1898 conflict with Spain, U.S. troops faced a devil's division of cholera and malaria ten times deadlier than the antiquated arms of Spanish soldiers. A jolted Congress acted fast to expand the budget and purview of the Marine Hospital Service to investigate infectious diseases and other "matters pertaining to public health." Among the beneficiaries of these funds was the army research physician Walter Reed, who in 1901 identified the mosquito species behind yellow fever.

Government research contracts grew again during World War I, focusing on a new set of technologies. Wilson established a wartime National Research Council to enlist academic and industry partners in crash programs spanning chemical weapons to radio. Many of the resulting inventions would transform the peacetime economy. But even as the government was dispersing German intellectual property, it lacked a coherent patent policy to organize wartime contracts with U.S. companies. As a result, private contractors walked away from wartime partnerships with patents that provided the foundation for, or strengthened, the very same monopolies that were deemed liabilities and national security threats when the next war arrived.

The wartime expansion of federal power led progressive journalist and critic Randolph Bourne to observe that "war is the health of the state." But the state was not yet much interested in health. This is surprising, given the conflict's overlap with the great influenza pandemic of 1918–19. In a curious lag between pandemic and policy, it would take another decade, and another flu strain, to launch federal infectious disease research into the modern era. The 1928–29 flu and pneumonia season killed fifty thousand people, many

of them in the nation's capital. This was the epidemic trigger for the Ransdell Act of 1930 that hatched the National Institutes of Health (NIH) from
the sleepy Marine Hospital labs on Staten Island. "The Ransdell Act established the principles for all future federal science agencies," says physicist
and science policy historian Michael S. Lubell. "The 1929 flu broke through
strong political resistance to coordinating research by a large health bureaucracy. It marks the first serious recognition that the government could fund
medical research, not just at institutions it ran, but also research carried out
elsewhere."

The timing was poor, however. The NIH was stillborn into the Great
Depression. A pet project of Herbert Hoover, the original vision for the new
agency had been grand in the style of the Roaring Twenties. The president
promised gleaming research facilities that would produce medical breakthroughs to rival those of the most storied European state laboratories. The
new agency instead arrived in a grim reality of skeletal federal budgets and
impoverished citizens. The senator whose name adorned the bill that created
the NIH, Joseph Ransdell of Louisiana, took to the road to rally support for
the disappointing initiative, delivering upbeat lectures to corporate and medical audiences. In a 1931 speech before an audience of radiologists, Ransdell
proclaimed the administration's unwavering commitment to "preventing and
curing disease with its awful train of suffering and colossal economic losses
to the world."

A year later, Franklin Roosevelt replaced Hoover in the White House.
A polio victim, the new president was known to be a strong supporter of
government science and infectious disease research. Under normal circumstances, Hoover's project would have found a strong champion in FDR. But
there were more pressing matters.

It was a British economist and a Nazi tyrant, not an American scientist or politician, who reignited the stalled project of government research. First, John
Maynard Keynes changed Washington's thinking on deficits and spending;
a little later, Hitler focused the New Dealers on the need to accelerate scientific innovation if the United States was to defeat a technologically advanced

enemy. This need covered weapons as well as medicines. The specters of 1898 and 1918 haunted war planners as they prepared for unconventional weapons in Europe and tropical diseases in Asia.

After the attack on Pearl Harbor, the White House established two crash research projects under the direction of an agency called the Office of Scientific Research and Development (OSRD). One program focused on weapons research and development, the other on treating wounds and preventing disease. Together the OSRD oversaw hundreds of research projects that employed twenty thousand scientists and technicians spread across a dozen federal agencies. Thousands more worked in laboratories run or contracted by the research fiefdoms inside the War and Navy Departments.

The U.S. wartime research complex was of unprecedented size and scope, dwarfing the combined science outlays of every president since Jefferson bankrolled Lewis and Clark. It was all built with breathtaking speed. When Hitler annexed Austria in 1938, the U.S. research budget totaled less than $100 million, or roughly one-third what private industry spent on R&D. On the day Paris was liberated in 1944, the number approached $2 billion, dramatically inverting the ratio of public to private R&D spending.

As during World War I, private-sector contractors received about fifty cents of every wartime research dollar. The government approach to patents on wartime inventions was also similar to the last war. The OSRD and the military allowed contractors generous opportunities for staking private claims on government-funded and collaborative projects.[14] (The OSRD programs to build the atom bomb and produce industrial penicillin were major exceptions that proved the rule.) A Senate investigation after the war showed that among all wartime contracts issued by the War Department, Navy Department, Reconstruction Finance Corporation, and the OSRD, 90 percent of contracts left patent ownership with the contractor. The government received, at most, a nontransferable royalty-free license.

---

14. In the few cases where government and industry both claimed rights on the result of a wartime collaboration, conservative judges decided in favor of the contractor, in one case denying the government even a nonexclusive license on an invention it had underwritten in full.

The policy left a bad taste in the mouths of the New Dealers. During the last war, some of the companies who stuffed their pockets fullest with government science were later revealed to be unscrupulous profiteers; the largest industrial concerns, including Alcoa, used federally funded research to build the very cartels with Nazi industry that now threatened war production.

The war profiteering scandals of World War I kept the patent issue in partial public view during the 1920s. Wilson and his fellow reformers judged these wartime schemes to be far more serious than the misdeeds of a few businessmen. Rather, they were symptoms of a lethal systemic rot that demanded a national reckoning over the relationship between public and private power, one rife with implications for antitrust and patent policy. Such a reckoning, Wilson said, amounted to "nothing less than a fight over whether the U.S. economy would remain free or become shackled by totalitarianism." The reckoning sought by Wilson never happened. By the end of the decade, a scab had formed over the memories of scandal and the Progressive calls to action. This scab was ripped off in 1934 when *Fortune* magazine published an investigation revealing the full magnitude of profiteering during World War I, a conflict that minted an estimated twenty thousand American millionaires. Not eight years later, Missouri senator Harry Truman would gain fame as the scourge of a new generation of war profiteers that he called merchants of death. As many New Dealers predicted, Truman's targets included second-time contractors who had benefited handsomely from the generous government patent policy of the last war.

On the eve of the World War II, it was obvious that Wilson's wartime research policies contained flaws resulting in predictable outcomes. Given the heavy corporate presence on the National Research Council and the War Production Board, the two groups responsible for administering contracts, those bodies naturally adopted oversight and patent policies that served the interests of monopoly-minded contractors. Now another war had arrived and with it an opportunity to avoid the same mistakes.

U.S. patent policy during World War II did not reflect New Deal ideas about patents and public science because FDR did not put a New Dealer in charge of the policy. The man he selected for the job of research czar, Vannevar Bush, was a lifelong Republican with extensive personal and business ties to industry and a commitment to deepening the corporatization of academic research. He was also an unquestionably brilliant scientist and science administrator. For Roosevelt, this trumped politics. The OSRD job would be central to winning the war and required someone of extraordinary ability and depth of knowledge.

Not even his enemies denied Bush's brilliance. As a hometown boy wonder, he earned a PhD in electrical engineering at the Massachusetts Institute of Technology in 1916 and returned as a professor three years later. While in his twenties, he built a "thinking aid" called the differential analyzer that is today recognized as the first analog computer. Another of his early inventions, the "rapid selector" machine, advanced cryptography and prefigured the internet by addressing the information glut posed by the rise of microfilm. An early advocate and researcher of alternative energy, Bush was building solar-powered irrigation pumps in his basement workshop decades before most people ever heard the term *solar power*.

Bush was never enamored by the ideal of the "pure" scientist. He was doubtful such purity existed, and if it did, it was not native to the United States in the twentieth century. The modern scientist, he believed, should not apologize for taking advantage of, as he put it, the "possibilities for serving the needs of a complex civilization." Bush engaged these possibilities with gusto. Before turning to science administration—first as a dean at MIT, then as president of the Carnegie Foundation—he "devoted a considerable portion of his oversized energies to business," writes his biographer G. Pascal Zachary. "Seeking fame, he would settle for money." As a newly minted PhD, he accepted a professorship at Tufts over a research position at Bell Labs because academia allowed more freedom for private-sector consulting.

Bush has been called the most politically influential American scientist since Franklin. On the subject of intellectual property, they are a study in contrasts.

In the early 1920s, Bush became research director for the American Radio and Research Corporation, a young company seeking to break into the radio market by producing affordable tubes. His first entrepreneurial venture ended when the company was crushed by larger competitors with key patents in the emerging field. Bush parlayed the patents held by his failed company into roles and shares in other companies, including a fledgling electrical engineering outfit called Raytheon. When the Depression hit, Bush's shares in Raytheon and a thermostat company kept him in comfort. His wealth would increase steadily, and sometimes exponentially, until his death in 1974.

Bush was not an aristocrat by birth, but he was a natural elitist. His conservative politics never wavered following the stock market crash in October 1929; if anything, the crisis and its fallout further chilled his attitude toward populist economic policies and the Democratic party. When he became vice president of MIT and dean of its engineering school early in the Depression, Bush groused that "the making of a large profit has been frowned upon." He professed sympathy with the hungry and the unemployed and was open to criticisms of corporate excess and unregulated finance. But he never approached these issues as a small-d democrat. He described the labor-led New Deal coalition as a "blind mass rush[ing] on."

Bush's first clash with populist science policy involved the issue that would occupy much of his life: the dispensation of patent rights on government-funded research. In 1933, Bush and MIT president Karl Compton sought a $250,000 grant from the newly formed Tennessee Valley Authority to study methods for extending electrical transmission past the standard three hundred miles. The TVA was finalizing the grant when Bush and Compton added a requirement that MIT retain rights to any useful inventions resulting from the federally funded project. The TVA's director, a New Dealer named David Lilienthal, rejected the clause outright. He countered that the government was underwriting the project and thus had a legitimate claim on resulting inventions. Moreover, it would use these rights to ensure those inventions were widely available and diffused throughout the economy. The TVA's quarter-million-dollar outlay, he wrote Bush, was extended on behalf of "the whole people and, in my judgement, the policy should be that any results should be available to the whole people."

Bush carried an animus toward public patent control into the presidency of the Carnegie Foundation in 1938. The position placed him at the lofty heights where national science policy is made by leaders from industry, academic science, and the government. The move completed Bush's transformation into what Zachary calls a "public entrepreneur," a hybrid of policy expert, businessman, and public servant.

Bush never pretended to fit in with the New Deal crowd by echoing its views on patents and monopoly. Shortly after his arrival in Washington, he was invited to address a TNEC hearing on the state of American research, economic concentration, and patent law. FDR's patent commissioner Conway Coe asked Bush his thoughts on data showing the eclipse of individual invention by corporate research laboratories, which now accounted for half of all patents. For Coe, this required government policies to prevent "the poor inventor, and through him the public" from suffering "the onslaught of mighty corporations" that blocked off entire fields of research with patent thickets. Bush diplomatically conceded that the rise in patenting by industrial research teams was troublesome, but he rejected Coe's proposed political remedy. Any reforms or actions that reduced corporate power would be counterproductive, he offered. "As fine as these cooperative groups [corporations] may be and as necessary as they are to our general progress in this country, they do not cover the entire field," said Bush. He concluded by assuring the committee that, overall, the system remained "decidedly democratic."

Bush's appearance before TNEC raised his profile in Washington and won him glowing national press. But it did little to endear him to the New Dealers. They did not trust the genteel Bush or his industry pals to define "decidedly democratic."

As the wartime chief of the OSRD, Bush instituted an industry-first approach to patents that overwhelmingly benefited the biggest firms in the economy. A similar skew favored elite coastal universities with established links to the government, notably Bush's MIT, which received more OSRD money than any other academic institution. The New Dealers from Midwestern states were especially irked by this imbalance and set to work on a postwar policy to spread federal research dollars more evenly across the country.

Carrying the New Deal torch and observing Bush closely was a rotund first-term senator from West Virginia named Harley Kilgore. For his dogged work in Truman's profiteering investigations, Kilgore was rewarded in 1942 with the chairmanship of the Subcommittee on War Mobilization and Military Affairs. Beginning on Kilgore's first day in that post, and lasting until the establishment of the National Science Foundation in 1951, Kilgore and Bush conducted a political war over philosophies as different as their physical forms. Bush was decorous, austere, and considered his words carefully between puffs on a straight wood pipe that seemed to live in his left hand. Kilgore, a gum-chewing former provincial criminal court judge, was an earthy backslapper whose aides did their best to keep him on a leash when the press was around. He embodied everything Bush found distasteful about populism, but was never intimidated by Bush's stature, education, and brilliance; nor did he ever lose confidence in his own formidable mind in his own sharp intelligence. Upon his death in 1956, Kilgore was remembered as the last of the Democratic Party's "idea men."

In early 1943, Kilgore attempted to get a jump on postwar patent policy by introducing an audacious science bill. It proposed to retroactively reverse Bush's wartime patent policy, and extend a policy of public patent control into peacetime. The postwar science agency proposed by Kilgore would engage in basic "blue-sky" research as well as science focused on applying general discoveries to practical use and product development. In keeping with the thrust of the TNEC recommendations, patents would be licensed broadly by the government to spur competition and keep the channels of scientific research open. Kilgore's plan reflected the bedrock New Deal belief that concentrated economic power was metastatic and the natural enemy of democratic government. To keep public research and invention from enabling such power, they must be held in public trust. One of the most dependable voices for organized labor in the Senate, Kilgore's ideas tracked closely to those promoted by the AFL-CIO and the local unions that formed the backbone of his Senate campaign. Kilgore's bill was introduced in the House by his friend and fellow friend of labor Wright Patman of Texas.

In March 1943, Kilgore opened hearings with a fiery testimonial from Roosevelt's antitrust enforcer, Thurman Arnold. Operating on all cylinders, Arnold enraptured the committee and assembled media with true-life horror stories about patent-hoarding U.S. companies obstructing war production and the monopolies that were sure to strangle the postwar economy if contractors were granted exclusive rights on public research. Alert as ever to the opportunity for a good headline, Arnold hailed Kilgore's bill as "the Magna Carta of science."

Arnold's enthusiasm was not shared by Bush's opposing coalition of blue-chip executives, military brass, and academic elites. Everyone had their reasons for opposing the Democratic bill. The military feared political control of science policy and the loss of control over its research institutions.[15] Universities like MIT, which received the lion's share of government contracts, did not like the idea of sharing them with public universities in the South and Midwest. America's research-based industries wholly supported government financing of basic science—which amounted to a massive running subsidy that relieved them of conducting the most costly and high-risk stages of research—but were alarmed by the idea of state competition in applied science. The patent issue, meanwhile, unified the university deans and industry players who were now accustomed to operating enormously profitable drug monopolies. Of all the pieces in Kilgore's bill, it was default government ownership of publicly funded inventions they were most determined to murder in the crib.

The patent divide was familiar to anyone who had been following the university research and drug patent debates of the 1920s and '30s. Kilgore used the old ethical language when he described his patent policy a safeguard against U.S. research being "perverted to private ends by monopolies and other interests at the expense of the common good." Bush and industry countered that Kilgore's "perversion" was in fact the motor of all progress. They wanted a continuation of the OSRD policy that restricted the government stake to limited, noncontrolling shop rights, with exceptions reserved for sensitive technologies related to national security.

---

15. Bush supported many of the military's criticisms of the Kilgore bill and worked closely with each branch. In 1946 he was appointed director of the Joint Research and Development Board of the War and Navy Departments and later became the first chairman of the Research and Development Board of the Defense Department.

After Kilgore distributed the full draft of his bill, Bush fired the opposition's first salvo in an essay titled "The Kilgore Bill" that sprawled across the first seven pages of the December 1943 issue of *Science* magazine. Written in the form of an open letter to the senator and his New Deal allies, Bush begins in a congenial tone by expressing his wish to "give you my thoughts in a constructive manner." But try as he might, Bush fails to suppress his patrician contempt for Kilgore and everything in his proposed legislation. This contempt ran deep, with origins in what Bush's biographer describes as "an almost unreasoning fear that the mob—unions, the poor, the political left and sundry other 'do-gooders'—would seize control of the nation's research agenda and wreck the scientific community."

Bush spends much of the letter dissecting Kilgore's "radical departure" from past and current government patent policies. He warns the senator that any meddling with patents will be "vigorously fought by those persons and organizations opposed to the theory that the Government should be the owner and custodian of all inventions made . . . under contracts whereby the Government has contributed any money, credit, physical facilities, or personnel." He further argues that the patent question should be left alone until the end of the war, and restates his personal view that the country's success owes much to the "sound patent system stemming from the Constitution." Any revisions to that system should be made "deliberately and with great care" to ensure its fundamentals "are not injured." Rash measures enacted in the name of competition and democracy, Bush concludes, risk a situation where "most industrial units would not wish to perform any substantial amount of their scientific work under government contract."

Bush closes the letter by saying he looks forward to working with Kilgore on a compromise bill. Subsequent events and scholarship would prove this to be as disingenuous as it sounds. When Kilgore's bill stalled and was withdrawn for revisions shortly before Roosevelt's death in 1945, Bush arranged for the ailing and preoccupied president to sign a letter publicly requesting the OSRD director's views on postwar science policy, including the matter of patents and "spinoffs." The familiar language used in the letter has led historians to suspect Bush drafted it himself, with an eye on the future uses of Roosevelt's signature and implied respect for his counsel.

Bush issued his report to the president in July 1945, three months after Roosevelt's death and two months after V-E Day. The title was a political masterstroke of its own: *Science—The Endless Frontier,* striking a forward-looking chord that resonated with one of the country's most powerful, sentimental, and malleable myths. Addressing the report to Roosevelt's successor, Harry Truman, Bush restated the ideas contained in his *Science* article. A year and a half later, these ideas carried the considerable weight of their association with Roosevelt and Bush's commanding position as a national war hero. Within a month of the report's publication, he would be hailed as the mastermind of the Manhattan Project and the man who brought an early end to the war in Asia.

The day Bush released his report, two Republican bills closely modeled on *Science—The Endless Frontier* were introduced in the House and the Senate. Bush had secretly been working with their sponsors for weeks. Kilgore was blindsided. When he called Bush's office to confront his wily opponent, a secretary informed him that the OSRD director was traveling and unavailable.

Before drafting *The Endless Frontier,* Bush put together a small handpicked advisory committee of elite deans and corporate executives. Two of these companies represented, Bell Telephone Laboratories and Standard Oil, were monopolies known for patent hoarding and thicketing. The report's proposal for federal science fellowships and scholarships—in effect, a labor subsidy for industry—was the personal brainchild of committee member and pharmaceutical CEO George Merck.

On every point of conflict with the New Dealers, Bush's *Science—The Endless Frontier* advanced the industry positions supported by the committee. In Bush's plan and the bills based on them, the government could only engage in basic science and was required to contract applied science to university and industry partners, mindful of its proper place and committing to never "operate any laboratories of its own." According to Bush, the "simplest and most effective way" for the state to strengthen applied research and advance industrial progress was to provide funding and get out of the way. On the question of postwar government patent policy, Bush was forcefully clear: "There should certainly *not* be any absolute requirement that all rights in such discoveries be assigned to the Government."[16]

In October 1945, joint congressional hearings began on the Republican bills modeled on *The Endless Frontier* and the Democratic alternative introduced by Kilgore. The battle lasted five years, bouncing between Truman's veto on one side and, starting in 1946, the first Republican-controlled Congress in fifteen years on the other.

In 1947, Kilgore benefited from the publication of a five-hundred-page study commissioned by the wartime attorney general and, later, Nuremberg judge, Francis Biddle. Presented as a set of recommendations to guide Truman's thinking on patent policy, the report examined the economic, political, and social arguments for keeping science funded by the U.S. Treasury under public control.[17] At multiple points, the authors repeated the commonsense observation heard during testimony on behalf of the Democratic bill: the policy so ferociously opposed by industry was a mirror image of its own. In the private sector, rights, as a matter of routine, reverted to the firm paying for the research. Why, it asked, should Washington "adopt a policy less favorable to itself as an employer than the policy adopted by private industrial employers"?

Republicans did their best to dodge the question for three years as the dueling science bills were repeatedly bottled up, withdrawn, tweaked, reintroduced, and pocket vetoed by Truman. Bush, meanwhile, observed the back-and-forth at a growing distance from public life. Although he remained as the placeholding director of a largely inactive peacetime OSRD, he was more focused on resuming his consulting career at a level reflecting his new

---

16. After the war, Bush advocated making an exception for nuclear technology. "This highly difficult matter can be handled in the future much more readily if there are not strong industrial interests involved," he wrote in a wartime letter to the head of the Manhattan Project.

17. In a case of literal genealogy tracking with intellectual genealogy, Biddle was a direct descendant of Owen Biddle, a colleague of Benjamin Franklin and fellow advocate of open science and a republican conception of knowledge.

stature. In 1947 he joined the board at AT&T. Two years later, he reunited with several OSRD colleagues on the board of directors at Merck Pharmaceuticals, a body he would eventually chair.

Like Bush, AT&T and Merck took an active interest in the contest to decide the fate of federal science and patent policy. Both companies were members of the Committee on Patents and Research at the National Association of Manufacturers (NAM), a group comprising R&D chiefs from the country's leading research companies. During the long contest between science bills, the committee took the lead in steering NAM's political and messaging strategy against Kilgore and the Democratic coalition. This required some tact. Kilgore's bill enjoyed the support of the same small businesses that constituted most of NAM's membership. As the Democrats pounded home on the Hill and in the press, the New Deal patent policy—open, distributive, counter-monopolistic—would benefit smaller firms otherwise at the mercy of the larger ones who could expect to win the most government contracts and, under the Bush-Republican plan, enjoy exclusive access to the resulting patents. Small firms understood that patent thickets and patent pools were instruments used by the strong to crush the weak. They wanted to institutionalize a more competitive distribution of public science.

The conflicting interests of corporate America and small business was a running theme throughout the five years of hearings. In 1946, secretary of commerce Henry Wallace warned a subcommittee on public health that the Republican plan held no benefit for "small and independent business enterprises" and was designed to entrench the power of "large and well-equipped laboratories which already have a tremendous advantage over their small competitors by virtue of the scientific and technical improvements which they alone can afford to develop and to patent." Where the Democrats' bill would diffuse knowledge and encourage competition, the Republican plan would "lead to further industrial concentration, lessened competition, and the stifling of small business and new enterprise."

Small business associations could and did speak for themselves. A postwar report prepared by the Smaller War Plants Corporation cited direct experience with how a nonassertive government patent policy served to concentrate monopoly power and benefit big enterprises at the expense of the small. Continuing the OSRD patent policy would have predictable consequences, the group testified: "The large corporations which carried on the great bulk of the federally financed wartime industrial research will be its chief beneficiaries [and] have control, through patents, of the commercial applications of that research . . . which will be enormous."

Organized labor and academic science supported these arguments with appeals to old republican ideals and virtues. A representative for the Congress of Industrial Organizations asserted during one packed hearing that the Bush-Republican bill "offends American democratic principles." Horace M. Gray, dean of the graduate school at the University of Illinois, elaborated on this theme before Kilgore's committee, declaring,

> It is really quite unthinkable that the Federal Government should tax the citizens of this country to secure funds for scientific research, on the ground that such research promotes the general good, and then turn the results of such research over to some private corporation on an exclusive, monopoly basis. This amounts to public taxation for private privilege and violates one of the basic tenets of our democratic faith. There is no escape from the simple and fundamental truth that new discoveries derived from research supported by public funds belong to the people and constitute a part of the public domain to which all citizens should have access on terms of equality.[18]

One of the Republicans' most-used counterarguments echoed a warning Bush issued in his 1943 *Science* letter: if contractors were denied controlling rights on publicly funded inventions, industry would simply refuse to collaborate with the government. Democrats found this logic especially irksome.

---

18. Kilgore's supporters included a number of figures associated with the elite institutions. Among those who opposed Bush's proposals were prominent figures at Harvard and MIT, including J. C. Hunsaker, the head of aeronautical and mechanical engineering at Bush's home institution.

When a pioneering biotechnology researcher with the Rockefeller Institute named Philip R. White was presented with this argument during a hearing, he reminded the room that the country contained plenty of companies who will always be happy to perform well-paid government contracting work, especially when, as is often the case, it comes sweetened with subsidized technology transfer. If a self-respecting government patent policy were to result "in hesitation on the part of large industrial concerns to participate in the work," said White, "this will be all to the good, since such concerns do not need Government support, and small businesses and the general public stand only to gain from a rigorous patent policy."

The prolonged duel over the shape of postwar science overlapped with the first years of the Cold War and related shifts in the tenor and substance of Democratic politics. In 1946, the diplomat George Kennan wrote his "Long Telegram" from Moscow outlining a policy of containment against the Soviet Union. The following year, a Republican Congress overrode Truman's veto of the anti-labor Taft-Hartley Act, which forced union leaders to sign affadavits swearing they did not belong to any radical political organizations.This provision of Taft-Harley echoed another 1947 law that mandated loyalty oaths for federal employees as part of a screening program to detect Soviet sympathies. Within a matter of months, the industry-Republican coalition behind the Bush-inspired science bill rolled off its back foot and found itself in possession of a shiny new offensive weapon: red-baiting. Inverting the accusations of monopolistic treason leveled at Nazi-linked industry during the war, the NAM Patent Committee scripted a campaign to cast the Kilgore science bill as a "Soviet-style" power grab—Joseph Stalin in a lab coat.

Some farsighted members of the NAM Committee on Patents had anticipated this shift before it occurred. In early 1945, R. J. Dearborn, the president of Texaco and the committee's chair, told his fellow members that "everything possible should be done to direct public attention to the importance of keeping science and research free of government domination." By 1946, the committee's messaging was increasingly driven by what it called the threat of "collectivism." A NAM position paper from that year unearthed by historian Daniel Lee Kleinman reveals a playbook centered on dark warnings about the future of free enterprise and the creeping threat of global communism.

"[I]f competitive and cooperative capitalism is to survive," the NAM memo reads, "cooperation, whether voluntary or compulsory, must not invade those basic areas of competition that constitute the most distinctive factor in our nation's economic growth." The association spread this message through mass-produced pamphlets that described Kilgore's bill as "a comprehensive plan for the most ambitious project to socialize industrial research and technical resources that has ever been proposed in the United States Congress."

Screaming "Communism!" at a proposed billion-dollar research subsidy for corporate America and small business was a brazen play. It was also effective. In May 1950, Truman betrayed the New Deal commitment to public science under public control and signed a competing Senate bill introduced by New Jersey Republican Alexander Smith. The law officially disbanded the OSRD and founded the National Science Foundation. The bylaws of the new institution included a "loose" patent regime that allowed agency chiefs to determine patent policy on a project-by-project basis. As a practical matter, writes Kleinman, both sides understood the law "virtually guaranteed that business would be able to enjoy monopoly rights to inventions resulting from government-supported research."

This was the result sought by Alexander Smith and his most important constituent and patron, George Merck, chief executive of the eponymous Rahway, New Jersey–based drug giant. Smith had been working with Merck on the details of the bill since the Republicans captured the House in 1946 for the first time since 1930. Their official collaboration began when Merck invited the senator to a dinner at the members-only University Club in Manhattan to meet with a little-known group called the Directors of Industrial Research. Composed of R&D chiefs from the country's largest chemical, energy, pharmaceutical, and technology companies, the group had been meeting socially to discuss science policy since 1923, when war profiteering scandals threatened to sour the public on public-private monopoly conveyer belts like the one managed by the War Production Board during World War I. In a private letter written after the 1950 passage of the Republican science bill, the senator described the group's influence on the final text. "I found [the corporate R&D chiefs] all unanimous in insisting that this [science] measure be limited to research in pure science, and not in applied science," wrote Smith. "We actually took the words 'scientific development' out of the bill for this reason."

Bush had declined Merck's invitation to join the dinner with Smith and the directors, citing matters of decorum and appearance. "I do not believe that I should definitely plan to join such a meeting until I know that it is quite in accord with what is fitting and proper on my part, for I am still head of OSRD which is not yet dissolved," he wrote in apology. This might have been true, and it might have been a convenient out for avoiding an evening with an unctuous senator whose bill he'd written years ago with the people who paid the directors' salaries.

A month after Truman signed the Republican science bill, the Supreme Court decided a patent case called *Automatic Radio Co. v. Hazeltine*. The suit involved claims that a radio company, Hazeltine, was bundling patents in an unfair and abusive licensing arrangement with a smaller firm, Automatic. The court's decision to uphold Hazeltine's tactics put the liberal justice William O. Douglas in a nostalgic mood. In his dissent, he recalled the anti-monopoly legacies of Brandeis and the Republican chief justice Harlan F. Stone, who often sided with Brandeis in patent-related cases.

"We are, I think, inclined to forget," mused Douglas, "that the power of Congress to grant patents is circumscribed by the Constitution. Article I, § 8 . . . [as a] statement of policy limits the power itself. The Court in its long history has at times been more alive to that policy . . . due in large measure to the influence of Mr. Justice Brandeis and Chief Justice Stone. They were alert to the danger that business—growing bigger and bigger each decade would fasten its hold more tightly on the economy through the cheap spawning of patents and would use one monopoly to beget another through the leverage of key patents. They followed in the early tradition of those who read the Constitution to mean that the public interest in patents comes first, reward to the inventor second."

Douglas understood this tradition was already fading, a process marked by a Democratic president ceding the principle of keeping public science under public control. What the justice could not have foreseen were the attacks on this tradition soon to be carried out by the last professions to maintain scientific republican ideals with something approaching Franklinian purity.

Six

THE BIRTH OF BIG PHARMA AND THE GHOST OF REFORM

I N MAY 1962, VANNEVAR BUSH RETURNED TO WASHINGTON ON A familiar mission: to defend private patent power against the democratic claims of a populist senator from the South. His new adversary was Estes Kefauver of Tennessee, Harley Kilgore's longtime protégé on the Subcommittee on Antitrust and Monopoly. Since inheriting the committee scepter upon Kilgore's death in 1956, Kefauver had proven himself a worthy successor, both in his dedication to the anti-monopoly cause, and in his ability to draw forth the pipe-puffing disdain of corporate executives and patrician elites in the Vannevar Bush mold.

A Chattanooga lawyer born on a family farm in rural east Tennessee, Kefauver entered Congress in 1939 as a New Deal loyalist and the most liberal member of his state's delegation. A decade later he beat a Memphis party boss in an upstart Senate run that drew attention for the candidate's signature coonskin campaigning cap. Like Kilgore, his speech was simple and direct and his hatred of monopoly pure. He forged his national profile with a successful effort to weld shut loopholes in the Clayton Antitrust Act of 1914 that allowed companies to raid the assets of weaker competitors under the guise of horizontal mergers. His follow-up crusade, a two-year traveling investigation into organized crime, made him one of the first political celebrities of the television age. His closest allies in preserving the anti-monopoly politics of the New Deal were Wright Patman in the House and his Senate colleague Russell B. Long, son of the populist governor and senator Huey "Kingfish" Long.

Bush appeared before Kefauver's committee to offer testimony in an investigation the senator launched in 1959 into the drug industry's patent and pricing practices. The former OSRD director was now seventy-two and no longer active in Washington power circles, but his celebrity had taken on the weight of legend. This had less to do with his role in the war than it did his new reputation as a prophet-scientist whose inventions anticipated the Jet Age and chimed retroactively with the optimistic futurism of the Kennedy administration's "New Frontier" mythos. "Our transition from an economy of scarcity to an economy of plenty is directly traceable to the prescience of Vannevar Bush," declared the author of *The Scientific Age*, a popular science book of the era.

Bush did not appear before Kefauver's committee in this capacity. He was doing his duty in the final months of his term as chairman of the board at Merck and Co., a position he'd held since 1957. He was there to put the force of his name behind the drug industry's organized opposition to the patent reform bill. That bill, S. 1552, was aimed at the heart of an industry that had completed a metamorphosis from the "ethical" business of the nineteenth century into the rapacious and monopolistic one of the twentieth.

This new industry would have been unrecognizable to old gatekeepers. Spending on misleading and crass marketing, once as controversial as patents, had overtaken many firms' research budgets. Fleets of salespeople known as detail men haunted waiting rooms to sell physicians on the advantages of expensive trademarked products over generics. The taboo against medical monopolies had turned into a race to collect and defend, by hook or by crook, the seventeen-year patents that had become the coin of the pharmaceutical realm. The huge markups these patents enabled made U.S. drug prices the highest in the world, producing corporate profit margins unique to the postwar economy, double and often triple those found in other manufacturing sectors.

Kefauver opened the committee's first hearing in 1959 with an Upjohn-patented anti-inflammatory steroid sold at a markup of 1,118 percent over the cost of production. In the subsequent two years leading up to Bush's appearance, Kefauver had sparred with a rogues' gallery of drug company CEOs over much larger markups of 2,000 to 3,000 percent. Within these numbers was the story of an industry that had shed its former identity as a self-consciously ethical actor and become a caricature of socially destructive greed.

The drug industry began the postwar era riding high. Wartime research had accelerated a so-called therapeutic revolution that produced a steady march of breakthrough medicines with wide application, spanning antibiotics, steroids, and antidiabetics. U.S. drug firms introduced, on average, fifty new products every year during the 1950s—twice the rate of the previous decade. But these blockbuster drugs were marketed under a profusion of pricey trademarks through advertising campaigns designed to push pills in ways once associated with "patent-medicines" of the previous century. The result was a very profitable state of public and medical confusion leading to systematic overprescribing and misuse. People died. One case that later came to light involved the innovator of "ethical" patenting, Parke-Davis. After the company was granted a monopoly on the antibiotic chloramphenicol in 1949, the Detroit drug maker marketed it as a cure for common conditions it had no known activity against. Its marketing efforts persisted after the drug was linked to hundreds of cases of aplastic anemia, a fatal blood disease.

As in the case of Aspirin at the start of the century, Americans knew they were being gouged. By 1953, more than 60 percent of Americans thought drug prices were too high. That year the Federal Trade Commission authorized an investigation into cartel behavior and price-fixing in the booming antibiotics market. After languishing for two years, the probe finally got underway in 1955, the first ever government probe of the industry not related to the safety and purity of its products.

Harley Kilgore, who died a year into the FTC probe, would have relished the showdown with Bush over the postwar drug industry. The West Virginia New Dealer had, after all, predicted the patent abuses that were beginning to come to light. The industry's explosive growth during the 1950s was based largely on monopoly profits derived from inventions that benefited from government research and tech-transfer programs; even the industry's in-house research capabilities were built on a foundation of wartime contracts and subsidized tech-transfer. Under the New Deal plan championed by Kilgore, many of these monopolies, and the outsized economic and political power they conferred, would not have been possible.

Kefauver understood this, but had taken an indirect route to his confrontation with Bush. After inheriting Kilgore's chairmanship of the Subcommittee on Antitrust and Monopoly in 1957, he announced major investigations into price-fixing and anticompetitive behavior in a number of industries suffering what Brandeis called the "curse of bigness"—Big Auto, Big Steel, even Big Bread came in for the Kefauver treatment. In his statements and introductory remarks, Kefauver delivered Brandeisian denunciations of industrial collusion and economic giantism as mutations of capitalism that threatened the nation's experiment in self-government. "It is only a step from the loss of economic freedom to the loss of political freedom," Kefauver warned at the start of his hearings. A "third great merger movement" was underway, powered by the "competitive avarice of certain giant corporate enterprises."

Cold War politics had complicated Kefauver's ability to replicate Thurman Arnold's approach to manhandling American executives. But he was steadfast in his belief that it was they, not the anti-monopolists, who raised the specter of "statism followed [by] the seizure of economic and industrial power." Though the business press cast him as a would-be southern-fried Soviet commissar—seeking to institute "Komplete Kefauver Kontrols," in the words of a 1960 article in *Sales Management* magazine—he never flinched. During his five years of investigative hearings, he dragged dozens of the country's most powerful executives through tough interrogations that began with the assumption they were the enemies of democracy and free enterprise.[19]

---

19. Kefauver had guts. He faced down mob bosses Frank Costello and Mickey Cohen in his organized crime hearings, and in 1960 risked his reelection in a southern state by supporting desegregation and civil rights.

The idea of extending the "Big" hearings to drug companies belonged to Irene Till, an FTC staff economist who was married to Walton Hamilton, the Yale law professor who authored the 1941 TNEC report on "Patents and Free Enterprise." Kefauver was excited by the idea, had been thinking along similar lines, and hired Till to help prepare and oversee the drug industry investigation. She brought with her another FTC economist, John Blair, who had led the commission's mid-1950s investigation into the antibiotics market that dredged up evidence of rampant patent fraud, patent abuse, and price-fixing.

The FTC investigation had not helped the industry's image, but its findings rarely landed on the front page, and it failed to change any laws. The companies were just starting to relax, believing the matter behind them, when the letters arrived from Kefauver's office requesting their appearance on Capitol Hill. In December 1959, Big Pharma became the last industry to take its turn under the bright lights of the Senate Subcommittee on Antitrust and Monopoly. "We've led a sheltered life for years," an anonymous drug company official told *The New York Times*. "But we're really in for a bad time now."

The FTC's 1955 probe into the antibiotics market ended the drug companies' long run of avoiding federal attention to their patent and prices practices. Not many research-based industries had been so lucky. The year before, Dwight Eisenhower's Justice Department came to terms on a historic consent decree with AT&T, ending a suit initiated by Harry Truman in 1949 related to patent hoarding and anticompetitive behavior by AT&T's research company, Bell Labs. The company's intellectual property vault formed the basis of the Bell System phone monopoly controlled by AT&T and Western Electric. It had also come to form a massive bottleneck to multiple emergent fields of research. By forcing Bell Labs to issue hundreds of licenses on early solid-state transistor and laser technology, the consent decree effectively seeded the nation's computer and high-technology industries. Eisenhower was nobody's idea of a crusading agrarian populist, but his antitrust and patent policies shared more in common with the late New Deal than the

Republican-Mellonist administrations of the 1920s. During his two terms, Eisenhower's Justice Department enforced more than one hundred judgments against American companies resulting in the compulsory licensing of some forty thousand patents. In his final State of the Union, Eisenhower expressed what sounded like genuine pride in this record.

The drug companies began the 1950s with ambitious goals and a plan to achieve them. Uniting them was a shared desire to enlarge the legal scope for claims on what the U.S. Patent Code called products of nature. This had always been a murky legal area for medical patent claims. The companies understood that the next stage of the "therapeutic revolution" involved new antibiotics and other medicines based on microbial cultures and processes found in soils, molds, and fungi. But in order to lock in long-term monopoly profits, the patents needed to be accessible and, once claimed, bulletproof. Before 1952, the language of the U.S. Patent Code and court precedent left ample room for rejecting claims on drugs deemed to be "products of nature," or that insufficiently reflected a "flash of creative genius."

"There was very little creativity in what [the drug companies] were doing and the products themselves were basically gifts of nature," writes the historian Graham Dutfield. "What they sought was blanket patent coverage."

The leading drug companies hired the New York State Bar Association to draft a bill to change the problematic language. In consultation with the industry's patent lawyers, the NYSBA wrote a bill that replaced the "creative genius" threshold with one lower to the ground: "non-obviousness." The legislation also stretched the definition of "novel compositions of matter" (patentable) to encompass a greater share of claims likely to be rejected as "products of nature" (unpatentable).

Whatever the companies paid the New York Bar and its lobbyists, it was money well spent. The industry's Republican allies pushed the bill through Congress and Truman signed it toward the end of his term to little fanfare or criticism. The 1952 law was a milestone in the industry's self-awareness and confidence as a political agent. It was also a demonstration of something other industries had known for a century: in patent policy, offense is better than defense. By the end of the 1950s, the biggest companies were selling well over a hundred antibiotics under five hundred trademarks in a $330 million market. Name-brand molds and bacteria brought the capitalization of U.S. firms within passing distance of the mighty Germans.

The companies failed to achieve so clear a victory against the ever-present risk of a return of patent populism, however. The locus of industry concern was a cabinet-level agency created in April 1953 called the Department of Health, Education, and Welfare, or HEW. Even after the Republican victory in shaping the National Science Foundation and postwar science policy generally, agency chiefs still had the option of retaining title on government-funded inventions. The stakes of this choice were enormous when it came to HEW: its position on the federal science flowchart gave its secretary power to decide the dispensation of rights on medical research conducted in a fast-growing network of hundreds, soon to be thousands, of labs funded by the National Institutes of Health. In 1955, the agency's first secretary, Oveta Culp Hobby, realized the sum of all industry fears by announcing a patent policy that retained exclusive rights on all NIH-funded research and invention for the government. HEW would pursue a generous licensing policy with low royalties to encourage broad access and maximum diffusion of publicly financed science. The HEW bylaws also required prompt publication by NIH-sponsored researchers, a slap against the growing practice of monopoly-minded drug companies pressuring university partners to maximize competitive market advantage.

The HEW policy was not ironclad. In rare cases where exclusive rights were deemed critical to the commercial development of an important medicine, HEW empowered the surgeon general to make special deals known as Institutional Patent Agreements, or IPAs. The exclusive licenses allowed under the IPA program were conditional on the contractor making the invention available to the public on "reasonable terms."

By twenty-first-century standards, the money involved when Hobby announced the policy was small. But it was, like everything else in the postwar economy, growing by the day. Between 1947 and 1957, the NIH budget ballooned from $8 million to $183 million. Some of this money funded inventions whose titles ended up in industry hands through the IPA program. In

the first five years of HEW's existence, two surgeon generals granted eighteen IPAs to universities and private companies.

The HEW policy was not the only patent fire that required tending in
the mid-1950s. The monopolies on many of the blockbuster drugs developed
in the early 1940s were set to expire at the end of the decade.[20] If companies were to avoid this looming patent cliff and maintain their stratospheric
postwar growth, they would have to find new patented blockbusters—either
through in-house R&D or the IPA exception—and defend the scope and
duration of their patents.

One thing the pharmaceutical industry did not need at decade's end
was public scrutiny. The opening of the Kefauver hearings in 1959 was, like
all of Kefauver investigations, a media event. The press would get its first
sustained look at the guts of the post-ethical drug industry; the most dramatic findings would land in the papers, if not beamed directly into millions
of American living rooms. For more than two years, Kefauver and his staff
lifted the hood on industry claims that monopoly prices were the necessary
cost of innovation and progress; a cost that did not reflect greed, but the
expense of engaging in complex and socially vital R&D. Often featuring former industry insiders and whistleblowers, the hearings revealed an industry
spending three times more on marketing than on research. The thrust of
this research did not match the picture presented by squirming executives.
Much of it focused on tweaking old drugs to make new ones that were redundant in everything but the new patent number. The industry's biggest
recent breakthroughs were habit-forming drugs of dubious benefit to public
health: amphetamines and a new class of sedative marketed as tranquilizers. To Kefauver and many Democrats, all this amounted to a strong case
for closer regulation, especially of the $2.5 billion prescription drug market.
By the end of 1961, after two years of continuous hearings, Kefauver began
drafting a bill touching on every aspect of the industry, from patents to advertising and safety.

---

20. Between 1864 and 1994, U.S. patents lasted seventeen years. How that number was
extended, and continues to grow, is a subject explored in subsequent chapters.

The Pharmaceutical Manufacturers Association and its affiliated Advertising Club responded with a campaign attacking Kefauver's subcommittee as "a kangaroo court" that threatened medical progress and American freedoms. A November 1961 editorial cartoon in the *St. Louis Post-Dispatch* depicted a hand-rubbing pharmaceutical executive huddled around a lab beaker with a gaggle of company scientists. "We've got it!" the executive exclaims. "A tranquilizer for Kefauver!"

When Bush finally appeared before Kefauver's committee, the investigation was winding down. The resulting bill, S. 1552, proposed a slate of deep reforms to the Federal Food, Drug, and Cosmetic Act based on nearly eleven thousand pages of testimony. If passed, it would cut the term of drug patents from seventeen years to three; require drug companies to license their drugs to all qualified domestic and foreign competitors, with royalties capped at 8 percent; and ensure patents were reserved for genuinely novel inventions by establishing a higher legal standard of "meaningful molecular difference." The bill contained rules to encourage the prescribing of generics; added teeth to FDA oversight of drug testing and approval; and set limits on pharmaceutical advertising that harkened back to the now-antiquated AMA code of ethics.

Kefauver knew his bill faced an uphill battle despite strong Democratic majorities in the House and Senate. Many of the staunchest old New Dealers were gone; their replacements were made of softer stuff, and cautious about being seen as too hard on a system the industry's public relations firms spent heavily promoting as "the free market" and the "American way." The Kennedy administration had its hands full with crises in Berlin and Mississippi, and sent word that the president could not be counted on to support Kefauver's attempt to restructure the pharmaceutical industry.

Bush knew about Kefauver's weak political hand on the spring morning in 1962 when he took his seat in the marble-walled Senate chamber beside John T. Connor, the wartime general counsel of the OSRD now working as the president of Merck. Connor was no stranger to the chamber. He'd been trading barbs with Kefauver in person and in the press since the start of the hearings, which he'd recently declared "a masterpiece in the art of propaganda but the reverse of what thoughtful citizens expect in a democracy." Bush had no history with Kefauver and had not publicly commented on the hearings before his appearance.

Bush opened his remarks with a joke about the lighting in the chamber, suggesting the Senate find a new electrical engineer. Kefauver frostily informed Bush the lighting arrangement was requested by the camera crew in the back of the room, which was filming the proceedings on behalf of the Pharmaceutical Manufacturers Association. Bush then turned to his prepared statement. To fully appreciate the malign impact of the reforms being proposed, Bush told the committee, it was necessary to recall the miseries and horrors of premodern medicine. If future generations were to see the medicines of 1962 as equally primitive, it was essential to protect the integrity of the seventeen-year drug patent. "You gentlemen have a blunt instrument in your hands," said Bush. "If you use it, you will do great harm [to] a complex organism . . . We are embarked on a great adventure to make life more healthy and sane. Our progress must not be slowed down now."

To heighten the emotional impact of this point, Bush evoked an even more gruesome nightmare than conscious surgery: the thermal wounds endured by the theoretical survivors of a third world war.[21] "A nuclear war would be far more terrible than any war in history," said Bush, who oversaw the programs that developed napalm and the atom bomb. "In addition to hydrogen bombs with their burns and radiation, we might also meet a still more appalling weapon in the hands of men with no conscience: biological warfare. This is no time to weaken our medical system, or the pharmaceutical industry which supports it. Compulsory licenses for all comers are bound to prevent the very kind of healthy competition in discovering new products that now characterize the industry."

There is no record of Kefauver's reaction to Bush's use of atomic anxiety

---

21. Leaving aside its relevance for the patent issue, Bush was likely sincere in his preoccupation with the horrors of nuclear war. As director of OSRD, he advocated for the collective management of nuclear knowledge by the major powers and international agencies. He also opposed the decisions to test the H-bomb and develop hypersonic missiles.

as an emotional cudgel wielded in the defense of drug patents. But the senator may very well have rolled his eyes at Bush's lack of imagination. The Soviet threat and nuclear war had been recurring tropes in the testimony of drug executives throughout two years of hearings, most of them lifted straight from the industry's updated Cold War playbook. In 1958, the Pharmaceutical Manufacturers Association hired the public relations firm Hill & Knowlton to develop a campaign that positioned patent-based drug companies as symbols of a free society and bulwarks in the fight against global communism at home and abroad. "Probably through no other industry can the superiority of our American competitive system be demonstrated so impressively," declared the PMA chairman in 1960. The message was repeated across thousands of booklets and magazine ads sponsored by the PMA, which asked readers to ponder the question, *Who's winning the human race?* The campaign painted the industry's critics as un-American and warned that reforming the patent-monopoly system could only result in a Soviet-ruled Dark Age of primitive medicine, if not the irradiated hellscape invoked by Bush.

When Bush finished his brief statement, Kefauver dismissed the familiar bait of a hypothetical third world war. He preferred to talk about the second. There appeared to be a mismatch, noted the senator, between the argument that only private drug monopolies can spur medical progress, and the former OSRD director's wartime role in producing history-making generic penicillin.

"Dr. Bush, I have here the Federal Trade Commission's report on antibiotic manufacturers of June 1958, which sets forth how you arranged for the licensing, manufacture, and sale of penicillin," said Kefauver, tapping the government tome. "Were you in favor of the patent title going to the companies, and not to the Government?"

Grasping the trap Kefauver had set, Bush appeared uncharacteristically flustered, to the point of pretending not to understand the question. "I don't quite get the point," said Bush. "You are talking about the handling of penicillin during the war?"

After some back and forth, Bush resigned himself to the senator's determination to talk about the wartime penicillin project.

"Yes, during the war," said Bush. "The story there is a very interesting one, indeed."

In the spring of 1943, while Allied generals planned the initial thrust into Axis-occupied Europe, British soldiers were practicing a different sort of thrust. In the brothels of Algiers and Tunis, they contracted venereal disease by the thousand. The infected included many of the commandos and paratroopers scheduled to spearhead the imminent invasion of Sicily. Officers watched with alarm as elite troops fell sick from the same bacteria that had plagued Roman imperial legions when they occupied the same African cities: *Neisseria gonorrhoeae*.

Howard Florey, the Oxford University pharmacologist and future Nobel Prize winner, was flown to Morocco and debriefed on the situation. He carried with him a small but precious amount of a gray mold called *Penicillium*, discovered in 1928 by Alexander Fleming in an overloaded laboratory sink at London's St. Mary's Hospital. Florey was part of the three-man team at Oxford that isolated the active molecule and proved its clinical application. In 1941, he started working on an Anglo-American effort to produce penicillin at industrial scale. When he toured the African field hospitals, that puzzle remained unsolved, and he had to be stingy with his small-batch supply. But even after proving its efficacy against gonorrhea, he needed the go-ahead from a priggish British officer corps that hesitated to sanction use of the mold to treat the "self-inflicted wounds" of venereal disease. The blushing indecision eventually reached up the chain of command to an exasperated Winston Churchill, who personally gave the order to use the penicillin immediately. To maximize supply, Florey recycled the urine of each patient. It proved just enough. The healed commandos opened the second European front on July 10, 1943.

Meanwhile, the Anglo-American program to crack the code of penicillin's industrial production was making progress in the American Midwest. The effort dated to 1941, when Florey and his scientific partner, Ernst Chain, traveled to the United States and convinced officials that penicillin could be scaled up. They showed the Americans everything they knew about the miracle mold, and shared their ideas about using fermentation to increase yields. Three years later, the program spanned nearly forty labs employing 1,500 scientists. Its size was second only to the Manhattan Project.

The breakthrough occurred at a Department of Agriculture laboratory in Peoria, Illinois, where government scientists had been working on deep fermentation technology since the 1930s. This work provided the base for a process resulting in a penicillin mold eighty times more potent than the small batches cultivated by the Oxford team. The effort was directed by the chair of the OSRD's Committee on Medical Research, Alfred N. Richards. In his initial meetings with pharmaceutical companies, Richards convinced skeptical executives that the project had a high chance of success and would repay their investments. The deals were sealed with promises of large cost-plus contracts and government-funded technology transfer overseen by the army. The OSRD and the War Production Board organized the supply chains and cleared any bottlenecks to facilitate a rapid, smooth production ramp-up. The biggest contracts went to Squibb, Merck, and Pfizer. On D-Day in June 1944, nearly twenty firms were producing fermented penicillin. A year later, they were manufacturing a combined six hundred billion doses of penicillin every month. The army could finally reduce its budget for propaganda posters warning against "Booby Traps" that spread gonorrhea and syphilis.

At every stage, the U.S. government licensed out the technology involved on a royalty-free basis to all qualified applicants to accelerate and maximize production. The buck stopped with Bush, the OSRD director, who considered the program uniquely important—on par with the Manhattan Project—and blocked contractors from seeking controlling rights to the products or processes involved. This suited the scientists, managers, and officials at the Department of Agriculture who organized the program's key laboratories. Agriculture retained historical and geographical connections to Midwestern populism that made it culturally hostile to patent monopolies in a way that was unique among federal agencies. Under Harding and Coolidge, the department was helmed by Henry C. Wallace, a spiritual and political descendant of the Grange and the Populists. So, too, was Wallace's son, the New Dealer Henry A. Wallace, who ran the department for seven years preceding his election as vice president in 1940.

For Democrats opposed to Bush's general OSRD policy of allowing contractors to claim title on wartime inventions, penicillin stood as a powerful counterexample. Public universities and research centers had been given a job and performed a medical breakthrough in record time. The government had partnered with industry contractors, both large and small, in mutually beneficial arrangements. For New Dealers, it was a demonstration test of self-respecting, competition-minded government patent policy in action. Here was public science serving the public good.

Socialism the penicillin program was not. Government contractors benefited in two ways: along with the steady profits earned by fulfilling cost-plus contracts for a guaranteed market, they were recipients of a transformational technology-transfer operation that "propelled the U.S. pharmaceutical industry into one of the country's most successful sectors," according to the medical historian Roswell Quinn.

Many contractors understood the getting was good and milked the opportunity for all it was worth. Cost overruns were often suspiciously large—some penicillin plants were billed to the government at three times the initial estimate—and the slow pace of construction by firms with the most resources was a common complaint of government progress reports. Investigators with the War Production Board noted early on that contractors were installing subsidized equipment at a peacetime pace with an eye for appearances, resulting in private facilities "in every detail equal to any industrial building built before Pearl Harbor." Attention to luxurious design details, wrote one WPB official, "makes one wonder whether they have heard a war is being fought."

Of greater concern were suspicions that the largest contractors—including Pfizer, Squibb, and Merck—were intentionally failing their contractual obligations to place all of their research and know-how in a common technology and knowledge pool that had been established to ensure collaboration and transparency. "As far as we are concerned here at Peoria, it has been largely a case of giving all our information and receiving very little," R. D. Coghill, a scientific director with the Department of Agriculture, wrote in a 1942 letter to the OSRD in Washington. Coghill's letter was addressed to Alfred Richards, director of the OSRD's medical committee, who was himself rumored to be intentionally shelving such reports and running cover for the companies, above all Merck, which employed him as a consultant prior to the war.

All this was overshadowed by the magnitude of the program's success. Among those who believed this success held lessons beyond the war was Vannevar Bush, who wrote in a 1958 letter to Alfred, "One can draw numerous lessons from the [penicillin] experience, which apply to relations between industrial units, and between these and government, in time of peace."

Kefauver pressed Bush on whether the lessons of the penicillin program weren't obvious, and if they were, why he felt they no longer applied. How did he square his wartime management of penicillin with his current position crediting patents as the source of all innovation and progress? Was not the requirement of pooling and cross-licensing, the senator said, "an important factor in distributing penicillin?"

"We were fighting a war, Mr. Chairman," replied Bush. "When you are fighting a war, you do a lot of things that you don't do in peacetime. We had a collaboration that was extraordinary. It showed that pharmaceutical companies could put their personal and private affairs aside in the public interest. They collaborated in the best way possible. Under those circumstances, we did what was fair and reasonable. That does not in any way apply to the situation in peacetime."

Bush's admission that drug companies' "private affairs" might be at odds with "the public interest" was candid. But from a man of Bush's intellect, the larger argument was jumbled. The penicillin project did not succeed due to a temporary suspension of private-sector greed, but because academic and government scientists in Oxford and Peoria did their jobs, and their governments fulfilled their constitutional mandates to diffuse science for the public good. The result was a competitive peacetime market for an essential medicine. When the U.S. government reverted after war to subsidizing research, granting monopolies, and stepping away, the antibiotics market was quickly cartelized by the same companies. Given the easily comparable results, Kefauver believed something closer to the wartime model should be the rule, not the exception.

Penicillin wasn't the only recent public science success story involving a breakthrough antibiotic. In 1948, an organic chemist named Selman Waksman discovered a powerful soil-based antibiotic, streptomycin, in a publicly funded lab at Rutgers University. Waksman was baffled that U.S. law would allow the monopolization of a microbial by-product of common soil. The Rutgers administration agreed and proceeded to patent streptomycin as a "novel composition of matter" to prevent it from ever becoming a private monopoly. The university licensed the medicine to all comers, domestic and foreign, for a nominal royalty. The effects were similar to those of the penicillin program: competition and downward pressure on prices. The two antibiotics had something else in common: the drug companies hated them and everything they stood for. John McKeen, a painter in Pfizer's Brooklyn factory who rose to become company CEO, growled to a reporter in 1954, "If you want to lose your shirt in a hurry, start making penicillin and streptomycin."

Nobody was going bankrupt selling broad-application antibiotics, but McKeen's fellow targets in that decade's FTC price-fixing probe—American Cyanamid, Olin, Upjohn, and Bristol Myers—surely caught his drift. Compared to patented "wonder drugs" like tetracycline, Aureomycin, and Terramycin, the profits on penicillin were negligible—so small the bigger companies shifted most of their output into animal feed.

There was, however, one last remaining avenue for making something like monopoly profits off generic penicillin: cornering the medicine markets in countries too poor to make their own.

In 1946, India was on the verge of achieving independence from Britain. But within the Indian National Congress, celebrations were tempered by an awareness of the monumental task of nation building that lay ahead. The country's public health needs were particularly urgent: nearly 400 million Indians lived in extreme poverty, and two centuries of export-oriented colonial rule had left the country with little health or industrial infrastructure. The poor country was starting from scratch. A year before the official declaration of independence, prime minister Jawaharlal Nehru sent a team of scientists on a tour of European and North American pharmaceutical plants. They returned with a plan for the domestic manufacturing of essential drugs and medicines, beginning with antibiotics, antimalarials, and sulfa drugs.

One of these was given special priority following the post-independence war with Pakistan. In 1949, Nehru announced the Penicillin Project.

At the time, drug patents had no legal standing outside the borders of the nation that issued them. In just about every case, this meant they had no legal standing outside the borders of the United States. But U.S. drug companies enjoyed a structural advantage that could play a role similar to patents. The newly independent nations of Africa, Asia, and Latin America had no native capacity to make medicines. Foreign firms exploited this dependence by targeting domestic elites with prices that were often higher than those in the company's home country. The most direct way to end this dependency was by building up domestic manufacturing capacity, a process that required north-to-south technology transfer. The problem was the same then as it is in the age of COVID-19: the most technologically advanced drug companies had no interest in helping developing nations achieve self-sufficiency. When tech transfer did take place, the foreign firms dictated the terms, usually maintaining strict control over local production and pricing, thus undermining sovereignty and development.

This was the dilemma facing Nehru as he issued the tender for India's first penicillin plant in 1949.

Nehru began by aiming high: his goal was a state-owned manufacturing plant under the control of Indian scientists and technicians. The bids that he received in return offered humiliating variations on the proposal. Companies were eager to provide penicillin, but not transfer the latest fermentation technology or train Indian scientists in the know-how needed to run the factories. In the bids submitted by Pfizer and Glaxo, Nehru's proposed factory was reduced to a refining and bottling center for bulk penicillin shipped directly from the companies' U.S. factories.

The best of the bad offers belonged to Merck. The company offered to build a full-cycle penicillin factory in India, conditional on the payment of burdensome royalties extending for decades. The company attempted to sweeten the pitch by dangling access to a certain proprietary "trade secret" that only its technicians possessed. Providing a partial description of this "secret," Merck officials claimed that it would reduce local prices in the long term and thus take the sting out of the long-term royalties clause. Indian scientists determined that the "secret" manufacturing method in question was not Merck's, but the subject of a recent article in *Industrial Engineering Chemistry*, a journal available at Indian libraries.

The inventors of the process were two University of Wisconsin scientists who had worked on the Department of Agriculture's wartime penicillin project. After the war, one of them took a research job at Merck. The other went to work for the newly established health agency of the young United Nations. As it happened, in the fall of 1950, this very agency, the World Health Organization, was in the process of devising a plan to blow up Merck's India deal, which Nehru was leaning toward accepting in the mistaken belief that nothing better was on the way.

After its founding in October 1945, the United Nations began developing a program to assist the decolonizing countries of what became known as the global south. The agencies at the center of this program were the Children's Fund (UNICEF), established in 1948, and the World Health Organization (WHO), established in 1949. Bringing the new "wonder drugs" of the West to the rest of the world was a primary concern; one of the WHO's first actions was to set up an expert panel on antibiotics.

Officials within UNICEF and the WHO had been monitoring the situation in India closely since Nehru announced the Penicillin Project. When it appeared the country was fated to accept the Merck offer a year later, they decided to intervene. A delegation was dispatched to New Delhi with a proposal for the Indian government: the UN would provide $1.2 million in grants to pay for the construction of a large-scale penicillin plant, as well as the technical support, know-how, and trainings necessary to operate the plant after the UN technicians departed. What the UN asked in return was a negative print of the Merck offer. "All that the UN required of India in return was an open-door scientific policy and a commitment to supply penicillin at no cost to Indian children through publicly funded health programs," writes the economic historian Nasir Tyabji. The offer also stipulated that India "agree not to establish links between the plant and commercial firms that might wish to keep manufacturing methods secret and, furthermore, would agree to operate the plant as part of a network of international antibiotics research and training centers that UNICEF and WHO were in the process of establishing."

In every detail, the UN proposal aligned perfectly with Nehru's internationalist views on south-south solidarity and broader Gandhian notions of self-reliance and internal development. Still, some of Nehru's advisers urged caution, and worried that the UN did not possess enough technical expertise to guarantee success. Merck played on these anxieties by making new promises about access to its "trade secrets." The UN countered by deploying scientific luminaries who supported the project to build nonprofit drug sectors and research hubs across the global south. Those sent to India to vouch for the UN's competence included Howard Florey and Ernst Chain, the Nobel Prize–winning developers of penicillin.

But perhaps the most decisive role belonged to the British biochemist Edward Mellanby, a man whose disdain for the American embrace of monopoly medicine was both deep and deeply personal.

In 1919, Mellanby gained fame for isolating vitamin D and identifying its deficiency as the cause of rickets. Like Britain's scientific and medical establishments, he was dumbstruck and made livid by Steenbock's "sunshine" patent and the merging of academic research and monopoly represented by the WARF. As the secretary of Britain's Medical Research Council during World War II, he maintained a strict no-patent policy. When Ernst Chain urged Mellanby to patent some of the methods for producing penicillin cultures, if only as a defensive measure, he refused. He would not follow the Americans into the gutter of post-ethical science and medicine. After the war, U.S. firms would win process patents based on research conducted by Chain and Florey at Oxford, further curdling his loathing of the U.S. pharmaceutical industry.[22]

In the summer of 1951, Mellanby met with Nehru and finalized India's acceptance of the UN offer. The Englishman could only have relished the chance to check the spread of a monopoly system he loathed. But the satisfaction he felt was deeper than the sort accompanying an isolated tactical victory. Mellanby knew the significance of the UN project went beyond a single penicillin factory "free from any private interest." The construction of Hindustan Antibiotics in the city of Pune was intended to provide the cornerstone for a public drug sector designed as part of a global counter-system to the one symbolized by Merck. For the next two years, Mellanby remained in India to help build this system as the founding director of the Central Drug Research Institute in Lucknow, India's first national research laboratory.

The portent of India's first step to pharmaceutical self-sufficiency did not escape drug companies with global ambitions. An Indian firm capable of fermenting penicillin today would be able to reverse-engineer other medicines tomorrow, and manufacture them at scale for export across the global south.

Merck's defeat left the industry alarmed about its future beyond U.S. borders. The company had been isolated and blocked out of a major market, without a friend in the world; even Truman's State Department supported the UN project. The idea of an international legal regime protecting U.S. drug patents abroad, meanwhile, was closer to the era's science fiction than an imaginable reality. This feeling of being alone and against the ropes only intensified mid-decade with the launch of the 1955 FTC probe, followed by

---

22. The bitterness this engendered still lingers. In a graduation speech to the class of 2020, Oxford University vice-chancellor Louise Richardson defended patenting the university's COVID-19 research for the public good, so as to avoid repeating "the mistake of the early forties when Oxford academics discovered penicillin but handed all rights off to American companies."

the emergence of the first celebrity scientist of the television age, an American Mellanby whose achievement rivaled penicillin, named Jonas Salk.

For sixty years, poliomyelitis was a fearsome and democratic stalker of American children. Diphtheria thrived in crowded tenements; poliovirus could strike anywhere, from the slums to the country estates of the rich. It rolled through the country in regular but unpredictable waves, each time sending thousands of children aged five and younger through a terrifying progressive illness that caused asphyxiation, paralysis, and death.

The vaccine that ended polio in the United States was developed with public funds in the most literal sense. Unlike the government, which funds science through Treasury-issued debt, the National Foundation of Infantile Paralysis (NFIP) built a direct pipeline between the wallets of ordinary Americans and the laboratories conducting the research. It was constructed from thousands of cardboard boxes and glass jars full of spare coins and dirty dollar bills.

The campaign began in January 1934 when the NFIP raised $1 million through six thousand community-organized "birthday balls" thrown to honor the nation's most famous polio victim, Franklin Roosevelt. The next polio drive benefited from celebrity spokesmen Bud Abbott, Lou Costello, and Eddie Cantor, who in 1938 suggested the idea of a permanent loose change campaign called the March of Dimes.[23] Boxes with coin slots, marked with the NFIP logo, popped up in every conceivable public space, movie theaters especially, bringing in enough money to underwrite polio research in leading institutions. In 1947, the March of Dimes funded the multimillion-dollar construction and staffing of a two-floor laboratory at the University of

---

23. The CEO of theater chain Loew's Inc., Nicholas Schenck, threw his support behind the campaign in part to burnish his company's image as a good corporate citizen. Schenck was in the midst of a federal antitrust suit to block his acquisition of what became Metro-Goldwyn-Mayer studios.

Pittsburgh Medical School. It was in this lab that Jonas Salk developed his novel "dead virus" polio vaccine.

Only hours after the vaccine was announced a success on April 12, 1955, Edward R. Murrow interviewed Salk on *See It Now*, the country's highest rated primetime news show. Toward the end of the segment, Murrow turned to a subject Americans were beginning to hear and think more about: medicine patents. Leaning forward, the legendary newsman fixed a piercing stare on Salk and put the question, "Who owns the patent on this vaccine?" Salk paused briefly before stammering, "The people, I would say. There is no patent. Could you patent the sun?"

Salk was not the first person to invoke the sun as a symbol for the scientific commons. His comment echoed the ancients who believed knowledge was as indivisible as the natural elements ("as common as air"), the republican founders ("Every invention or improvement of science, as universal as the influence of the sun"), and the medical gatekeepers of the mid and late nineteenth century ("It would seem to me like *patent sun-light*"). Twenty years earlier, Morris Fishbein had criticized the vitamin D monopoly by saying, "the sun in the sky should be freely available to all who wish to use it."

It's possible that Salk had Fishbein's words in mind when he answered Morrow's question. (If knowledge is meant to be shared, so are metaphors and quips.) Wherever Salk drew his inspiration, the reaction to this expression of the classical view of knowledge suggests the public was already souring on the country's still-young post-ethical pharmaceutical industry.

The humble hero of open science and antipode to drug industry greed was never quite as pure as the myth. As a young researcher investigating influenza at the University of Michigan in the early 1940s, Salk was the subject of laboratory gossip overs rumors he was entertaining a consulting deal with Parke-Davis. His boss at the time, acclaimed virologist Thomas Francis, stepped in and squelched the deal. It was becoming common for scientists in public labs to accept consulting side gigs, but Francis maintained the old ways. The arrangement would have obligated Salk to provide the company with data and patents on his inventions in return for royalties flowing from their successful commercialization. Salk had been conflicted over the offer, but with a growing family to support, he allowed himself to rationalize the temptation. After moving to Pittsburgh to begin full-time work on polio, Salk accepted another offer from Parke-Davis to consult on the development of adjuvants, a component of vaccines that boosts potency. When Salk started to achieve fame in the early 1950s, the company threatened the relationship by using Salk's name in promotional materials that falsely implied that Parke-Davis was involved in his polio research.

There's no evidence that Salk anguished much over his moonlighting for the private sector. But it did inform his lifetime skepticism about the industry's reliability and trustworthiness. This surfaced in 1953 during the NFIP's search for companies to produce vaccine for the following year's nationwide field trial. More than anyone else in the organization, Salk anticipated problems with money-minded contractors. He strongly advised against giving one company control over production, and instead advocated for a pooling approach that enlisted "all those who are interested in helping solve the problem of poliomyelitis." Salk comprehended that "drug manufacturers were entrepreneurs, not academic scientists; they occasionally ignored the 'Minimum Requirements' and made cost-saving decisions," writes his biographer, Charlotte DeCroes Jacobs.

Salk's vaccine formula was complex, expensive, and required following his protocol with precision. Each of the protocol's hundreds of steps, he knew, presented opportunities and temptations to cut corners. Along with opening up the process to multiple companies, Salk insisted the companies not be entrusted with testing the finished batches. Salk's boss at NFIP, Basil O'Connor, at first resisted the idea of adding a fail-safe testing layer, but eventually consented to random screening by the National Institutes of Health's Laboratory of Biologics Control.

Events justified Salk's concerns. The NFIP contracted six companies to produce the industrial-scale batches of vaccine required for the field trial: Pitman-Moore, Sharp & Dohme, Wyeth Laboratories, Eli Lilly, Cutter Laboratories, and Parke-Davis. Each firm was paid 300 percent over production costs; their request that NFIP pay for upgrades to their facilities was rejected.

"Without the customary protection of secret formulas and patented proce-dures, the manufacturers had to rely on speed and efficiency to give them a profitable share of the potential market," notes Jacobs. This fed Salk's primary fear. His unease mounted early in the production process when he sensed many of the corporate lab chiefs were planning to tweak or fudge items in his detailed instructions. The biggest red flag on Salk's radar involved Parke-Davis. As Jane S. Smith writes in her history of the polio vaccine, "Salk suspected a subtle form of sabotage. He thought Parke-Davis was trying to discredit his inactivation process so the company could switch to a method of virus inactivation with ultraviolet radiation on which it held a patent."

Whatever the motivations, his fears came true when a number of batches rolled out by the companies were found to contain live polio virus. In April 1955, several states reported cases of children contracting polio imme-diately after receiving the shot. Salk knew there was nothing wrong with his vaccine. There had never been issues with batches produced by his lab, nor had there been any such reports out of the field trials underway in Canada and Denmark. He suspected, correctly, that the contractors were not follow-ing instructions, for reasons of greed or incompetence. During a pause in the trial, investigators traced more than one hundred polio cases, including five deaths, back to the California factory of Cutter Laboratories.[24] A technical audit showed the company had cut corners and failed to follow protocols. After its government contract was terminated, the company faced ruin, its name forever synonymous with the scandal known as the Cutter Incident. An NIH audit followed multiple other botched lots back to the factories of Parke-Davis and Eli Lilly. Unlike Cutter, the drug giants were cleared of in-tentional wrongdoing and given valuable second chances. Eli Lilly, the main contractor, made $30 million in profit during its first year producing polio vaccine for the U.S. government.[25]

---

24. In the 1970s and '80s, as a subsidiary of Bayer, the company would be tied to numer-ous blood products tainted with HIV.

25. The cost to the government was the subject of a second scandal around Salk's polio vaccine. On three occasions in the late 1950s, five companies, including Merck,

When the field test resumed in May, Salk faced no resistance when he insisted every batch undergo mandatory screenings by the National Institutes of Health.

The Cutter Incident was seven years old but not quite forgotten when Kefauver introduced his reform bill to the Senate in July 1962. Despite his committee's investigative work over nearly three years of hearings, and despite all the scandals and systemic corruption it dredged up, the bill was delivered dead on arrival. Heading into an election year, Democrats felt stretched on other issues; few were in the mood to antagonize financially powerful drug companies over patents, even if, as many told Kefauver in private, they agreed with him on the substance. House and Senate versions of the bill were all but lying in state when, as happened in 1906, a drug safety scandal changed the course of events.

In late July, *The Washington Post* published a front-page report detailing links between a tranquilizer called thalidomide and thousands of stunted-limb birth defects throughout Europe, where pregnant women were given the drug to treat anxiety. The U.S. licensee had planned to introduce the drug into the American market in the winter of 1960, the *Post* explained, but had been held up by the brave and determined stubbornness of a newly hired FDA medical staffer named Frances Kelsey. Citing large holes in the company's toxicity data, Kelsey refused to green-light the drug. For two years she stood her ground in the face of industry and internal agency pressure to approve the sedative as a harmless anxiety treatment for women.

The *Post* report made Kelsey a national hero, hailed as a model public servant and awarded a medal for Distinguished Federal Civilian Service. The scandal shocked life back into Kefauver's bill. Its proposals to expand FDA

---

quoted the same price to federal, state, and local agencies. The FTC charged them with price-fixing and criminal conspiracy involving $54 million in government purchase orders. A federal judge later dismissed the case on appeal, citing a lack of evidence.

regulation of drug testing and safety now seemed prescient, commonsense, and overdue. No such reconsideration, however, attended the patent reforms at the core of the legislation as drafted by Kefauver.

On the morning of October 10, four days before a U.S. spy plane identified Soviet missiles in Cuba, Kennedy signed a revised version of Kefauver's bill. It was gutted of every reform that touched the post-ethical industry's business model, and which had been based on years of investigation and testimony. The 1962 Amendments to the Federal Food, Drug, and Cosmetic Act contained no mention of patents, prices, competition, or marketing. Its narrow focus was limited to strengthening the FDA's capacity and purview to test, monitor, and regulate drugs. In remarks that accompanied his signing of the bill, Kennedy seemed to acknowledge the tortured history and whittled ambition of the law remembered as the Kefauver-Harris Amendments, named for its original drafter and its House sponsor, Arkansas Democrat Oren Harris.

"We want to pay particular appreciation to Senator Kefauver for the long hearings which he held," said the president. These hearings "permitted us to have very effective legislation on hand when this matter became of such strong public interest."

With the receding of the thalidomide scandal, Kennedy assumed that the patent issue of such concern to Kefauver, and Kilgore before him, was no longer "of strong public interest." This was not a point that Kefauver was willing to concede in what turned out to be the last year of his life. After his party erased his bill of every mention of patents, he started work on a book aimed at a popular audience based on his drug industry investigation. In his Senate subcommittee, he carried the fight for public control of public science and its spoils into new terrain. His final sentence in the Senate record was a statement delivered from the floor during an August 1963 debate over amendments to the Communications Satellite Act of 1962, which created the nation's first commercial satellite company. In the middle of his statement, Kefauver paused and excused himself, saying he did not feel well.

"After taking a short break, he recovered sufficiently to denounce the corporation as 'a private monopoly,'" writes the historian Daniel Scroop in his account of the senator's death from a ruptured aortic aneurysm. "Within

48 hours, Kefauver, the most prominent and persistent critic of monopoly in the immediate postwar era, and the man for whom business lobbyists coined the phrase 'In Kefauver we anti-trust,' was dead."

Surviving him was a defiantly reprobate drug industry determined to avoid further challenges to its power, wealth, and monopoly birthright.

Seven

THE MAKING OF A MONSTER

THE DRUG COMPANIES DODGED A CANNONBALL IN 1962. DESPITE the damning evidence presented over the course of two years of Senate hearings, followed by a high-drama thalidomide scandal that confirmed Kefauver's lowest and most unforgiving estimation of post-ethical pharmaceuticals, the new law did not leave so much as a scratch on the industry's core business model. In ways that Kefauver did not foresee, new FDA standards actually increased the power of the industry's worst actors by forcing smaller firms out of business. As Merck CEO John Connor told an audience of conservative doctors shortly after the law's passage, many of the reforms had long been advanced by the biggest companies. "In many ways," concludes historian Dominique Tobbell, "the pharmaceutical industry gained more than it lost." On the determining matters of patents and pricing, it lost nothing at all.

This does not mean the industry was happy with the law. It was rattled by the FDA's new oversight powers, and it bristled at the new safety requirements attached to drug approval, even if they did raise the cost of market entry for generic competition. Previously, the industry had been bound only to the minimal labeling and safety requirements mandated by the 1906 Pure Food and Drug Act and its sequel, the 1938 Food, Drug, and Cosmetic Act. Now it had to satisfy trial criteria overseen by newly hired divisions of federal scientists and bureaucrats. The companies were also troubled by the impact of the extended public vivisection that Kefauver performed on the industry, revealing a system in which profits were eerily unconnected to normal price factors like production costs, supply, and demand. The hearings had failed to curtail drug patents, but they had shown the country things that couldn't be unseen and wouldn't be soon forgotten.

The industry responded in the early 1960s by deepening strategic alliances with two communities with their own concerns about government regulation. One was the world of academic research, in particular younger scientists who lacked memory of the old rules and were seen as more alert to the growing opportunities for commercial reward. The second and more important alliance was with the house of medicine. In the nineteenth and early twentieth centuries, the drug companies had been allied with orthodox medicine in opposing the many faces of unscientific and unprofessional greed: patents, trademarks, marketing, secrecy, and deceit. During the 1930s and '40s, organized medicine and the drug companies reunited in struggle against government healthcare, and helped each other negotiate the identity crises brought about by the rise of "ethical patenting" and industry-academic partnerships. In the 1960s, they would walk as allies in defense of the very things they once defined themselves against, two of the most dexterous and fearsome agents of reaction in postwar America.

Even during its "ethical" golden age, organized medicine evinced signs of moderate schizophrenia. In its view of science, knowledge, and medicine, it was proudly communistic. But when it came to *healthcare*—the administration of medicine—it was fiercely capitalistic and antisocial. When national insurance emerged as a Progressive cause in the early twentieth century, the AMA opposed calls by reformers to, in the words of Edward Devine, "devote the fruits of abundance to the health of all." This opposition surfaced something deep-rooted in the profession. Sociologist of medicine Robert K. Merton gently referred to this as medicine's "ambiguous situation . . . in which the socialization of medical practice is rejected in circles where the socialization of knowledge goes unchallenged."[26]

---

26. "From the earliest days of their profession, physicians had organized their practices

This ambiguity was clarified during the AMA's mid-century partnership with a drug industry in the process of resolving its own contradictions.

With the exception of two state chapters—Wisconsin and Pennsylvania—the AMA stood unified against social reform before World War I. It removed all dissenters from state leadership positions and continued its opposition with one voice after the war, opposing the creation of private group insurance pools as well as public health initiatives and programs. During the 1920s, the AMA successfully lobbied to overturn a 1921 law that funded the creation of the nation's first women's health clinics. The doctors believed that the centers, which focused on prenatal and children's health, were an unacceptable intrusion onto its turf. Following a sustained AMA pressure campaign, Congress closed the clinics in 1927.

When the Depression hit, the AMA expanded its political operation. It continued to reject any form of collective healthcare and correctly anticipated that the Democrats would push for government insurance as a crisis measure. In its attacks on the early New Deal, the AMA updated the red-baiting strategy that it deployed during the Red Scare that followed the Russian Revolution of 1917. The hysterical tone of red panic—the opposite of the calm and reassuring physician—marked the AMA's response to a 1932 report by an independent group called the Committee on the Costs of Medical Care. In a *Journal* editorial presumably written by Morris Fishbein, the AMA did not merely state its disagreement with the committee's endorsement of private insurance pools—it denounced the report as "incitement to revolution." The newly elected Democratic president noted the tone of the backlash with care. The doctors' "extreme reaction," writes Paul Starr in *The Social Transformation of American Medicine*, "confirmed the suspicions of many that it was risky even to advocate voluntary health insurance. Coming just as Franklin D. Roosevelt took office, the controversy over the [report] helped persuade the new administration that health insurance was an issue to be avoided."[27]

---

in the individualistic, fee-for-service, free-enterprise pattern," writes historian Monte Poen. "They had always been businessmen as well as public servants."

27. Just as the NAM patents committee's policy during the Bush-Kilgore debate went against the interests of the majority of NAM members, the AMA policy during the

When Roosevelt made the decision to exclude healthcare from the Social Security Act of 1935, he mollified healthcare hawks on the administration's Committee on Economic Security by promising to push for government insurance in the near future. In the meantime, the New Dealers landed at least one body blow in return. In August 1938, Thurman Arnold opened a grand jury investigation into the group's attempted sabotage of a voluntary insurance pool organized by federal employees. Evidence gathered by the FBI showed the AMA had attempted to deny pool members access to local hospitals and threatened member physicians who accepted payments from the pool with expulsion and censure. The group's leadership lambasted Arnold in the press for "promoting socialized medicine and perverting the antitrust laws." In 1943, the Supreme Court issued a unanimous decision upholding the Justice Department's fines against the AMA and an affiliated D.C. medical society.

As it waged an unsuccessful appeal of the Supreme Court ruling, the AMA opened its first office in the capital. It was home to a new body called the Council on Medical Services and Public Relations, created to lead the counteroffensive against Roosevelt's expected second push to add government insurance to an expansion of the Social Security Act. From its suite downtown, the AMA Council coordinated with the National Physicians Committee, a freshly established doctors' group funded by the AMA's old friend turned invigorating ally in the fight against activist government: the pharmaceutical industry.

The AMA and the drug companies were prepared when Roosevelt listed health insurance in the "Second Bill of Rights" he announced in his State of

---

Depression hurt the average physician struggling to keep their practice afloat. Rejecting Democratic calls to subsidize demand (i.e., pay people's medical bills) as un-American, the group instead put a squeeze on supply. AMA president Walter Bierring's call for half of the medical schools in the country to be shut down was never realized, but between 1934 and 1940, medical schools sharply reversed years of rising enrollments. In his account of the policy, Paul Starr notes that it reduced the number of medical personnel available for the war and worsened a critical shortage of doctors in rural parts of the country.

the Union Address on January 11, 1944. The inclusion took many Democrats by surprise. Less than a year before, the president was still resisting pressure from the left to take on the AMA, telling one Democratic senator, "We can't go up against the State Medical Societies. We just can't do it." After Roosevelt's death in April 1945, the job of resisting that pressure fell to Harry Truman, who in September of that year announced his support for a second Bill of Rights that included "the right to adequate medical care and the opportunity to achieve and enjoy good health." Two months later, Truman sent a long message to the seventy-ninth Congress in its final weeks of Democratic control. "The time has arrived for action," said Truman. "The benefits of modern medical science have not been enjoyed by our citizens with any degree of equality. Nor will they be in the future—unless government is bold enough to do something about it."

Truman emphasized that his proposal was not socialized medicine. Doctors and patients would still have freedom of choice, with the "all-important difference" that patients getting "the services they need would not depend on how much they can afford to pay at the time." Polls showed the plan had overwhelming support. Chipping at that support would not be any easier than weakening support for other popular social programs of the New Deal. But the healthcare plan had not yet been passed, and the first winds of postwar anti-communism were blowing in the direction of the AMA and its old friend, the drug industry.

After retaking Congress in 1946, Republicans began parroting AMA scripts that described government insurance as, in the words of Ohio senator Robert Taft, "the most socialistic measure this Congress has ever had before it." A Republican House subcommittee, meanwhile launched an investigation of Truman's promotion of health insurance to determine if "known Communists and fellow travelers within Federal agencies are at work diligently with Federal funds in furtherance of the Moscow party line."

This was something more than the AMA resistance foreseen by Roosevelt. By fanning the first flickers of anti-communist hysteria, Truman had played sorcerer's apprentice to the politics that allowed the opposition destroy the popular Roosevelt policy he'd adopted as his own. When

Truman won reelection in 1948, the AMA added fresh coal to its red-baiting engine. Collecting an additional $25 in annual dues from membership, it set in motion the costliest lobbying and public relations campaign in the country's history. The AMA's $1.5 million effort, writes Paul Starr,

> used pamphlets, the press, public speakers, and private contacts to stress that voluntarism was the American way and to persuade private organizations—1,829 of them according to its count—to endorse the AMA position. "Would socialized medicine lead to socialization of other phases of American life?" asked one pamphlet, and it answered, "Lenin thought so. He declared: 'Socialized medicine is the keystone to the arch of the Socialist State.'" (The Library of Congress could not locate this quotation in Lenin's writings.) . . . As anticommunist sentiment rose in the late forties, national health insurance became vanishingly improbable.

An AMA-led alliance that included the drug companies and the Chamber of Commerce accomplished more than just block national health insurance. By stripping the 1950 Social Security Act of an amendment to expand coverage to include people who had become totally disabled before reaching retirement age, it also defeated the first attempt to pass national disability insurance. By then, the AMA was spending more than $2 million annually to "educate" Americans about the evils of national social and medical insurance. Drug industry money funded many of the ad buys that saturated print and radio with corporate propaganda cloaked in the cultural authority of the family doctor.

The post-ethical AMA-pharmaceutical alliance developed into the 1950s as patent reform displaced government insurance as their most pressing menace. Though medicine was not directly threatened by patent reform, its relationship with the drug industry had become symbiotic. They increasingly shared the financial spoils of monopoly, and these spoils were the foundation of their political power. After the Kefauver hearings ended with patents secure, the alliance shifted again—this time back to the insurance front, where

Democrats were pushing for programs to insure the poor and elderly, soon to be known as Medicaid and Medicare.

"Organized medicine received large contributions from pharmaceutical firms to fight health insurance, in addition to the revenues from pharmaceutical advertising in AMA journals," writes Starr. "The doctors received this support in part because of the strategic location they held in the marketing of drugs; their gatekeeping function allowed them to collect a toll for use in political agitation."

Compared to the drug companies, the AMA was slow to revise its ethical codes on patents. While the major pharmaceutical associations had updated their charters with conditional benedictions of intellectual property by World War II, the AMA did not overhaul its Principles of Medical Ethics until 1955. Henceforth, its member physicians could patent and profit from their medical inventions—so long, the new code stipulated, as research and access were not impacted. But these were empty words. The moral and political tensions within organized medicine had been resolved in the direction of business and profit—of "mammon and dishonor," as Nathan Smith Davis, one of the AMA's founders and twice its president, once put it. Edward Hyde had consumed Dr. Henry Jekyll.

And yet, there were holdouts. Within academic medicine and even industry research, influential pockets of refuseniks clung to the old ways. These dead-enders expressed their concerns privately to university officials and publicly in the press and in Senate hearings, where they lambasted the new order of industry consulting, academic patent profiteering, and deepening medical journal dependence on ads for medically dubious prescription drug monopolies. What made them dangerous wasn't their number but their status. They were medical school deans, senior faculty, and national laboratory directors. They made eloquent testimonies on Capitol Hill that used the old ethical language to attack patents and advocate for regulation and government healthcare. "The academic prigs . . . these therapeutic nihilists . . . are our most severe critics and must not be ignored," an executive with Wyeth Laboratories told a November 1964 gathering of the Pharmaceutical Manufacturers Association.

In her book *Pills, Power, and Policy*, Dominique Tobbell recounts the influential classification of the postwar establishment by a Wyeth executive named Daniel Shaw. The largest group of academic physicians and researchers consisted of what Shaw called friendly neutrals that could easily be molded into "one of our most prized assets." A majority of midlevel and even senior medical researchers he also considered unthreatening and winnable, being either pro-industry or indifferent to politics. Only the last and smallest group, the "academic prigs," worried Shaw. If they could not be co-opted, they would have to be made irrelevant.

The prigs represented the old order; Shaw was the archetype of the new. His employer, Wyeth Laboratories, began its history as a member of the Philadelphia establishment during the mid-nineteenth-century crown and height of ethical drug manufacture. A century later it was a boundary-smashing pacesetter, and the Wyeth "detail man" the representative figure of a monopoly-based industry. The Wyeth man was known by his sharp suits, generous expense account, and a leather satchel bag filled with freebie samples of the company's bestselling drug: a shield-shaped pill called Equanil.

The world's first tranquilizer and the engine of Wyeth's postwar growth came from an unlikely source: a committed socialist steeped in the idealism and traditions of the European university. A German-speaking Czech Jewish immigrant, Frank Berger arrived in the United States after the war faithful to the idea that medical research should benefit and belong to all. In an interview with historian Andrea Tone, he described fleeing Nazi-occupied Czechoslovakia in 1938 and settling in Britain, where he made key contributions to the transatlantic penicillin project, refining and extending the shelf life of mold samples he received from Alexander Fleming. Just as Fleming discovered the antimicrobial properties of penicillin with a chance observation of a pile of unwashed petri dishes, Berger's research produced a serendipitous stumble of his own. While investigating penicillin preservatives, he noticed that one of his candidate compounds appeared to produce an abnormally relaxed state in lab mice. Berger isolated the compound, mephenesin, and after the war it was developed as a treatment for muscle-control conditions such as Parkinson's. In line with his personal code of ethics, he published his research quickly "so that no commercial exploitation may deprive any human being" of its benefits.

After settling in the United States after the war, Berger turned down multiple offers to consult for drug companies and accepted a research job at the University of Rochester. Only after he was rejected for a life insurance policy due to high blood pressure did he revisit the company offers. The Communist Party takeover of Czechoslovakia hadn't changed his broadly socialist politics, but it did cost him his savings and property. In 1949, he doubled his former university salary by accepting a job as president and medical director of Wallace Laboratories, the new research division of a little-known company called Carter Products. In the 1870s, the firm had been a leading seller of patent medicines, its star product a laxative called Carter's Little Liver Pills ("Wake Up Your Liver Bile!"). Its owners wanted to replicate this success in the new century, and the fastest way to do that was to get their hands on a patented blockbuster prescription drug.

Ensconced in Wallace Laboratories' well-supplied New Jersey research center, Berger returned to his wartime experiments with nerve relaxants and sedatives. Within two years, he'd developed a molecule that had effects similar to his earlier discovery, mephenesin, but lasted longer and carried less debilitating side effects. Berger named it meprobamate and saw its effects in high-minded terms. "He regarded excessive anxiety as an impediment to clear thought and reason, the hallmarks of enlightenment and progress," writes Andrea Tone in her history of tranquilizers, *The Age of Anxiety*.

It was both a risky and auspicious moment to introduce a novel sedative. In 1951, the government brought a hammer down on the over-prescription of barbiturates, the first synthetic. Berger believed meprobamate was safer and less prone to abuse than barbiturates, but its main effect—rapidly depressing the central nervous system—was strikingly similar.

Introduced under patent to the U.S. market by German firms in the early 1900s, the first barbiturates were sold under a number of trademarks that suggested their use as sleeping aids: Seconal, Luminal, Nembutal. All were perennial blockbusters. By the late 1930s, Americans were consuming more than a billion barbiturates annually. Industry materials described the drugs as modern descendants of opiates and chloral hydrates, the "shotgun" sleeping aids of the nineteenth and early twentieth centuries. The marketing did not mention barbiturates' rapid production of tolerance, high rates of addiction, and overdose risk.

Barbiturates' alleged link to juvenile crime and an overdose epidemic led Congress in 1951 to pass a bill regulating what editorialists and reformers called the devil's capsules. Henceforth, barbiturates would be sold only with a doctor's order, and they became the first drug class ever required by law to display the phrase "prescription only" on its packaging. At a three-day meeting of drug makers held that year at the Biltmore Hotel, the lead lawyer of the Proprietary Association called the labeling requirement "a handmaiden of socialized medicine" that "jeopardizes the traditional right of self-medication and choice of remedies."[28]

The reputation of barbiturates was at its lowest point when Berger prepared the first human trials of what he believed to be his safer, less addictive, less toxic sedative. After seeing his data, regulators agreed. When meprobamate was approved for sale by the FDA in 1955, Carter Products turned its attention to finding a partner to license and produce what it called a "tranquilizer." (Paul Janssen, the future founder of Janssen Pharmaceuticals, coined the word over dinner with Berger.) The firm conducted this search in what should have been a receptive and hungry market. Between 1929 and 1939, the prescription drug business grew a thousandfold, and by 1949 accounted for more than half the entire drug market. But by the early 1950s profit rates had begun to slow; golden goose patents were expiring and generic competition was on the rise. To compensate, drug companies pumped money into marketing budgets and swelled the ranks of detail men tasked with maintaining "brand awareness." They also prowled the research landscape for the next patentable prescription blockbuster.

Strangely, the big firms all gave meprobamate a look and passed. There

---

28. The National Association of Retail Druggists, perhaps remembering the acetanilide deaths of the Aspirin wars, backed the reforms.

was no precedent for a prescription-only "anti-anxiety" medicine, no history of outpatient psychiatry at all. Wyeth Laboratories alone saw the potential. Among the major companies based in Philadelphia, Wyeth was always ahead of the post-ethical curve. The rise of detail men was industry-wide—between 1929 and 1959, the nation's drug sales force grew from two to fifteen thousand—but Wyeth blazed the trail. By 1950, its sales force of nearly one thousand had a first-in-class reputation. "Groomed to perfection," writes Tone, the Wyeth detail man "underwent an intensive eighteen-month training program [and] upheld an industry-wide code of style and comportment." Together with middle- and upper-rank Wyeth executives, they showered physicians with a largesse "akin to Roman splendor," according to one contemporary.

Wyeth's proposal to Carter Products reflected the firm's confidence in meprobamate. It offered to pay twice the production cost of the drug, plus 5 percent royalties, in exchange for an exclusive license to market the drug to doctors under an exclusive trademark. Carter would retain title and the right to sell meprobamate on the consumer market under a different trademark.

Both Wyeth's version of the drug (Equanil) and Carter's (Miltown) were runaway successes. Within a year of its 1955 release, Miltown had become not just a household name but a cultural totem. Associated with Hollywood glamour, it received unpaid celebrity endorsements from Milton Berle, Sugar Ray Robinson, and Aldous Huxley. After hearing reports that Salvador Dalí was a devotee, Carter commissioned the surrealist painter to create a Miltown-themed installation for the 1958 meeting of the American Medical Association. Wyeth was also printing money and struggling to keep up with orders from family physicians prescribing Equanil as an all-purpose treatment for depression, anxiety, insomnia, alcoholism, and "agitation."

The birth of popular psychopharmacology added sinew to what Dominique Tobbell calls the industry's "Cold War alliances" with practicing and academic medicine. The displacement of psychiatrists brought newly empowered family doctors closer to the drug companies, where they could be cultivated as the industry's "most prized assets," as Wyeth's Daniel Shaw put it. At the same time, the sudden appearance of prescription drug ads in medical journals created a dependency on the companies that rivaled Americans' developing reliance on the drugs themselves. A typical full-page, full-color Wyeth ad from the period touted three different forms of Equanil tablets, described as a "normotropic drug for nearly every patient under stress." The ad drew attention to the newest of the three designs: a yellow 400 mg tablet that "tranquilizer-conscious patients will not recognize." Another touted "acceptably flavored" liquid Equanil as the perfect solution for "children and the aged in anxiety and tension states."

The smash success of the tranquilizer created an instant scramble for the next mood-altering blockbuster. Within a year of Miltown's release, drug companies had redirected their focus to developing or scouting the next Miltown. In the sedative market, Hoffmann-La Roche trotted into the winner's circle in 1960 with the first benzodiazepine, Librium, followed in 1963 by a little blue pill called Valium. Stronger and with a faster onset than tranquilizers, Valium also mixed better with a martini. The unofficial emblem of Cold War suburban anxiety, it was the country's bestselling drug between 1968 and 1982.

Downers had competition in the billion-dollar anxiety management market: amphetamines. SKF patented the first pharmaceutical speed in the U.S. market, amphetamine sulfate, in 1937, and had retained first-mover advantage after the war. In 1947 the company rolled out Benzedrine and Dexedrine. In 1956, the Swiss firm Ciba struck gold in the United States by patenting methylphenidate, an amphetamine derivative trademarked as Ritalin and positionally marketed as "a happy medium in psychomotor stimulation." The company won its place in a crowded speed market with a positional marketing campaign touting "a happy medium in psychomotor stimulation."

The amphetamine market was another showcase for the symbiotic partnership between industry and medicine. Advertising amphetamine as a harmless weight loss treatment for women required AMA approval, which was granted, resulting in a flood of advertising buys in medical journals that pushed amphetamine sales through the roof. These profits, in turn, funded more and bigger ad buys, as well as juicier perks for prescribing doctors doled out by armies of detail men, who were hired with the profits of the prescription drugs being advertised so heavily in the journals and doctors' offices.

Around and around it went, creating greater profits and an ever-tighter union of interests and forces.

This cycle required all sides to dispense with the pretenses that defined the transitional phase of "ethical patenting" during the first half of the century. This could be seen in the case of SKF's patent on Dexedrine. As the expiration of its valuable monopoly loomed, the company patented one of the most profitable "me-too" drugs of all time: Dexamyl, a prescription combination of Dexedrine and the barbiturate Amytal. The patent and associated marketing campaign broke all the old rules of ethical patenting, beginning with its complete lack of molecular novelty. But it was a winner that dominated the pharmaceutical speed market well into the 1960s. Everybody benefited and few complained. The industry was not just printing money, it was spreading it around.

In January 1960, a bottle of Miltown tablets cost $3.25 in the United States versus 69 cents in Germany. The only entity strong enough to infringe on the Carter-Wyeth monopoly was the United States itself, which is to say the government that granted the patent and protected it in its courts. Occasionally, the industry would be reminded of this simple fact about intellectual property claims—that they exist at the pleasure of a sovereign, and on the sovereign's terms—as when the Pentagon imported generic meprobamate from Sweden in defiance of the Carter patent in 1961. At the time, the military was also importing off-label tetracycline, Pfizer's best-selling patented antibiotic.

On October 12, 1963, the nation's pharmaceutical executives awoke to disturbing news. Included in that morning's edition of the *Federal Register* was a four-page presidential memorandum directed to the heads of all executive departments and agencies. Hereafter, the proclamation read, "the government shall normally acquire or reserve the right to acquire the principal or exclusive rights to any inventions made in the course of or under the contract." John F. Kennedy, it seemed, had been sympathetic to the Kilgore-Kefauver position on public science and patents, after all. The executive order, issued just weeks before Kennedy's assassination, placed the federal research complex under a regime that reflected New Deal ideas about the importance of keeping democratic control of public knowledge and diffusing it for broad social benefit. The attempt to overturn the order policy would shape the drug industry's lobbying and policy agendas for the next two decades.

Under the terms of the Kennedy memorandum, private contractors could, in rare instances, be granted exclusive rights on federally funded inventions. But such cases were to be the exception, and only when such a course was deemed "most likely to serve the public interest." This applied across agencies, but the memo expressly called out research contracts connected to "exploration into fields which directly concern the public health or public welfare." All exceptions to the general policy, meanwhile, would be conditional on contractors fulfilling their obligation to serve the public interest. If the contractor made no progress toward the "practical application" of the invention within three years of being granted a monopoly, or if it failed to make it available to licensees on reasonable terms, the agency heads were instructed to assert their power and license the invention on a royalty-free nonexclusive basis. The memorandum specified this power be applied most liberally when needed to "fulfill a health need."

The memorandum cast a global eye, using a definition of the public interest that was both international and self-interested. Like Truman's support for Nehru's state penicillin project, and Eisenhower's offer to help the Soviets produce the Salk vaccine, Kennedy understood U.S. medicine as a priceless instrument of soft power on the world stage. The government must have control, Kennedy wrote, over "the sharing of the benefits of government-financed research and development with foreign countries to a degree consistent with our international programs and with the objectives of U.S. foreign policy." While paying lip service to the role of incentives "to draw forth private initiatives," it hewed more closely in spirit and letter to the strict policy advocated by the New Dealers than the loose, ad hoc policy supported by industry.

The order remained in force following Kennedy's assassination in Dallas on November 22. It was maintained with special rigor by the Department of Health, Education, and Welfare, which had been on similarly strict track since its founding in 1953. Following the Kennedy policy, the agency took an even stricter line. The IPA program, the wiggle-room mechanism established under Eisenhower to allow contractors in special cases to claim patents, was all but cancelled. In the five years following Kennedy's memorandum, the agency turned down thirty-four out of thirty-four contractor patent claims on publicly funded inventions.

But the number of contractors working with HEW was abnormally low during the mid-1960s. This is because displeased drug companies had responded to the Kennedy order by making good on a threat they'd been throwing around since the Kilgore hearings. It was a threat that was hard to square with their tireless claims of selfless patriotism: they announced a boycott of the United States government.

Screening programs involve testing long series of candidate molecules for a particular response. When NIH-funded labs screen the products of their research, they often pay outside contractors for the job. Sometimes the desired response is discovered; in other cases, molecules are found to have unintended applications that are pleasant surprises. The history of drugs is full of accidental discoveries resulting from screening candidates organized by a long series of numbers. Albert Hofmann discovered LSD-25 through a chance mishandling of the twenty-fifth molecule in a series of experimental treatments for uterine bleeding during childbirth. In the first months of COVID-19, it was a government screening of Gilead's molecular vault that led NIH scientists to flag GS-5734, later named remdesivir and trademarked as Veklury, as a possible therapy for COVID-19.

The postwar years witnessed a growing sophistication in molecular chemistry that resulted in greater opportunities for this kind of collaboration. The NIH conducted research and hired drug companies to help classify and identify promising molecules. Sometimes this work resulted in contractors claiming title on research in hopes of developing a successful commercial product and monopolizing its market. The Kennedy patent policy greatly reduced the scope for these claims. The companies were also concerned about the policy's implications for what it called contamination. If a contractor integrated an element of publicly funded research into an in-house project, the fusion would produce a hybrid product that the companies feared could be the subject of an ownership claim by the surgeon general. Given that nearly every medical invention of the past hundred years has relied on some measure of public science, the industry's fear of a public-interest standard being applied to "contaminated" or "related" inventions was rational. But their response was not, given the broad license they had to use public science and their high success rate in winning patents based on even the most dubious claims of "novelty."

The companies refused to play by the rules of the Kennedy policy. Following the release of the 1962 memorandum, they stopped signing screening contracts that reflected the new restrictions on contractor patent claims. A 1968 report commissioned by the Senate Subcommittee on Patents, Trademarks, and Copyrights described the results:

> The immediate effect of the drug firms' refusal to sign the amended patent agreement was their almost complete withdrawal from screening compounds resulting from NIH research . . . Having to do without the drug firms' screening services—which in their total range include specific screening, extensive test results, and concomitant development work—means to the academic investigator that the work on his compound that is necessary for ultimate utilization is cut off, in most cases, at the development stage.

The shock of realizing its dependence on a fickle and selfish industry could have led the U.S. government to expand its purview in the development of medicines, from basic science to trials. This was, in fact, the policy being pursued around the world, from Sweden to India. The United States did not follow this path, and the stalemate ended on the industry's terms. In 1969, Richard Nixon's secretary of HEW, Robert Finch, reversed the agency's suspension of the IPA "exception," and the drug companies resumed screenings and other forms of collaboration.

They had not spent the intervening seven years waiting idly for a Republican president. In 1964 the pharmaceutical and chemical industries came together to lobby for reversing the Kennedy policy, in HEW and every other government agency. The industries' strongest ally in Congress was conservative Arkansas Democrat John McClellan, chair of the Senate Subcommittee on Patents, Trademarks, and Copyrights. McClellan drafted a bill closely reflecting the agenda of the Pharmaceutical Manufacturers Association and its belief that Kennedy's approach to public health was perfectly backward. "When the purpose of a contract is to explore the fields of public health, welfare, or safety," stated the group, "we think it is even more important, rather than less important, to encourage the perfection and marketing of the inventions."

When McClellan's bill stalled in the House, the industry had five years before Nixon's election to think about what a truly pro-industry patent policy might look like. Such a policy would be partially realized in the waning days of the Carter administration, before being fashioned into the stuff of drug industry dreams under Ronald Reagan.

The midwives of this policy shift would perform burial rites over the Kennedy policy and the broader New Deal vision for public science. They would do so with a swagger born of a victory more momentous than the rollback of any law or decades-old executive order. They would do so as emissaries fulfilling an audacious intellectual project with roots deeper than the Kennedy policy and the New Deal itself. This project of ideas sought to reverse and repeal the legacy of mid-century liberalism the hard way: by rewriting history and rewiring the nation's most deeply held conceptions about democracy, monopoly, antitrust, and corporate power. It pursued this reversal under the claimed authority of a hybrid "science" unveiled in the inaugural 1958 issue of *The Journal of Law and Economics*. Published out of the University of Chicago, the *Journal* advocated ideas considered queer for their time, but it did so comfortably on the dime of two generous and well-fixed private backers. One was the Lilly family drug fortune.

Eight

BLACK PILL

Neoliberalism and the Chicago Turn

THE FRANKLIN ROOSEVELT OF 1932 DID NOT MUCH RESEMBLE
the populist who accepted his party's nomination four years later, thundering pugilistic promises to take on the nation's internal enemies. In his campaign against Hoover, Roosevelt sounded like the aristocratic liberal he was said to be, a mild-mannered governor lacking the fire and populist instincts of his distant cousin Theodore Roosevelt. And yet, when Republicans listened to Roosevelt's promise to relieve America's suffering farmers, they heard the voice of Eugene Debs. When they looked at his shadow, they saw the profile of V. I. Lenin. This conviction was shared by the leader of the Republican party, Herbert Hoover, who described Roosevelt in a 1932 letter as the latest challenger in a long contest "between the nationalists and what we now call 'bolsheviks.'"

Following Roosevelt's victory, the most hardline elements of the nation's business community responded in a way consistent with their warnings: by attempting to reverse the election by military coup. The plan came apart in the fizzled "Wall Street Putsch" of 1933, also known as the bankers' plot.

The conservative hatred for Roosevelt survived him, but the political project based on that hatred proved impotent against the institutions that were the New Deal's regulatory and social reform legacy. The New Deal institutions were so popular that they created a new middle lane running through both parties. Dwight Eisenhower, the first post–New Deal

Republican president, issued a famously withering dismissal of Republicans who fantasized about rewinding the political clock to the days when the business of America was business and Andrew Mellon ran the Treasury Department. These nostalgic and embittered conservatives, the president said, represented "a splinter group [of] a few Texas oil millionaires, and an occasional politician or businessman from other areas. Their number is negligible and they are stupid."

Eisenhower's description of this group as unmoored from reality was correct; no such political project stood a chance. But his summary of the cast was incomplete. It wasn't just a few blustery oilmen and nostalgic Rotary Clubbers wearing KEEP COOL WITH COOLIDGE buttons who sought to correct what they considered the error of the welfare state. At the time of Eisenhower's statement, a transatlantic school of well-funded and well-ensconced intellectuals was a decade into a project to bring about the return of classical liberal economics. This group was not delusional. Its members agreed with Eisenhower's assessment of their near-term prospects. They understood that lobbying and red-baiting could at best be used tactically, as in the defeat of health and disability insurance orchestrated by the AMA, the drug companies, and the Chamber of Commerce. Winning the long game would require more sophisticated methods, a dedication bordering on fanaticism, and patience.

"If the ideals which I believe unite us are to have any chance of revival," the man at the center of this group declared in 1947, "a great intellectual task must be performed."

Friedrich von Hayek was already famous within the economics profession when *The Road to Serfdom* made him a global celebrity. In the 1930s, the Austrian-born Hayek established himself at the London School of Economics as a leading theorist of pricing, monetary policy, and business cycles. He approached these subjects with a belief that the market was fundamentally self-balancing and all-knowing. This placed him in direct opposition to John Maynard Keynes, the economist and writer whose ideas dominated mainstream Western economic thinking before, during, and after the war.

Hayek's first public encounter with Keynes occurred shortly after his arrival in England from Vienna, when the two economists clashed over the benefits of government spending in the pages of the London *Times*. The letter exchange was a microcosmic preview of their transatlantic ideological conflict over the shape of the postwar economic order. Until Hayek's death in 1992, Keynes's fluctuating influence would serve as a real-time measure of his own; an indicator of Hayek's value, as the Austrian might have said.

Hayek's criticism of Keynes reflected the worldview he developed during the 1920s. In Vienna, Hayek had been an acolyte and colleague of Ludwig von Mises, the figure most responsible for the period's fringe revival of interest in the classical liberal economics of the nineteenth century. During the war, Hayek used these ideas to frame a contrarian theory of the rise of fascism. The prevailing view in the United States and Britain was that fascism was a phenomenon of the right, emerging in response to the threat liberalism and socialism posed to entrenched private power and traditional hierarchies. Hayek argued the opposite; that fascism was, in fact, a natural progression of the interventionist state, the predictable outcome of collectivism in all its forms. Priming demand with government spending, basic social insurance, macromanaging the economy in any way—these were not bulwarks against tyranny but steps on the "road to servitude," as Hayek first titled *The Road to Serfdom*. The strongest guarantor of individual freedom was the minimalist state described by the classical and neoclassical economists. Only by recognizing the inherently virtuous and self-calibrating nature of market forces could the likes of Adolf Hitler be avoided in the future.

The Road to Serfdom sold well in England upon its release in 1944, but it was the U.S. edition published a year later by the University of Chicago Press that changed the course of Hayek's life and much else. In April 1945, Hayek was touring the United States promoting the Chicago edition of *Serfdom* when *Reader's Digest* released a condensed adaptation. Overnight, Hayek's appearances became standing-room-only events, with crowds lining up to meet the formerly obscure academic. One evening early into Hayek's new fame, he was preparing to leave an event at the Detroit Economic Club when he was approached by a man named Harold Luhnow. The scion of a family manufacturing business in Kansas City, Luhnow was in the process of taking control of the family's sleepy philanthropic outfit, the William Volker Charities Fund. He had a clear vision to fund the dissemination and popularization of classical economic ideas, and to sponsor free market scholarship like Hayek's book. In Detroit, he proposed to fund another *Reader's Digest*–style edition of *Serfdom*, written at a basic level for a popular U.S. audience. Hayek politely demurred but wasn't quite ready to let Luhnow walk away. He countered with an idea of his own: a multi-year academic project focused on the great economic questions of the age. Luhnow assented on the spot. The following autumn, Hayek joined several conservative economists at the University of Chicago to launch a five-year study program. Its angle was in the name: the Free Market Study.

Though it was Hayek's idea, he would serve as only a part-time participant in the project. When it completed its course in 1951, the "free market" it championed would be transformed and greatly disfigured by the standards of the Austrian School. But by then, those were no longer the standards being used by adherents of what had become known as the Chicago School. The apple-pie version of liberal economic theory contained ingredients not found in the original strudel. The Chicago School developed a tolerance, and then an affection, for cartels, monopolies, and patents. A multidisciplinary laboratory cosponsored by the university's law school, business school, and economics department had nurtured Hayek's baby into a new kind of liberalism. In a word, neoliberalism.

The Free Market Study tackled a riddle: How to reconcile the theory of the nineteenth-century minimal state with the modern realities of economic concentration, cartelization, and monopoly?

For classical economists, monopolies and cartels—seemingly inevitable and intractable features of modern economies—presented an impossible choice. Option one: violate a core tenet of classical theory and accept the suppression of natural price movements and other anticompetitive distortions resulting from the existence of metastatic concentrations of corporate power. Option two: risk an expansionist state by permitting it to develop and use far-reaching regulatory powers, justified on the grounds that such powers are necessary to protect the basic requirements of a functioning free market. There is no third option.

Ludwig von Mises, Hayek's mentor and father of the Austrian School, chose intervention. So, too, did his most influential students and colleagues, notably Hayek, Arnold Plant, Fritz Machlup, and Michael Polanyi. As a group, Austrian School liberals supported state action to prevent monopolies and maintain the conditions for a competitive economy. When it came to patents, a form of state-protected monopoly, the Austrians had a uniquely simple and elegant solution: abolish them.

Michael Polanyi, one of several scientists associated with the Austrian School, added a philosophical argument to the group's denunciation of patents. Patents, he wrote in 1944, "parcel up a stream of creative thought into a series of distinct claims, each of which is to constitute the basis of a separately owned monopoly. But the growth of human knowledge cannot be divided up into such sharply circumscribed phases . . . Mental progress interacts at every stage with the whole network of human knowledge and draws at every moment on the most varied and dispersed stimuli. Invention is a drama enacted on a crowded stage."

Hayek's theory of the economy as a giant information processor left little room for knowledge monopolies. The healthiest economy was the one that most efficiently facilitated the natural flow of knowledge. "If the economy is knowledge before it is property, then the question of how much of that knowledge should be made into property is of critical importance," writes economic historian Quinn Slobodian. "It follows . . . that if you privatize too much or incorrectly, knowledge could also be misallocated, blocked, or left stagnant." Hayek believed monopolies held an even greater danger than distorting prices and competition. The patent-based industrial combines of Nazi Germany demonstrated how monopolies can feed the growth of the state. In *The Road to Serfdom* Hayek approvingly cites the Temporary National Economic Committee's view that "the superior performance of large companies has not been demonstrated" and that "the monopoly is obtained by collusion and encouraged by the government."

The evils of patents was a recurring theme during ten days of meetings convened by Hayek at the Mont Pelerin mountain resort overlooking Lake

Geneva in April 1947. It was there that Hayek and thirty-nine like-minded scholars developed a critique of collectivism that had no place for monopolies on knowledge. "A slavish application of the concept of property as it has been developed for material things has done a great deal to foster the growth of monopoly," said Hayek. "Here drastic reforms may be required if competition is to be made to work."

One member of Hayek's audience had especially strong feelings on intellectual property. In 1934, University of Chicago economist Henry Simons had published a pamphlet, *A Positive Program for Laissez Faire*, regarded at the time as the definitive statement of the classical case against patents. "The great enemy of democracy is monopoly, in all its forms," wrote Simons. The political ends of economic policy were threatened unless the state acted against monopolists to preempt "a domination of the state by them." In later works, Simons extended this critique to the state's "shameful" allowance of "gross abuse of patent privilege for extortion, exclusion, and output restriction." In the assessment of historian Robert Van Horn, "Simons condemned the patent system because it enabled firms to restrict competition, both actual and potential, and thereby augment their monopoly power. [He] believed that just as free trade required equal and free access to markets, industrial research required equal and reasonable access, if not wholly free access, to technical knowledge."

Simons's view was shared by the group that launched the Free Market Study in 1946. Indeed, they were held to some degree by every major European and American conservative intellectual at the time, including Milton Friedman, the University of Chicago economist destined to become neoliberalism's public face.

Only one figure associated with the project dissented from this key tenet of classical orthodoxy. He happened to be the one holding the checkbook.

Harold Luhnow couldn't claim ignorance of the Austrian School position on patents. The *Reader's Digest* edition of *Serfdom* included Hayek's general views on the subject—illustrated by his praise of the New Deal TNEC investigation—and concluded with a warning that "great danger lies in the policies of two powerful groups, organized capital and organized labor, which support the monopolistic organization of industry."

For American conservatives like Luhnow, the Austrian School's focus on "organized capital" was disposable. A product of European trauma, maybe, a bias based on an understandable obsession with the role of industry in Imperial and Nazi Germany. But big business was not a threat in America. The political destination of Luhnow and his ilk was not nineteenth-century Holland—which rejected patents in favor of a "free trade in inventions"—but a second Gilded Age where corporate titans not only had a God-given right to patents but could do with them what they goddamn pleased. The conservative revival they envisioned had no place for valorizing the TNEC, and certainly not the antitrust crusade of Thurman Arnold, who continued to haunt corporate America's nightmares, a pen in one hand, the consent decree in the other.

Months before the Free Market Study was to begin, an unexpected event released the tension between classical liberal theory and modern American conservatism in Luhnow's favor. In June 1946, Henry Simons committed likely suicide by overdosing on barbiturates. A key figure in the development of monetarism, and generally considered the most brilliant of the Chicago conservatives, Simons was the Chicago group's antitrust conscience. He did not apologize for advocating the use of state power to maintain an even playing field as the precondition of a free market, and once described the Federal Trade Commission as the most important government agency. Heterodox but consistent, he hated Hoover as much as Roosevelt, and oligopolies and monopolies above all.

Luhnow knew Simons's views and understood the respect he commanded from the group's members, many of whom had been influenced by Simons's strict 1934 tract, *A Positive Program for Laissez Faire*.

Following Simons's death, Luhnow asked his friend and fellow Chicago economist Aaron Director to take over running the Free Market Study. In his book *Goliath*, Matt Stoller writes that Luhnow had been concerned with Simons's influence and hard-line position on monopoly, and believed Director to be "far more ideologically malleable."

For the next three years, not much changed, and Director maintained the Simons-Hayek line on monopoly and corporate giantism, which aligned with the views he expressed in an address to the 1947 meeting in Mont Pelerin. Current antitrust laws, Director had said, should be seen as "stopgap measures" on the way to more radical restrictions on corporate power. These included limits to the scope of corporate activity as well as "perhaps a direct limitation of the size of corporate enterprise." Director was equally clear in his condemnation of patents as the handmaidens of monopoly and called for dramatic reductions in their terms. Simons would have been proud.

Only when funding for the Free Market Study was set to expire, in late 1950, did Luhnow begin to express himself on the matter. According to historian Rob Van Horn, officials from "the Volker Fund went so far as to threaten to eject Director from his leadership role in the project because the Volker Fund refused to accept certain tenets of classical liberalism, namely, those espoused by the deceased Chicago economist Henry Simons."

The evidence suggests Director received the message loud and clear. Later that year, he began a steep public climbdown from his former, ideologically consistent opposition to monopoly. In a 1950 book review, Director argued that monopolies did not justify state intervention because the "corroding influence of competition" was their natural enemy and could be counted on to "destroy" concentrations of economic power. If the market produced monopoly-killing antibodies, then antitrust enforcement and patent reform were unnecessary.

At a Chicago conference on corporate law the next year, Director elaborated on his new beliefs. "The corporate form was ideal," he said, "because it did not contribute toward business monopoly." According to his updated views, anything that emerges from the market is by definition a natural expression of the market and therefore inherently less threatening and coercive than powers granted to government. "Less than five years after the FMS began," writes Van Horn, Director's belief that "concentrations of business power were relatively benign . . . became, for the Chicago School, an assertion of fact."

When the Free Market Study expired in 1952, its principal figures were all moving toward accommodating the new Chicago doctrine of benign monopoly. Completing this ideological journey would be the focus of the next Luhnow-funded project at the University of Chicago, called the Antitrust Project.

The Antitrust Project was designed to interrogate and revise the traditional legal and economic interpretations of monopoly in America and the antitrust movement that arose to challenge it. It aimed to achieve a "redefinition of the functions of the state," as Hayek said in one of his Sermons on the Mont. But its redefinition was not of the sort Hayek had in mind. Over the next several years, the Project produced a multivolume revisionist history of antitrust that reversed conventional legal and economic thought on the subject. The Project's breakout star was a young Chicago legal scholar named Robert Bork. A talented writer and polemicist, Bork produced some of the Project's earliest reappraisals of the Sherman Antitrust Act and related case law. His writings defending the legality and competitive advantages of vertical mergers were as fulsome as his condemnations of antitrust actions were withering.

Not to be outdone, Director produced articles targeting the most celebrated, least controversial antitrust suits in the country's history. These included the 1911 Supreme Court decision that dismembered Standard Oil, a judgment that Director dismissed as without merit and counterproductive. In a 1956 Project article that anticipated later theories about shareholder value, Director and Chicago law school dean Edward Levi argued that corporations benefited the wider economy by practicing exclusionary and anticompetitive behavior.

Hayek did not join his colleagues in this sharp ideological turn. He spent 1959, his last year in Chicago, writing a book that contained a forceful restatement of the Austrian School's traditional opposition to patents and all forms of monopoly. "Knowledge," Hayek wrote in *The Constitution of Liberty*, "once achieved, becomes gratuitously available for the benefit of all. It is through this free gift of the knowledge acquired by the experiments of some members of society that general progress is made possible, that the achievements of those who have gone before facilitate the advance of those who follow."[29]

---

29. In his final book, published in 1988, Hayek continued to espouse this view, and cites his fellow Austrian Fritz Machlup on the inherently anti-competitive nature of patents and copyrights.

✦

In October 1958, academic libraries across the United States and Europe received the debut issue of a new periodical published out of Chicago by figures associated with the Antitrust Project. Its title gave a name to the movement led by Director, Bork, and others to systematize their apostate beliefs on monopoly and patents. The first slate of articles in *The Journal of Law and Economics* included pieces on monopoly policy and prices in medicine, reflecting the ideological distance traveled by its editorial board in the previous decade, but also changes behind the scenes. The Volker Fund was no longer the only sponsor of the Antitrust Project, but had been joined by a second wave of funders. One was the family foundation of Eli Lilly, the Indiana drug giant. It was Lilly money that launched the *Journal*, a fact that likely inspired the young publication's interest in regulatory debates impacting the medical and pharmaceutical industries. Some of these pieces had the trappings of traditional scholarship; others read like screeds. Many fell somewhere in between, such as British economist D. S. Lees's attempt to "try and unravel, once and for all, the twisted logic that underlies the National Health Service" and its threat to "principles and aims consistent with the basic assumptions of a free society."

Until the late 1950s, the drug companies hadn't paid much notice to the arcane intellectual experiment at the University of Chicago. This changed when Kefauver announced he was extending his anti-monopoly hearings to include the drug industry. Their interest sharpened following the passage of the Kefauver-Harris Amendments in 1962, an event that demonstrated the limits of its skipping-record "drug story" public relations narrative and its Cold War–meets–Chamber of Commerce political strategy. The expansion of FDA powers placed the industry's product chain under the purview of a government agency for the first time, a development the public overwhelmingly supported. If not quite as worrying as attacks on its patent privileges, the regulatory state's new powers over drug development and sales was nonetheless serious. The industry's critics, meanwhile, viewed it as a work in progress. Before his death in 1963, Kefauver had cultivated and inspired a coterie of protégés, notably Gaylord Nelson, the liberal governor of Wisconsin who arrived in the Senate earlier that year.

The Chicago figure who most intrigued the industry was the economist George Stigler. A late arrival to the Antitrust Project, Stigler joined the Chicago faculty from Columbia University in 1958, just in time to contribute an article on economies of scale to the first issue of *The Journal of Law and Economics*. Like his new colleagues, Stigler was once a devotee of Henry Simons and had maintained a classical liberal's antipathy toward monopolies, cartels, and patents. In 1942, Stigler published a pro-competition treatise that endorsed the TNEC and the antitrust offensive of Thurman Arnold's Justice Department. In a 1945 speech to the American Economic Association, Stigler condemned monopolies as "an evil demanding correction" and called the case for reducing patent terms "irrefutable."

Stigler no longer believed this when he arrived in Chicago in 1958 and made regulation the focus of his work, with a special interest in the drug industry's travails with Congress and the FDA. During his first years in Chicago, Stigler developed the economic theory for which he is best remembered: "regulatory capture." Stigler argued that because industries targeted by state regulation have more at stake than the public or the agency overseeing the regulation, those industries will inevitably gain control of the process. The danger described by the theory was real enough, but the elder Stigler no longer advocated the countermeasures he embraced during the 1930s and '40s—namely, strengthening democratic oversight and checking the runaway growth of concentrated corporate power. The Chicago version of Stigler was a servant of corporate power and embodied neoliberalism's open animus to majoritarian rule. At a 1978 meeting of the Mont Pelerin Society, Stigler would recommend "the restriction of the franchise to property owners, educated classes, employed persons, or some such group."[30]

---

30. This aspect of Chicago-engineered neoliberalism, never well hidden, rushed into view when prominent figures associated with the movement signed on as advisers to right-wing police states in Chile and Argentina, justifying state torture as easily as they now justified state-protected monopolies.

The other solution to the phenomenon of regulatory capture was the one Stigler's friend and colleague Milton Friedman advocated in his weekly *Newsweek* column: abolish the agencies and leave regulation to consumers and the free market. Stigler saw Friedman's position as the media performance it was—good for chumming the waters of public backlash against the activist state, perhaps, but unrealistic and crude. Most important, he believed abolishing the agencies was unnecessary. If you believed in an industry's natural right to determine its own behavior, capture was not a problem. It was an art.

In his study of Stigler, the historian Edward Nik-Khah writes that the Chicago economist believed in "several ways to skin a cat," his chosen euphemism for gaining dominance over government regulators. As chair of the University of Chicago Business School's Governmental Control Project, and later his own fiefdom, the Center for the Study of the Economy and the State, Stigler theorized how major industries could go about skinning their particular regulatory cats while wearing Cheshire grins. He recommended that industries threatened with regulation go beyond traditional lobbying, and instead aim to control the mental frames and vocabularies used by regulators and the public. "What began as a study of the nature and extent of governmental control of the economy came to explore methods for how to control the government," says Nik-Khah.

If the ideas developed by Stigler during the 1960s seemed precision-engineered to help an embattled drug industry, that's because they were. As with every Chicago School project since the late 1950s, Stigler's policy shop was wide open for business. Preferring to work for "patrons uncontaminated by the egalitarian views of the government and the public at large," writes Nik-Khah, "Stigler found them in corporations and pro-market foundations. The topics Stigler settled on, studies of the economy and the state, had the virtue of appealing to a paying clientele."

To a pharmaceutical industry still recounting the same old "drug story" in pamphlets and *The Saturday Evening Post*, Stigler's blueprints for colonizing the brain and organs of government must have appeared visionary, if not futuristic. Stigler would teach the industry to control its own destiny, not by throwing red paint at the FDA and placing editorials calling for its abolition, but by reshaping the thinking and priorities of its administrators and affiliated scientists, politicians, and the public—all without them even knowing it was happening. The promised land described by Stigler was not regulatory capture, but cognitive capture.

For the drug companies, this opened up a number of possibilities. Some lines of attack were already underway and awaiting their support, such as Robert Bork's revisionist project to rewrite the histories of antitrust law and patent populism. Others remained in the planning stage, such as establishing quasi-academic research centers to produce papers and books. These centers would serve as "echo chambers" to ensure the industry's message rang continuously in the public square. It was Stigler's belief that, if crafted and disseminated with care, anything put through this system would in time be internalized by scientists, regulators, and the public.

In 1971, a small group of Pfizer executives visited Hyde Park to meet with the dean of the University of Chicago law school, Phil Neal. Like other companies with an interest in regulation, Pfizer was curious to know what funding opportunities existed to support the work of Stigler and other neoliberals working along similar lines (and providing similar services). The movement's biggest corporate funder at the time was General Electric, sponsor of the school's Government-Business Relations program as well as the work of Robert Bork, who had become a human antitrust revisionist tornado, bouncing between courtrooms and boardrooms in a crusade to make the world safe for monopoly.

If the Pfizer executives debriefed the law school dean about the enemies at the drug industry's gate, it may have been a long meeting. In 1967, Wisconsin Democrat Gaylord Nelson picked up Kefauver's mantle in the Senate Subcommittee on Antitrust and Monopoly and initiated hearings on "Competitive Problems in the Pharmaceutical Industry." He also revived Kefauver's mission to reduce the terms and scope of drug monopolies, and proposed a law to require the prescribing of generic drugs over their branded versions. Nelson and the cause of patent reform entered the 1970s with a new ally at their side: the national consumer rights movement. The face of this movement was a young lawyer named Ralph Nader, famous for challenging the automobile industry with the public safety argument described in his 1965 exposé, *Unsafe at Any Speed*.[31]

The industry's recent success in loosening the Kennedy patent policy at HEW, meanwhile, was a limited one. The Nixon administration adopted a relatively hard line on antitrust similar to its Democratic predecessors. In 1970, a deputy attorney general in the Justice Department announced a "watch list" of nine patent and licensing practices that would be prosecuted as anticompetitive restraints of trade. The list of "Nine No-Nos," as it came to be known, sat like bowling pins for the Chicago School's antitrust bowling ball, Robert Bork, for the remainder of the decade. In 1974, another of Nixon's assistant attorney generals declared private patent claims on government inventions "unconstitutional."

This was the backdrop to the two-day Conference on the Regulation of the Introduction of New Pharmaceuticals hosted by the law school during the first week of December 1972.[32] The agenda brought two worlds face to face: Professors affiliated with the Law and Economics movement delivered critical talks on regulation and the 1962 Kefauver-Harris Amendments.

---

31. Just as Kefauver's hearings featured cameos by veterans of the Kilgore hearings, Nelson's hearings contained a number of links to Eisenhower- and Kennedy-era hearings. More than a decade after Kefauver grilled Parke-Davis executives about their fatal over-prescription of the antibiotic Chloromycetin, Nelson summoned them back to answer reports that the company was continuing to promote use of the drug to treat conditions for which it had no known activity. When the executives admitted Parke-Davis was not using the warning labels on its U.S. packaging in exports targeting the markets of developing countries, Nelson told them, "I don't see how you people can sleep at night."

32. The university was an ironic location for this, having declared in 1944 a strict no-profit policy for its faculty members, based on the belief that "the advancement of scientific knowledge depends on the free interchange and use of the ideas and information between scientists and research workers within a university. The basic purpose of university research may be thwarted if the free exchange or use of such information is checked or prevented by the attempt of one or a group of faculty members to profit from patentable discoveries. By removing any such incentive, the patent rule of the University of Chicago insures that the cooperative search for truth is untrammeled."

Drug company executives and their research directors delivered papers of their own. Each reinforced an understanding of current FDA regulations as unnecessary and counterproductive. In most cases, the presentations were more political than scientific or scholarly, or the data they rested upon. When the conference papers were published as a book, *Regulating New Drugs*, it was roundly panned in the scientific press for advocating ideas "so at variance with the current thinking in this field that they will be subject to much criticism," as one reviewer put it. The book's critics did not yet understand that establishing a counternarrative at "variance with the current thinking" was the point of the conference.

The conclave of executives and neoliberal academics was a watershed event in the development of the modern drug industry. Over the course of the 1970s, alumni of the Chicago conference would build out an industry-funded pseudo-scientific echo chamber with the aim of setting the terms of political debate and "co-opting the experts with finesse," in words of an influential 1978 Stiglerian tract called *The Regulation Game*.

In 1974, conference participants became the first hires at the Center for Health Policy Research, a drug policy think tank funded with industry money at the American Enterprise Institute. Two years later, another conference alumnus, the clinical-scientist-turned-FDA-critic Louis Lasagna, started the Center for the Study of Drug Development at the University of Rochester.[33] Both centers were organized around the production of research designed to reset the drug debate. Success came quickly. One of the first memes produced by the CSDD was the "drug lag." This was the idea that excessive safety regulations were hurting public health by deterring investments in research and delaying the arrival of new drugs on the market. As Daniel Carpenter notes in his history of the FDA, the idea that regulations

---

33. After joining the neoliberal side of the regulation debate, Lasagna became a frequent writer for *The Good Drugs Do*, a public-facing newsletter published by the medical advertising agency headed by Arthur Sackler, who would later hire Lasagna as dean of the Sackler Graduate School of Biomedical Sciences at Tufts University.

stifled innovation emerged from these corporate-funded centers and quietly took root in public and academic debates. A key vector involved studies and articles funded by leading drug firms, which were then distributed without disclosures, leading to their citation in mainstream journals and use in clinical pharmacology and economics programs.

The new think tanks were publicity hives for finessing and packaging industry messages. Previous generations of industry publicists had allowed scripts to go stale; the post-Chicago machine was more dynamic. Even old standbys about patents driving innovation were updated and given shines. Some of these variations had more legs than others. One notable dud belonged to Edmund Kitch, a Chicago law professor and veteran of the 1972 conference, who published an article in 1977 praising patent monopolies for preventing "wasteful duplication" in the drug market. But there was always money to fund novel approaches to a genre that reached terminal rhetorical velocity in Michael Novak's 1996 Pfizer-funded philosophical essay on the moral and godly bases of patent monopolies, *The Fire of Invention, the Fuel of Interest.*

Half a century after this echo chamber hatched from an industry-academia networking and strategy event, it continues to perform the function Stigler imagined for it: shaping and policing the boundaries of the drug pricing debate, awaiting activation at key moments. In the early 2000s, the system released the meme of the "$800 Million Pill," cited by George W. Bush as a justification for signing away the government's right to negotiate drug prices in the 2003 Medicare Prescription Drug, Improvement, and Modernization Act. (The industry is constantly revising the meme, which at the time of writing is the "$2 Billion Pill.")

The drug industry network built in the mid-1970s—one able to produce propaganda and send it reverberating through the wider culture—served as a model for the tobacco and fossil fuel industries, who faced similar regulatory and political threats related to their impacts on public health. Oil companies were especially precocious students of Stiglerian ideas about co-opting experts with funding. Following a 1969 oil spill off the coast of Santa Barbara,

California, state agencies were dumbfounded when every local scientist with relevant expertise refused to testify against the companies, because every one of them was being funded in whole or in part by the industry.

With time, this echo chamber would learn to tarnish and weaken the impact of any findings and research that threatened industry interests. In the name of science, data wielded by critics would be dismissed as "adversarial" and fundamentally unserious. "The point of pharma's echo chamber was never to get the public to support monopolistic pricing," says Nik-Khah. "As with global warming denialism, which involves many of the same institutions, the goal was to forestall regulation by sowing confusion about the relationship among prices, profits, innovation, and patents."

He continues, "Stigler and those influenced by his work had very sophisticated ideas about how to audit and slowly take over the agencies by getting them to internalize [their] positions and critiques. You target public conceptions of medical science. You target the agencies' understanding of what they're supposed to do. You target the very thing inputted into the regulatory bodies—you commercialize science. Outside of Chicago, Stigler, his students, and those in their close orbit developed relationships with scientists, resulting in a variety of interlinked and coordinated research institutes spanning economics, politics, and the biomedical sciences."

Perhaps the slyest Stiglerian tactic of all was a trend that emerged following the economist's death in 1991: industry-funded academic chairs in bioethics. By the century's end, such sinister moves were routine practice, decorative touches, for what had become an expansive pharmaceutical idea factory. The base victory was won decades earlier with the triumph of the neoliberal obsession with "objective" cost-benefit analysis. This product of Chicago's laboratories was noted by the philosopher Michel Foucault in a lecture at the College of France in 1979. The defining and most effective characteristic of U.S. neoliberalism's "permanent criticism of governmental policy," said Foucault, was the reductionist use of quantification to

> test government action, gauge its validity, and to object to activities
> of the public authorities on the grounds of their abuses, excesses,
> futility, and wasteful expenditure . . . [It targets] the activity of the

numerous federal agencies established since the New Deal and especially since the end of the Second World War, such as the Food and
Health Administration [*sic*].

Foucault delivered this speech in March 1979. Whether he knew it or not, the
industry campaign that incubated this strategy was nearing an endgame in
Washington, D.C., where George Stigler and Milton Friedman would soon
be honored guests of a U.S. president who agreed monopolies were benign,
and that the drug companies deserved everything they ever wanted, and perhaps a few things more.

Nine

BAYH-DOLE AND THE REAGAN ACCELERATION

THE 1974 MIDTERM ELECTIONS ARE REMEMBERED FOR THE WAVE of fresh blood they brought into the Democratic-controlled House. The class of first-term Democrats—seventy-five in all, the youngest only twenty-five-years-old—were named "Watergate Babies" after the impeachment scandal that concluded the previous summer. Many were marked by a skepticism toward the national security state, and had campaigned on promises to curtail its power and abuses at home and abroad. Less discussed were their differences with Democratic economic traditions, especially on policies touching on regulation, antitrust, and corporate power. In an early sign of this generational break, Watergate Babies led efforts to strip Wright Patman of his chairmanship of the House Subcommittee on Banking and Currency. Together with Russell Long in the Senate, Patman was a vital living connection to the New Deal anti-monopoly legacy and vision for public science. Signs of impatience with liberal loyalties also marked the Congressional class of 1976 and Jimmy Carter's White House. A leaked strategy memo prepared in early 1977 by one of Carter's closest advisers, Pat Caddell, discussed how the administration could "adopt many of the [Republican] positions" and ignore the inevitable "rumblings from the left of the Democratic Party [who are] as antiquated and anachronistic a group as are the conservative Republicans."[34]

These shifting political winds were welcomed within the industry-Republican effort, now in its second decade, to replace the Kennedy patent policy with one granting contractors monopoly access to federally sponsored inventions. Since the successful NIH boycott of the mid-1960s, the effort had ground to a frustrating stalemate. A wall of opposition in Congress stopped cold every legislative attempt to reverse the policy. The federal agency chiefs appointed by Nixon and Ford, meanwhile, were of little help to the cause. It was Nixon's Justice Department, after all, who had codified the "Nine No-Nos" of anticompetitive practices.

In the end, it wasn't a political shift that gave enemies of the Kennedy policy the break they needed. It was an economic one. The prospects of the crusade to open federal science to private claims brightened when those of the national economy began to darken.

In 1971, the United States posted its first trade deficit since 1893. The March 1973 issue of *Newsweek* introduced Americans to a British term, *stagflation*, to describe the double bind of high inflation and unemployment. In 1975, the U.S. economy posted its first trade surplus in four years, but in the context of a full-blown recession. None of this was good news for any sector of the U.S. economy, but the research industries seeking movement on the patent issue sensed opportunity.

As the economy contracted during the Ford and Carter years, the anti-Kennedy policy alliance—grown to include venture capital and the nascent

---

34. Some figures from the New Deal who remained on the scene reappeared in a new guise. Alfred Kahn, the wunderkind theorist of New Deal patent skepticism, became the leading force in the deregulation of the airline industry. No longer interested in how patents retarded innovation and plugged up competition, he penned an influential book, *The Economics of Regulation*, credited with laying the basis for the undoing of his party's regulatory legacy, beginning with the Aeronautics Board established by Truman.

biotech industry—struck up a fresh rationale for bequeathing patents to government contractors. It centered on a new word in the country's political and economic lexicons: *competitiveness*. According to the latest script, government patent ownership not only inhibited commercialization, it undermined America's ability to compete with the recovered economies of Europe and Asia. Unless U.S. firms had exclusive access to the latest science to do with as they pleased on a monopoly basis, they would be crushed on the global stage by technological rivals. The sclerotic New Frontier policy of default government ownership must give way to a dynamic industry-first policy that incentivized innovation by handing inventions over to the private sector. Monopoly was not a threat to American strength, innovation, and global leadership; it was their precondition.

At a time of sliding trade balances and stagnant wages, stamping the Kennedy policy as weak and self-defeating was clever. It was also specious. The "competitive" argument was premised on the false assumption that public science was hidden away under lock and key. In reality, government science, especially the medical research coveted by the drug companies, was by definition available for licensing and use. Companies did not lack access to government science; they just wanted the right to deny that access to their competitors.

The argument broke down further when comparing the U.S. policy with those of the countries challenging America's technological preeminence. All of them had far weaker intellectual property regimes than the United States, especially when it came to medicines and public health. "The most formidable new rival to U.S. technological leadership, Japan, maintained a much weaker patent system, among other things requiring the licensing of most patents," says F. M. Scherer, the FTC's chief economist between 1974 and 1976. During Republican-led hearings on how the Kennedy policy was hurting the economy, Carter's Federal Trade Commission chair, Michael Pertschuk, explained there was "no factual basis" for Republican claims that government patent control slowed down the commercialization of government science. "The available evidence shows just the opposite," he told the red-faced senators.

There was no need to study the patent policies of Japan or Germany, because the best case against turning public science into private monopolies was the high-tech innovation surge on the cusp of transforming the U.S. economy.

The foundational technologies of the information economy—solid-state transistor circuits, lasers, fiber optics—had origins in three things: publicly funded research, liberal government licensing of that research, and above all, a 1954 Justice Department consent decree that forced open Bell Labs' patent vault and diffused its contents. Had corporate America's most notorious high-tech monopolist and knowledge-squatter been allowed to continue hiding its patented technology on bunkered shelves, the course of U.S. "competitiveness" in the twentieth century would have looked very different.[35]

The disco-era push to privatize public science also featured a Cold War trope most closely associated with the president whose patent legacy was under dispute. Just as Kennedy accused Richard Nixon before the 1960 election of allowing a "missile gap" to open up with the Soviets, the patent reform strategists blamed the Kennedy policy for allowing an "inventions gap" to undermine public health and threaten American "competitiveness." This "inventions gap" concerned an alleged mountain of government patents being blocked from productive development and use, each one a piece of progress lost to dogmatic statism.

The "inventions gap" meme was conceived in the summer of 1976 by Howard Forman, a former chemical industry patent lawyer serving as a deputy assistant secretary of commerce. Speaking before the House Committee on Science and Technology, Forman claimed the government was allowing twenty-eight thousand patents to languish (in his written testimony, the

---

35. An understanding of this history, together with the influence of psychedelics and the counterculture, contributed to the open science ethos of the young Silicon Valley.

number was twenty-six thousand). Each of these patents represented, in his telling, an invention kept from American industry and the public by a selfish and inept policy. "Whatever system we have been using is not helping to contribute to the promotion of the progress of the arts and sciences, because I understand that only about five percent of those twenty-eight thousand patents have been the subject of some kind of licensing action," Forman told the committee. "The greater majority of those patents are not getting into use, and they are doing no good to anyone."

Forman's argument—that by refusing to offer contractors monopoly rights to these inventions, the government was actively *suppressing* their diffusion and development—unsettled lawmakers in both parties. But it landed with a force proportional to their ignorance about how patents work. Where Kennedy's "missile gap" involved a quantifiable difference in the number of U.S. and Soviet rockets, Forman's "gap" involved subtler distortions of the truth, each constructed to exploit the innocence and insecurities of lawmakers and the public. The first distortion was the insinuation that most patented inventions are ever licensed for production, when the great majority of inventions, patented or not, interest no one. The U.S. Patent Office issues thousands of patents per day; only a tiny fraction ever result in applied technologies or new products. Making Forman's number even more meaningless was the fact that government-owned inventions are routinely used without anyone bothering to obtain a license, because the entire purpose of government ownership is to guarantee access and encourage the use of knowledge, not release hound dog patent lawyers to track the scent of infringement.

This was explained in the counter-testimony of a seventy-nine-year-old navy admiral named Hyman Rickover, then and still the longest-serving officer in the history of the U.S. armed services. The legendary founding director of the U.S. nuclear submarine program, Rickover was famously strict about keeping patent rights in government hands. He was also angered and baffled that anyone in Congress could think doing otherwise was a good idea. In testimony before a Senate subcommittee on the Constitution in June 1979, Rickover urged lawmakers not to fall for "the age-old arguments of the patent lobby." He dismissed Forman's statistics about government invention as sophistry, because

> Government agencies do not have a reason to search for patent in-fringement. The Government, unlike private parties, generally has no desire to prevent others from using its inventions. The reasons the Government should take title to these inventions are primarily to ensure the Government is not subsequently barred by someone else's patent from using the idea; to preclude the establishment of a private monopoly for a publicly financed invention; and to ensure the public has equal access to these inventions.

Regarding their claim that nonexclusive rights were blocks to progress, Rickover told the senators, "Truly good ideas tend to be used."

Forman's case was on thinnest ice regarding those industries with the most to gain: pharmaceuticals and biotech. In a review of HEW licensing practices between 1968 and 1978, the very decade Forman described as an "inventions gap" dead zone, law professor Rebecca Eisenberg found that the health agency licensed a full quarter of its roughly 350 patented inventions. This is more than double the licensing rate of universities who were granted patents under the IPA program during the same period. Between 1968 and 1981, companies who gained patents under HEW's IPA program licensed just nine, resulting in a grand total of four commercial products.

Still, the alliance pushed on with its arguments. Though the campaign was supported by the usual suspects—the National Patent Council, the Chamber of Commerce, the National Association of Manufacturers—it wasn't organized out of the private suites of industry and its lobbyists. Its messaging and political strategy was developed by a rogue brain trust of bu-reaucrats inside the Departments of Commerce, Energy, and—in the case of its most senior and influential member—Health, Education, and Welfare, the very fortress they were preparing to storm.

✦

Following Jimmy Carter's election in 1976, Forman, already at work on the "inventions gap," organized a few like-minded officials into an informal group called the Government Patent Policy Committee. Like him, they were mostly holdovers from the Nixon and Ford administrations who worried that HEW's grip on government research would tighten further under Carter's new man at HEW, Joseph Califano, a liberal Democrat who had helped Lyndon Johnson steer the passage of Medicare and Medicaid. Califano lived up to his reputation and confirmed their suspicions: during his first two years in office, HEW did not grant one patent waiver under the IPA program.

One member of the group was a fellow ex–patent lawyer named Norman J. Latker. Latker had served as general counsel to HEW since the early 1960s, forced to oversee a patent policy to which he was ideologically opposed. Over the next fifteen years, he privately developed working relationships with those at the center of efforts to undermine and overturn that policy. While on the public clock, Latker was legally obligated to enforce the policies set down by his boss. It was a double life.

The first patent bill advanced by the Forman-Latker circle was a swing for the fences. Introduced to the House in April 1977 by Arkansas Democrat Ray Thornton, not even the legislation's most passionate supporters—Barry Goldwater Jr. among them—denied it was a pure distillation of industry desire and its hatred of liberal science policy. In the words of Betsy Ancker-Johnson, a Boeing physicist who was active with the Forman-Latker group, Thornton's was a "patent policy as perfect as we could make it, one totally devoid of the shortcomings associated with political expediency."

It was also devoid of a snowball's chance in hell of becoming law, or even being reported out of committee in the Democratic-controlled House. In the Senate, Wisconsin's Gaylord Nelson convened his Subcommittee on Antitrust and Monopoly for the sole purpose of warning his colleagues not to consider introducing a Senate version of Thornton's bill. "If this group of Commerce Department employees has its way," said Nelson, "the government would end up giving away to a small number of companies the rights to every invention produced through government financed research." When asked about the bill, Russell Long snarled, "It's a beaut—what a real giveaway should be like. It doesn't leave even a sliver of meat on the bone. This proposed legislation is one of the most radical, far-reaching and blatant giveaways that I have seen in the many years that I have been a member of the United States Senate."

The humiliating defeat sent the patent lobby back to the drawing board. Despite decades of ideological sawing by Robert Bork and other Chicago figures, the anti-monopoly and patent legacies of the New Deal were proving stubborn and difficult to fell. It seemed unlikely a reform bill would get past a phalanx of old-guard senators and Jimmy Carter. But the oil shocks and deepening anxiety about the economy continued to put longshot policies in play in unpredictable ways. The reformers doubled down on the line that an attachment to liberal dogma was holding back progress and creating a strategic "inventions gap." They hoped the refrains—repeated in op-eds, think tank reports, and Senate hearings—would drown out the rebuttals and counter-evidence presented by FTC, Justice, HEW, and Defense Department officials.

Moving public opinion would not be easy. Drug companies and drug monopolies remained burdened by enormous baggage stored in the nation's collective memory. The pricing and safety scandals unearthed by the Nelson hearings were fresh in the public mind. Most Americans remembered the Kefauver hearings; anyone over the age of sixty was around for the TNEC, Arnold, and Kilgore investigations. This presented a challenge: How to pass a bill that expanded the scope for drug monopolies without triggering public suspicions about drug monopolies?

The patent lobby settled on a solution of elegant simplicity: Keep the drug companies out of the picture. If politicians and the public associated abusive pricing and anticompetitive behavior with the Mercks and the Pfizers, *don't mention the Mercks and the Pfizers.* Within weeks of the Thornton disaster, the Latker-Forman group began to work on a new bill defined by one major revision: it restricted patent claims on public science to small businesses and universities. The bill was crafted to draw attention away from the drug companies and exploit public ignorance about the rise of university patenting since the 1930s. Few understood that research universities were now in the business of maximizing revenue by licensing patents on exclusive terms to drug and biotech firms large and small. The new bill merely added an extra step on the way to monopoly, one that effectively pushed the companies into the shadows of the debate. This extra step was always conceived as temporary. Once an initial tear in the policy fabric was made, the law could be easily expanded to include the multinational drug majors.

But they still needed to pass the law. This daunting task would be easier with an effective champion in Congress, ideally one of a higher weight class than the lowly Representative Thornton. It turned out to be a brief search. One of the core members of the Forman-Latker group was on the staff of a reform-minded Democratic senator from Indiana, Eli Lilly's home state, named Birch Bayh.

To produce a draft of the bill, the group turned to Norman Latker, the HEW general counsel. Latker was the best person for the job, but he had to be very careful. Using federal resources to lobby for legislation was illegal. He had been investigated on similar suspicions in the past, and Califano did not trust him. To be safe, Latker wrote the draft by hand and outsourced the typing to a tech-transfer entrepreneur and friend of the group named Mick Stadler. Even without any proof connecting the draft to Latker's office typewriter, Califano got wind of rumors that his general counsel was again working against HEW policy on government time, and fired him in December 1978 without separation pay. Latker returned to a lucrative private practice in patent law.

With a draft in hand, the group turned to cultivating support for the bill. The most important link between the Forman-Latker group and the political side of the operation was a twenty-seven-year-old Bayh staffer named Joe Allen. When Bayh agreed to sponsor the bill, it was Allen who wrote the speech formally introducing the University and Small Business Patent Procedures Act in the Senate in February 1979. Until the vote more than a year later, Allen would draft nearly all of Bayh's written and oral remarks on the legislation, from pitches to skeptical labor groups to luncheon talks before friendly audiences like Patent Lawyers for Bayh and Eli Lilly executives. Allen crafted and stage-managed much of Bayh's advocacy with one of the senator's colleagues foremost in mind. "We hoped that limiting our bill to universities and small companies would avoid Senator Long's wrath," Allen said decades later.

The ploy showed early signs of success. More than fifty years after the rise of the Research Corporation and WARF, most people still did not know much about the industry represented by the Society of University Patent Administrators (now called the Association of University Technology Managers, Inc.) that lobbied heavily for the bill. "Universities' history made them seem more trustworthy than business firms: they would use their patents for public benefit rather than private gain," writes law professor Rebecca Eisenberg. "The perceived halos over universities lit the path to passage of the Bayh-Dole Act."

The university patent lobby had come a long way since the debates they sparked in the 1930s. By the 1970s, every major public and private research university had a patent office or hired a contractor to manage its intellectual property as a source of "nontraditional revenue." Their association adopted the line set down by Forman, with a focus on loosening restrictions on patenting federally financed research related to public health.

In Bayh's speech introducing the bill, Allen inserted the sensational allegation that the development of twenty-nine important medicines had been delayed by government indecision over the dispensation of patent rights. Repeated in the press, the unfounded claim heightened the fear factor around the bill: The Democrats' quaint and anti-business commitment to public science not only threatens American factory jobs, *it's killing our grandmothers. Do your elected representatives even care?*

The strategy was effective. Labor warmed to the idea that patents could drive growth and create jobs, a case made in a March 1979 letter to labor leaders drafted by Allen under Bayh's signature. "The most efficient patent policy possible," he wrote, "translates into more jobs for the American worker and a higher standard of living not only here, but throughout the world." These arguments resonated with Democratic lawmakers, who were announcing their support for the bill in growing numbers. In the spring of

1979, Gaylord Nelson signaled he would support the bill, following the lead of his fellow Wisconsin Democrat Robert Kastenmeier, whose congressional district included the University of Wisconsin and the WARF, a leader of the Bayh-Dole lobbying coalition. Whether Nelson was also swayed by this powerful home-state constituent, his about-face provided cover for other liberal Democrats. The Forman-Latker group was cautiously optimistic as it planned for autumn hearings in Bayh's Judiciary Committee.

One Democrat saw through the ruse and refused to go along. Louisiana's Russell Long, chair of the Senate Finance Committee, had spent three decades bringing hammers down on industry fingers reaching for patents on government science. From the day Bayh introduced the bill, Long smelled a rat, but as the lobbying campaign gained steam, his allies dwindled. One that never wavered was the only person in town who hated patent incentives in federal R&D more than he did: Admiral Hyman Rickover. "These inventions are paid for by the public and therefore should be available for any citizen to use or not as he sees fit," Rickover told a November 1979 hearing on the bill, now co-sponsored by Kansas Republican Bob Dole.

The addition of a public-interest provision to the bill—reserving "march-in" rights for the government to ensure the rights holder made products available to the public on "reasonable terms"—left Rickover unmoved. These rights tend not to be used, he noted, and it would be much simpler to retain the current law. But in making a perfunctory nod to the social obligations of patent holders, and reserving ultimate power for the government, the "march-in" clause provided cover to wavering Democrats looking for reasons to convince themselves the bill was more than a historic giveaway certain to result in more dug monopolies and higher drug prices.

A quirk of Senate procedure gave Long all the power he needed. Carter had lost his reelection, and in lame duck sessions, non-budget bills require a unanimous vote to proceed. As federal workers erected the last Carter White House Christmas tree, bedecked with five-watt energy-saving bulbs, nobody expected Long to do anything but murder Bayh-Dole with his own two hands.

Then, late one afternoon in early December, Bayh, who had also been

defeated, was packing boxes in his office when the phone rang. It was Russell
Long. After some chitchat, the elder senator delivered his goodbye gift. "Birch,
you can pass your damn patent bill," he said. "I'm really going to miss working with you." After brief floor debates in the Democratic-controlled House
and Senate, the bill was sent to the White House. On December 12, 1980,
the final day of the ninety-sixth Congress, President Carter signed the
bill, renamed the Patent and Trademark Law Amendments Act, into law.
Kennedy's flexible policy of default government title on government-funded
research was pulled inside out. The burden now lay with the government to
prove its possession of a patent would better serve the public than a private
monopoly.

Long left no record clarifying the mystery of why the Senate's most dedi-
cated guardian of public science changed his mind. Most accounts of Long's
decision ascribe it to senatorial comity—"a magnanimous gesture" according
to one contemporary observer—but that seems unlikely. A more probable
explanation is that Bob Dole offered Long something big in return, likely
related to Louisiana, paired with the assurance, which he also received from
Bayh, that the bill was not a Trojan horse for drug companies and would not
be expanded to include them.

Events soon confirmed Long's initial gut suspicion that the bill was a
fake out. Again, the Commerce Department played the key role. After clear-
ing out his desk in Bayh's office, Joe Allen briefly served as executive director
of the Intellectual Property Owners, Inc., a lobby group, before returning
to government to help Forman oversee the implementation of Bayh-Dole in
the department's Office of Science and Technology Policy. The position also
reunited Allen with Norman Latker, back in federal employ as director of
the department's patent office. The trio was effectively in charge of overseeing
the implementation and expansion of Bayh-Dole, and on their recommendation, Ronald Reagan signed an executive order in 1983 that expanded the
law to include corporations of all sizes. (The bill was officially amended to fit
Reagan's memo in 1984.) Having served its temporary purpose, Bayh-Dole's
stage-prop halo was removed and tossed out the window.

◆

The tradition that ended with Bayh-Dole—public science under public control—survived as long as it did because its champions understood that a democratic patent policy has political and economic spillover effects. "The general welfare, promised by the Constitution and still unrealized, is not blocked by nature and must not be blocked by the artificial barriers which man erects against man," wrote Walton Hamilton in his TNEC report in 1938. A decade later, the attorney general's report submitted to Truman argued that only a policy of public ownership "will assure free and equal availability of the inventions to American industry and science; will eliminate any competitive advantage to the contractor chosen to perform the research work; will avoid undue concentration of economic power in the hands of a few large corporations . . . and thus strengthen our American system of free, competitive enterprise."

The 1980s showed how fast, and how completely, generations' worth of public knowledge could be appropriated by invasive parasitic industries, in partnership with public institutions transformed by incentives and temptations introduced by changes in the law. For some observers, the only historical precedent for this process was the Gilded Age parceling of the natural commons. Former FDA commissioner Donald Kennedy describes Bayh-Dole as the "Homestead Act of the Endless Frontier," an unflattering reference to the 1862 law that divvied up the most prize tracts of the American West among land speculators and railroad barons.

Bayh-Dole opened up government science to business just as government science budgets exploded as a subset of Reagan's historically high defense budgets.

The 1980s upsurge in federal research outlays reflected broader reputational rebounds for science, technology, and even the concept of progress. From the mid-1960s through the late '70s, the early Space Age optimism of Camelot and *Star Trek* darkened and gave way to a more nuanced and critical accounting of technology's character and costs. Under the influence of the New Left, the counterculture, and the early environmental movement, the starry vistas of the Endless Frontier became crowded in the public mind with cancer-causing pollution, petroleum-jelly explosives, and research contracts for next-generation nuclear warheads. This suspicion of what Marxist and counterculture critics called technological rationality was among the targets Republican operatives had in mind when they attacked the "malaise" of the later Carter years.

That the techno-optimism current running through Reagan's "morning in America" was represented by Silicon Valley, an offspring of the counterculture, is not without irony. The emergent high-tech industries of the 1980s fed on the same military programs and foreign policies that informed the science skepticism of the 1970s.[36] The historic arms buildup of Reagan's first term pushed annual R&D spending past $86 billion in 1983, more than Europe and Japan combined.

As the administration pushed federal science spending to new heights, it continued to expand private-sector monopoly access to its fruits.

The decade of privatized science officially kicked off two months before the passage of Bayh-Dole, in October 1980, with Carter's signing of the Stevenson-Wydler Technology Innovation Act. Anticipating Bayh-Dole, the law required federal labs to create budget lines to help industry find partnerships and file patent applications. When Reagan opened Bayh-Dole to contractors of all sizes in 1983, the help centers mandated by Stevenson-Wydler in 1980 became insufficient, and in 1986 Reagan signed amendments mandating their expansion. The new centers were part of a wider program to facilitate "cooperative research and development agreements," or CRADAs. Crafted in part by Latker and Allen, the CRADA program turned what had been information booths into luxury suites. Federal laboratories would henceforth feature staff, services, equipment, and facilities to help make the acquisition of title on publicly financed science an easier, more pleasant experience.[37]

---

36. This shift was embodied in Silicon Valley hype men like Stewart Brand, publisher of the *Whole Earth Catalog*, who traded in his back-to-the-land philosophy for a spastic digital utopianism.

37. As of this writing, the NIH website defines the CRADA program as "an exciting opportunity for NIH investigators to join with their colleagues from industry and

✦

These CRADA red carpets realized the kind of futuristic nightmare Morris Fishbein might have had during the controversy over Steenbock's vitamin D patent. From a commitment to the open pursuit of knowledge, a free-flowing exchange of ideas, and unrestricted publication, public universities had adopted the perspectives and interests of industry, including those conflicting with once-sacred norms around publishing and secrecy.

It is important to recall how new these norms were even within the research divisions of the largest pharmaceutical companies. In 1949, Merck's executives triggered an internal company revolt by pushing a policy of delaying publication of research related to new drugs for five years after the patent filing. The company's outraged senior scientists quashed the idea as "incomprehensible, detrimental to the company, and totally unacceptable," in the words of one Merck researcher quoted by Dominique Tobbell. The same pressures that transformed industry publishing norms in the 1950s were now pressed on academic laboratories to the same result. As early as 1983, a report published by the Twentieth Century Fund, titled "Midas in the Academy," would note the suddenness of this change and lament, "The stage has perhaps been reached at which almost every biological advance discovered in American universities is made by, or made known before publication to, someone who has a possible commercial interest in keeping it secret."

The post-Bayh-Dole university lab was the subject of a deeper investigation published the following year, David Dickson's 1984 *The New Politics of Science*. A veteran Washington correspondent for *Science* and *Nature*, Dickson painted the era's defining portrait of Bayh-Dole's impact on the culture of academic research. "In pushing for the new legislation, universities

---

academia in the joint pursuit of common research goals. Government scientists can leverage their own research resources, as well as serve the larger mission of NIH, to facilitate the development and commercialization of healthcare pharmaceuticals and products. Companies also can leverage their own R&D efforts while collaborating in state-of-the-art NIH research."

argued strongly that patents could generate a source of much-needed income," he wrote. This income, however, was premised on parceling up "the results of research programs into a form over which private companies could exert direct—and usually exclusive—control, an essential step in securing scientific knowledge for the private marketplace."

Few of the old "ethical" holdouts from the first wave of university patenting remained on the sidelines as opportunities for profiting off industry involvement grew over the decade. In 1934, Harvard adopted a policy of dedicating all patents related to "therapeutics or public health" to the public domain. Fifty years later, it specialized in partnerships that allowed corporations to set the terms. Harvard president Derek Bok directed the university's embrace of what he called a new breed of "speculative" deal, while at the same time conceding the "dangers to academic science seem real and severe."

Dickson marveled at how quickly Bayh-Dole had eroded the deepest of academic research conventions. By the end of Reagan's first term, university officials no longer denied or apologized for suspending or revising centuries-old open-publication norms under pressure from corporate partners. Drug companies were likewise done apologizing; they saw their new power as an entitlement. In a 1982 address to the nation's medical school deans, a senior Johnson & Johnson executive informed his audience that "patents are a must." Prigs who criticized delaying publication to protect corporate advantage, he said, must abandon this "narrow view."

The "wider" view on publishing delays was dutifully adopted by universities under the advice of their tech-transfer officers. When Dickson started researching his book in 1981, the longstanding scientific norm of publishing "without delay" had been adjusted to "within two months," or enough time to file and win a patent claim. When he submitted his manuscript in 1984, the norm had been loosened to four months or more. A subsequent study conducted by Massachusetts General Hospital found that nearly 60 percent of leading life-science firms contractually required academic partners to delay publishing any data for at least six months.

The cause of this sea change was not a mystery. The Bayh-Dole policy of default private claims on public science created new incentives and dynamics wherever that science was produced. Universities and newly ensconced and empowered companies and speculators conspired to rewrite the rules around scientific production to maximize their respective shares of the gains. That a melding of values followed is not surprising. When asked in 1982 about the impact of Bayh-Dole, University of California immunologist Leon Wofsy shrugged, telling a reporter, "The motive force of the universities is the pursuit of knowledge; the business of business is to make money."

Ten

THE MOST EXPENSIVE DRUG
EVER SOLD

Generics, AIDS, and AZT

W HEN ESTES KEFAUVER DIED IN 1963, HE WAS WRITING A BOOK about monopoly power called *In a Few Hands*. Early into Reagan's first term, the industry must have been tempted to publish a gloating retort titled *In a Few Years*. Between 1979 and 1981, the drug companies did more than break the stalemate of the 1960s and '70s—they smashed it wide open. Stevenson-Wydler and Bayh-Dole replaced the Kennedy policy with a functioning framework for the high-speed transfer of public science into private hands. As the full machinery was built out, the industry-funded echo chamber piped a constant flow of memes into the culture: *patents alone drive innovation . . . R&D requires monopoly pricing . . . progress and American competitiveness depend on it . . . there is no other way . . .*

In December 1981, the drug companies celebrated another long-sought victory when Congress created a federal court devoted to settling patent disputes. Previously, patent disputes were heard in the districts where they originated. The problem, from industry's perspective, was the presence of so many staunch New Deal judges in key regions like New York's Second Circuit. These lifetime judges often understood patent challenges not as threats to property rights, but as opportunities to enforce antitrust law. Local circuit judges appointed by Republicans could also be dangerously old-fashioned in their interpretations of the "novelty" standard. By contrast, the judges on the new patent court, named the Court of Appeals for the Federal Circuit, were appointed by the president. Reagan stuffed its bench with corporate patent lawyers and conservative legal scholars influenced by the Johnny Appleseed of the Law and Economics movement, Robert Bork. Prior to 1982, federal district judges rejected around two-thirds of patent claims; the Court of Appeals has since decided two-thirds of all cases in *favor* of patent claims. Reagan's first appointee, Pauline Newman, was the former lead patent counsel for the chemical firm FMC.

The Supreme Court also contributed to the industry's 1979–1981 run of wins. When Reagan entered office, one of the great scientific-legal unknowns involved the patentability of modified genes. Similar to the uncertainty around the postwar antibiotics market—settled in the industry's favor by the 1952 Patents Act—the uncertainty threatened the monopoly dreams of the emergent biotechnology sector. The U.S. Patent Office was against patenting modified genes. In 1979, its officers twice rejected an attempt by a General Electric microbiologist to patent a modified bacterium invented to assist in oil spill cleanups. The GE scientist, Ananda Chakrabarty, sued the Patent Office, and in the winter of 1980 *Diamond v. Chakrabarty* landed before the Supreme Court. In a 5–4 decision written by Warren Burger, the Court overruled the U.S. Patent Office and ruled that modified genes were patentable, as was "anything under the sun that is made by man." The decision was greeted with audible exhales by the players in the Bayh-Dole alliance. "*Chakrabarty* was the game changer that provided academic entrepreneurs and venture capitalists the protection they were waiting for," says economist Öner Tulum. "It paved the way for a more expansive commercialization of science."

But the industry knew better than to relax. It understood that political victories could be impermanent and fragile, and it had the scar tissue to prove it. Uniquely profitable, uniquely hated, and thus uniquely vulnerable—the companies could not afford to forget that their fantastic postwar wealth and power depended on the maintenance of artificial monopolies resting on dubious if not indefensible ethical and economic arguments that were rejected by every other country on earth. In the United States, home to their biggest profit margins, danger lurked behind every corner in the form of the next crusading senator eager to train years of unwanted attention on these facts. Not even Bayh-Dole, that precious newborn legislation, could be taken for granted. This mode of permanent crisis was validated by the return of a familiar menace in the early 1980s. Of all things, it was the generics industry, an old but weak enemy of the patent-based drug companies, that reappeared and threatened to ruin their celebration of achieving dominance over every corner of medical research and the billions of public dollars flowing through it.

As late as the 1930s, there was no "generic" drug industry to speak of. There were only big drug companies and small ones, some with stature, others obscure. They both sold products that were, in the parlance of ethical medicine, "nonproprietary." To be listed in the *United States Pharmacopeia* and *National Formulary*, the official bibles of prescribable medicines, drugs could only carry scientific names; the essential properties of a good scientific name, according to the first edition of the *Pharmacopeia*, were "expressiveness, brevity, and dissimilarity."

The naming of drugs and medicines formed the other half of the patent taboo: branding a drug evidenced the same knavishness and greed as monopolizing one. The rules of "ethical marketing" did permit products to include an institutional affiliation—Parke-Davis Cannabis Indica Extract, or Squibb Digitalis Tincture—but the names of the medicines themselves (cannabis, digitalis) did not vary. "The generic name emerged as a parallel form of social property belonging to all that resisted commodification and thereby came to occupy a central place in debates about monopoly rights," writes Joseph Gabriel.

As with patents on scientific medicine, the Germans gave the U.S. drug industry early instruction in the use of trademarks to entrench market control. Hoechst and Bayer broke every rule of so-called ethical marketing, aggressively advertising their breakthrough drugs under trademarks like

Aspirin, Heroin, and Novocain. The idea was to twine these names and the things they described in the public mind so tightly, the brand name would secure a de facto monopoly long after the patent expired.

The strategy worked, but the German firms did not reap the benefits. The wartime Office of Alien Property redistributed the German patents and trademarks among domestic firms who produced competing versions of aspirin, creating the first "branded generic." During the patent taboo's extended death rattle of the interwar years, more U.S. companies waded into the use of original trademarks to suppress competition. As they experimented with German tactics to avoid "genericide"—the loss of markets after patent expiration—they were enabled by court decisions that transformed trademarks into forms of hard property, similar to the way patents were reconceived in the 1830s.

After World War II, branding and monopoly formed the two-valve heart of a post-ethical growth strategy. The industry's incredible postwar success—between 1939 and 1959, drug profits soared from $300 million to $2.3 billion—was fueled in large part by expanding the German playbook. While branding monopolies with trade names, the industry initiated campaigns to ruin the reputations of scientifically identical but competing products. The goal was the "scandalization" of generic drugs, writes historian Jeremy Greene. The drug companies "worked methodically to moralize and sensationalize generic dispensing as a dangerous and subversive practice. Dispensing a nonbranded product in place of a brand-name product was cast as 'counterfeiting'; the act of substituting a cheaper version of a drug at the pharmacy was described as 'beguilement,' 'connivance,' 'misrepresentation,' 'fraudulent,' 'unethical' and 'immoral.'"

As with patenting, it was the drug companies that dragged organized medicine with them into the post-ethical future. As late as 1955, the AMA's Council on Pharmacy and Chemistry maintained a ban on advertisements for branded products in its *Journal*. That changed the year Equanil hit the market, opening the age of branded prescription drugs as a leading source of income for medical journals and associations. "Clinical journals and newer 'throwaway' promotional media now teemed with advertisements for Terramycin, Premarin, and Diuril rather than oxytetracycline (Pfizer), conjugated equine estrogens (Wyeth) or chlorothiazide (Merck)," writes Greene. In 1909, only one in ten prescription drugs carried a brand name. By 1969, the ratio had flipped, with only one in ten marketed under its scientific name.

In another echo of the patent controversy, the rise of marketing and branded drugs produced division and resistance. By the mid-1950s, an alliance of so-called nomenclature reformers arose to decry trademarks as unscientific handmaidens of monopoly and call for a return to the use of scientific names. These reformers—doctors, pharmacists, labor leaders—made regular appearances before the Kefauver committee beginning in 1959. Their testimony on how the industry used trademarks to suppress competition informed a section in Kefauver's original bill requiring doctors to use scientific names in all prescriptions. The proposed law reflected the norms that reigned during ethical medicine's heyday, and would have allowed doctors to recommend firms, but not their branded products. Like most of Kefauver's core proposals, however, the generic clause was excised. The only trademark-related reform in the final Kefauver-Harris Amendments placed limits on companies' ability to rebrand and market old medicines as new breakthroughs.

With the passage of Medicare and Medicaid in 1965, prescription drug costs became a federal and state budget issue. Calls for generic substitution laws grew louder, and in 1967, Louisiana's Russell Long and New Mexico's Joseph Montoya championed a Senate bill to amend the Social Security Act to require and incentivize generic substitution. The bill failed, but the issue lived on. In May 1967, Wisconsin's Gaylord Nelson opened a decade of hearings on drug industry practices in the familiar setting of the Senate Subcommittee on Antitrust and Monopoly. Nelson's hearings began where Kefauver had left them: directly over the target of patents and trademarks. "This is a shocking business," he told the chamber. "I don't know of any other area in the marketplace where competing items are available, and where this kind of [price] disparity would last one day. It wouldn't last a day in this case, either, if the consumer knew the whole story."

The Nelson hearings put the nomenclature reformers back into public view. One of the hearing's revelations involved how the drug companies had subverted the original goal of scientific naming—simplicity and easy recall—by purposefully choosing complex, overly syllabic names that were unpronounceable by design. This touched a nerve with the public and became something of a cultural punchline. A 1969 *New Yorker* cartoon depicted a woman telling her pharmacist, "No expensive brand names, if you please. Just give me a few milligrams of phenylpropanolamine hydrochloride, with a touch of chlorpheniramine maleate added."

The AMA and the drug companies weren't smiling. They launched an initiative to preempt state-level generic substitution laws across the country, led by state AMA chapters provided with scripts from the national office that scandalized generics as threats to public health. The drug companies, meanwhile, turned to their longtime communications guru Arthur Sackler to orchestrate a campaign highlighting the alleged dangers of "drug counterfeits" and "the fallacy of generic equivalence." The efforts enjoyed a success as rapid as it was complete. By 1970, all fifty states had passed anti-substitution laws.[38] At the same time, the companies exercised leverage at the highest levels of federal power. In August 1969, *The New York Times* ran a front-page story about John Adriani, a supporter of generic prescribing whom President Nixon's FDA chief planned to appoint director of the agency's Bureau of Medicine. Sources told the *Times* that Nixon quashed the appointment because industry opposition was "too great for the administration to bear." Adriani told the paper, "It's a sad commentary when the pharmaceutical industry doesn't let the Commissioner of the FDA appoint his man to protect the public."

The substance of the industry campaign to discredit generics, however, was bogus. According to expert testimony by the editorial board of

---

38. The campaign anticipated the fifty-statehouse strategy of the corporate-funded American Legislative Exchange Council, founded in 1973 with pharmaceutical industry contributions.

the *National Formulary* and the *United States Pharmacopeia*, biological inequivalence—differences in the way two chemically identical drugs operate in the body—had been detected in only a small handful of generic drugs compared to their branded equivalents. One of the experts, Dr. Edward Feldmann, said he "would be hard pressed to name more than even a few—less than five—well-conducted clinically acceptable studies which have demonstrated significant differences between two or more products clinically where they have met all of the chemical and physical standards as provided by the official compendia." He noted that similar differences were sometimes found within the same batch of any drug, branded or not, saying, "[F]rom a technical standpoint there really is no such thing as complete 'drug equivalence.'"

The industry responded to evidence that generic drugs were not inherently inferior to branded drugs in a strange fashion: by conceding the point. As William C. Gray, the public relations head of the Pharmaceutical Manufacturers Association, explained to Nelson's committee in 1974, "there is really no such thing as a 'generic drug,' just different drugs of different merits that reflect the reputation of the manufacturer." If this was true, then the companies should have welcomed a return to the days of Squibb Digitalis Tincture. They didn't, of course, because branding twinned to monopoly multiplied the power of each. If they could not win on the superiority of branded drugs, they would die defending their right to profit from the corruption necessary to maintain the illusion.

The industry beat back Nelson's mid-decade push for national generic-substitution legislation, but again failed to bury the issue. In 1976, the FTC launched a probe into the AMA-orchestrated state-level industry-AMA anti-substitution laws, concluding that they "impose substantial unwarranted costs on consumers by unduly restricting price competition in the multi-source prescription drug market." A more definitive judgement was delivered by the alliance of consumer groups, organized labor, and the AARP that overturned the anti-substitution laws in forty states. The successful pushback operation hastened a reckoning with a larger failure: The right to prescribe generics has meaning only to the extent generic drugs are available on the market to prescribe. Toward this rub the battle now turned.

✦

The drug companies feared senators. They feared the consumer movement. They feared the AFL-CIO and the AARP. They feared the FTC, the FDA, and the general public they served. One thing they did not fear was the generics industry. Small, underfunded, and poorly organized, the country's off-patent drug companies lacked even a trade association to speak on their behalf when Nelson began his hearings on generic substitution in 1969.

"The vast majority of generic manufacturers were family businesses into the 1980s," said Alfred Engelberg, the founding counsel for the Generic Pharmaceutical Industry Association. "Of the eight companies in the generic trade association in 1980, five or six of them were Jewish families in the greater New York area. The husbands had chemistry degrees and made the drugs while their wives managed the books. They couldn't afford the FDA trial requirements, so it created perpetual natural monopolies for the big drug companies, who could continue charging obscene prices on branded drugs with expired patents and no threat of generic competition."

The generics industry took its first steps toward mobilizing on its own behalf in the mid-1970s. Helping them was a crusading ex-Kefauver committee staffer named William Haddad. In meetings in New York and Washington, Haddad coached the ragtag group of generics executives into a *Bad News Bears*–style underdog counter-drug lobby. The focus of their efforts: reforming the FDA drug application process to lower the barriers to generics entering the market.

The group gained traction in Congress throughout the early 1980s, led by a California "Watergate baby" named Henry Waxman who became Haddad's closest ally. By 1983 there was broad support for streamlining the FDA drug approval process—last updated in 1970—so that generic drug manufacturers only had to prove their products performed the same as branded drugs once in the body, known as bioequivalence. To move the issue forward in the Senate, Waxman teamed up with Utah Republican Orrin Hatch. The two found support in both chambers, suggesting the Nelson hearings had prepped the political ground for generics reform, so long as the bill did not touch the political third rails of patents and mandatory substitution.

Framed as pro-competition and budget-serious, the bipartisan drive to reform the FDA process was a slow-moving knuckleball for an industry used to fastballs. For decades, it had maintained that patents and monopolies were the only drivers of progress. But the Waxman-led effort to update FDA rules left both untouched. It imposed no new regulations on the brand name industry. On what grounds, then, were the drug companies opposed? Was the Progress Clause not premised on the eventual diffusion of new knowledge, once the patent term had expired?

Lacking answers to these questions, the companies responded by grabbing what they could out of a bad situation. As if by instinct, they started talking, apropos of nothing, about patents. Specifically, longer drug patents. If the generics industry was going to get an abbreviated path to market, they demanded a longer term of exclusivity. In July 1981, the industry's friends in the Senate introduced a bill to extend drug monopolies from seventeen to twenty-four years. "The industry argued that new drug patents were entitled to longer life to compensate for the time lost in obtaining FDA approval," says Engelberg. "It was a nonsensical claim. Whether a patented product is ever sold, for how long, and under what circumstances, is governed by a host of commercial factors. A patent does not create an affirmative right to sell a patented product at all, let alone for the life of the patent."

After the bill passed the Senate and moved to the House, Engelberg said as much before Tennessee House Democrat Al Gore's Committee on Science and Technology. "The claim that patents create an affirmative right to sell a product at all, let alone for a given amount of time, has no legal basis," Engelberg testified. "A patent only grants the right to exclude others from selling that product during its term. In an unrigged free market, the public is entitled to the benefit of competition from lower cost generic drugs without paying for that right by granting longer monopolies to brand name drugs."

When the patent-extension bill came within five votes of passing the House, the two sides agreed to negotiate. "It was clear that longer drug monopolies would be the political price for permitting the abbreviated generic drug approval process," Engelberg recalled decades later. The original proposal to trade patent term extension for the expedited generic approval was developed by Waxman in late 1983 and early 1984. Haddad served as the principal negotiator for the generic side.

The resulting compromise bill formalized the trade-off: the FDA would approve generic drugs that demonstrated bioequivalence without independent proof of safety and efficacy, and patented drugs would be eligible for an extra five years of market exclusivity. The deal included a last-minute sweetener for the brand-name companies: ten years of additional market exclusivity for all drugs introduced between 1982 and the bill's passage in September 1984. "Just to make sure their projected earnings for the decade were not adversely affected," says Engelberg.

The Drug Price Competition and Patent Term Restoration Act of 1984, better known as Hatch-Waxman, was controversial among the drug majors. Some companies were furious at their colleagues for not fighting the low-born generics industry to the death, on principle. The hard-line bloc was led by Hoffmann-La Roche, the U.S. division of the Roche Group based in Basel, Switzerland, a country that did not issue drug patents until 1977. In the wake of the bill's passage, Hoffmann-La Roche's CEO Irwin Lerner is said to have personally orchestrated the removal of the Pharmaceutical Manufacturers Association's president, Lew Engman, for the crime of conspiring with the enemy.

What kind of industry can weather the rise of competition that undercuts its prices by 65 percent, on products accounting for 40 percent of its market, and not only maintain its profit margins, but actually increase them? An industry with monopoly control of the remaining 60 percent.

In the six years after Hatch-Waxman, a flood of non-branded drugs entered the market and forced prices down on de facto prescription drug monopolies. Yet aggregate spending on prescription drugs increased over the same time frame, because the drug companies responded by jacking up prices on products still protected by the (now expanded) monopoly term.

The drug companies wiped out the country's savings on generics in two ways. In the near term, it simply raised prices. Next, it went to work innovating anticompetitive practices that remain standard operating procedure. The bluntest of these methods are "pay to delay," where brand-name companies grease the palms of generic firms to delay their generic FDA applications, and the "blow-off," in which the big companies refuse to provide samples and otherwise block necessary information from being available to scientists at generic companies. This latter strategy was connected to the industry drive to strengthen legal protections around "undisclosed information" in the Uniform Trade Secrets Act of 1985, a subject of this book's final chapter.

Post-Hatch-Waxman, the drug companies also put new energy behind developing the patent law practice known as evergreening. This is when a company that is facing a patent cliff, usually on a blockbuster drug, artificially resets the patent term, sometimes more than once, by submitting a new application based on extremely minor or cosmetic tweaks to the original product, or on advances in the manufacturing method made during the first patent term. By "going back to the well," the companies erect barriers to the arrival of generics without increasing the therapeutic value of the drug under extended patent protection. In many cases, new patent terms have been granted for changing the color of a drug or tweaking the language on the label. Even the most outrageous and legally vulnerable evergreening tricks serve a purpose by raising the cost of entry to competitors, who must either file and fight an expensive challenge or proceed with manufacture at the risk of being targeted with an infringement suit by a multinational company with bottomless resources and a field army of patent lawyers.

The rise of evergreening was captured in a first-of-its-kind study published in 2021 by Robin Feldman, director of the Center for Innovation at the University of California Hastings College of the Law. Using thirteen years of patent data beginning in 2005, Feldman built a database that shows how pharmaceutical companies have deployed minor tweaks and marketing rebrands to prolong patents and delay generic competition. Many of the deftest practitioners of the art are the same companies posing as heroes for their roles during the COVID-19 pandemic. AstraZeneca leads the pack with six drugs among the top twenty with the most additional protections—providing an additional *ninety years* of monopoly on drugs that treat common diseases such as diabetes. Johnson & Johnson has been granted 167 protections on fourteen patents related to its HIV drug Prezista, effectively delaying generic competition for sixteen years over the original patent term. Gilead is using similar tactics to artificially extend monopolies on the HIV drugs Truvada and Viread.

Feldman identified a mutation of evergreening that she calls "product hopping," in which modified versions of already evergreened products are rolled out to restart the clock yet again. "Look at the way AstraZeneca product hopped Prilosec to become Nexium, with all of the protections piled onto Nexium. They are essentially evergreening their evergreens."

"Patents are supposed to come to an end—they are intended as time-limited government grants of market protection to incentivize the innovation of new, lifesaving medicines," says Feldman. "But that's not what we are seeing. The database shows how the industry takes advantage of the patent system by blocking competition to protect their prices and revenue. These drug tweaks may be enough to get these companies past the patent office, but they may not mean much in terms of a benefit to patients. Society is lavishing expensive rewards on minimal improvements."

Feldman's findings reinforce a 2018 study by the research group I-MAK that showed the twelve top-selling prescription drugs in 2017 had an average of thirty-eight years of patent protection designed to block generic competition. "This is nearly double the 20-year monopoly intended under U.S. patent law," says Tahir Amin, the group's co-executive director. "Over half of the top twelve drugs in America have more than 100 attempted patents per drug, and prices have increased 68 percent on average since 2012 for 11 of these 12 drugs. These figures reflect an explosion in patenting rates. Between 2005 and 2015, the number of pharmaceutical patents granted in the U.S more than doubled."

In 1985, Engelberg left his law firm to work full-time challenging the validity of branded drug monopolies. He used some of the proceeds to found an institute for the study of innovation and intellectual property at the New York University School of Law. "I told the Gore committee in 1982 that extending drug monopolies will produce higher prices and less innovation," says Engelberg. "That's exactly what happened—an ongoing payoff to a highly profitable industry has wiped out the savings generic drugs should have produced. Generics now fill 90 percent of U.S. prescriptions, but we're still spending up to three times more on prescription drugs than other developed countries. Why? Because the remaining 10 percent account for 80 percent of all prescription drug spending, and no other developed nation allows pharmaceutical manu-facturers to abuse their monopoly power by price gouging."[39]

AIDS broke through to widespread public consciousness in 1985. It was the year of Rock Hudson and Ryan White; the year of the first reliable test for HIV antibodies. At a press conference on September 17, the president of the United States said the word *AIDS* for the first time. Reagan proclaimed the epidemic a "top priority" for his administration, even as it prepared a budget for 1986 that cut AIDS research funding by 11 percent.

In April of that year, a play opened Off Broadway at New York's Pub-lic Theater that cast a literal spotlight on the administration's miserable response. The twelfth scene of Larry Kramer's autobiographical play, *The Normal Heart*, finds Dr. Emma Brookner, a crusading AIDS researcher, alone in her wheelchair on an otherwise dark stage. Told that her request for an AIDS research grant has been denied on budget grounds, she delivers a wrathful monologue aimed at unseen government officials. "Five million dol-lars doesn't seem quite right for some two thousand cases. The government spent twenty million investigating seven deaths from Tylenol," she says.

> We are now almost into the third year of this epidemic. Your Na-tional Institutes of Health received my first request for research money two years ago . . . The paltry amount of money you are mak-ing us beg for—from the four billion dollars you are given each and every year—won't come to anyone until only God knows when. Any way you add all this up, it is an unconscionable delay and has never, never existed in any other health emergency during this entire cen-

---

39. In 2010, a Democratic Congress passed a Hatch-Waxman lookalike bill called the Biologics Price Competition and Innovation Act. It replicated the Hatch-Waxman tradeoff, establishing expedited approval for generic biologic drugs in exchange for giv-ing companies new pathways to delay competition and defend market exclusivity, which the bill guarantees for twelve years.

tury. While something is being passed around that causes death. We are enduring an epidemic of death.

Kramer's rage at the Reagan administration was well targeted, but perhaps too narrow. The failure to fund AIDS research extended to a private drug sector that no longer cared about infectious disease. Such diseases weren't eradicated after World War II—tuberculosis and dozens of tropical viruses killed and maimed tens of millions of people every year—but they were increasingly marginal to the interests of an industry focused on blockbuster prescription drugs and chronic disease treatments targeting the richest markets.

As recently as 1967, dozens of U.S. companies maintained infectious disease divisions and vaccine-manufacturing facilities. The rapid disappearance of both became an issue of official concern at the end of the 1970s, on the cusp of the first reports of an unusual and fatal pneumonia spreading through San Francisco's gay community. "The apparently diminishing commitment—and possibly capacity—of the American pharmaceutical industry to research, develop, and produce vaccines may . . . be reaching levels of real concern," concluded a 1979 report by the Office of Technology Assessment. Six years later, the nonprofit Institute of Medicine warned that the industry's vanishing investments in infectious disease threatened the nation's ability to address future epidemics, and possibly to suppress those already thought to be eradicated by science. "Reliance on market incentives to ensure vaccine availability may lead to a failure to meet public health needs [and] may not result in optimal levels of vaccine innovation," concluded the institute.

The industry did not dispute the economic logic driving the disinvestment. In an address to Congress in 1986, the president of Merck, Douglas MacMaster, said that his company might be forced to close down one of the industry's last major infectious disease and vaccine programs, due to the "profitability of such products."

The stigma surrounding AIDS only reinforced the industry's decision to keep its money at a safe distance from the new disease. Three years into the epidemic, not a single pharmaceutical firm had announced a research project to crack its mysteries or develop a cure or treatment. This intensified a sense of obligation in some quarters within the federal research establishment, which was never quite the apathetic bureaucratic monolith depicted in Kramer's dramatization. Within the National Cancer Institute and the National Institute of Allergic and Infectious Diseases, senior figures understood they would have to take the lead in a less than hospitable political climate.

The key figure was Samuel Broder, the newly appointed forty-year-old head of the Cancer Institute's clinical oncology program. Of the many NIH institutes, NCI was best positioned to develop experimental treatments in-house. For half a century, it had been amassing an archive of drug candidates drawn from thousands of federally funded projects across the country. "It is the only group at the NIH that actually had become a 'pharmaceutical company' working for the public, in difficult areas where the private sector either could not or would not make a commitment," Broder explained in an official NIH history.

Following the 1984 identification of HIV as the virus that causes AIDS, Broder and a team of NIAID and NCI researchers developed a system for measuring the effectiveness of experimental molecules in blunting HIV's potent attack on white blood cells. They then deployed the test to screen candidate drugs stored at research centers in a dozen states. Hundreds failed the test before one showed promise: azidothymidine, or AZT, an anti-cancer drug developed at Wayne State University and the Detroit Cancer Institute during the 1960s and '70s using NCI grants. The drug was abandoned as a dead end in 1974 after it proved incapable of reversing the growth of tumors. But the test developed by Broder demonstrated AZT's activity against an enzyme that drives the replication of HIV. When *The Normal Heart* premiered in late April 1985, Broder's team was finalizing preparations for the first human trial.

With a promising candidate molecule in hand, Broder began to search for an industry partner to codevelop and eventually manufacture the drug. He did not find any takers. The self-proclaimed defenders and champions of public health, the brave risk-taking firms who drive and deliver innovation—none of them wanted anything to do with the government effort to address the exponentially growing epidemic. As Broder later explained to *The*

Washington Post, the companies "weren't sure it would be worth the financial risk and the risk of having live viruses around. We needed companies to see that there was money to be made here."

The first candidate to nibble at the government tender was the U.S. subsidiary of the British drug giant Burroughs Wellcome. It seemed like a good fit. The company had a virology program attached to a modern laboratory just off the Duke University campus. But the company was hesitant to sign a contract that would obligate its researchers to handle AIDS samples. To entice the company off the sidelines, Broder offered everything he could, telling the company, "my entire lab [is] at your disposal." In exchange for its cooperation, the NCI would lend the company staff and pay the costs of trials.

Even after signing on as the contractor, the company held the AZT project at arm's length. "They refused to accept live virus, and at one point refused to accept patient samples," Broder later recounted. "They basically put the entire onus for the Phase 1 pharmacokinetics and related issues on NCI."

During the preparations for the initial trial, the company's bureaucracy blocked an internal transfer of a key AZT ingredient, thymidine. The NCI kept things on schedule by shipping its own supply of thymidine across the country to the Burroughs Wellcome factory. When the trials began, government staff conducted all the testing on hospitalized AIDS patients.

The public learned of the first trial results the following summer, in July 1986, when *The New England Journal of Medicine* published trial data. The article was followed by growing rumors of a fast-track FDA approval that could have AZT on the market as early as winter. AIDS patients weren't the only community heartened by the news. Overnight, Burroughs Wellcome became the "single-most-attractive major capitalization recommendation of pharmaceutical companies based anywhere in the world," one Wall Street analyst told *The New York Times*.

AZT was a front-page medical story, not a patent story. If anyone was thinking about the patent, they likely assumed the government owned it. And why wouldn't they? The government had invented and rediscovered the drug, then overseen its development as an AIDS treatment, up to and including the management of human trials. In March 1987, the government announced a plan to distribute $100,000 worth of the drug on an emergency basis, and launched a public information campaign to make doctors aware of the novel treatment.

But the government did not own the rights to the drug. The same day the FDA granted fast-track authorization of AZT, Burroughs Wellcome announced the cost of a yearlong course at between $8,000 and $12,000. Before it hit the market, the first AIDS drug became the most expensive drug in the history of world.

Most insurance plans did not cover drugs at the time, effectively pricing out many of the estimated 1.5 million Americans infected with the virus. As with branded hepatitis C drugs thirty years later, the price threatened to snap Medicaid and Medicare budgets already straining under Reagan's budget cuts. It also became an early rallying cry for the young New York City activist group ACT UP, the AIDS Coalition to Unleash Power, whose members organized a series of direct-action protests and blockades targeting the Food and Drug Administration federal building, Burroughs Wellcome's corporate offices, and the New York Stock Exchange.

The group drew national attention to the pricing scandal, but Burroughs Wellcome held on tight to its patent. The company evinced no sign it intended to license competition. The government showed no sign of doing anything about it.

How did this happen? From the start of AZT's development process, the government could have claimed ownership of the invention under the public health provisions of the Bayh-Dole Act. This would have allowed the NIH to license multiple manufacturers and drive down the price, and even produce the drug itself. That was the first of multiple possible fail-safes. When the price was announced, the government could have invoked its "march-in" power under Bayh-Dole—or the U.S. Code governing patents, or the Constitution's "takings clause"—to authorize competition. Instead, it did nothing.

When legislators and AIDS patients demanded to know why Burroughs Wellcome had been allowed to claim exclusive rights on a drug developed almost entirely in the public sector, the government played dumb. Assistant Secretary of Health and Human Services Lowell T. Harmison, who oversaw the AZT project, said the agency's plan to claim the patent and produce a competitive AZT market had been stymied by the speed of his contractor—"Burroughs got there first," he told *The Washington Post*. In the same interview, he described the AZT program as a successful example of "the way the capitalist system is supposed to work."

Broder fell into line. "The Burroughs Wellcome price was not something anyone could have anticipated," he told the *Post* in 1987. "We didn't pick up fast enough on the cost issue."

This was an absurd comment from a top official at the very heart of the post-Bayh-Dole federal health bureaucracy. Eight years of patent and tech-transfer reforms had been designed to produce precisely this outcome. The law at the center of the AZT joint project, the Technology Innovation Act of 1980 (better known as Stevenson-Wydler; expanded in 1986), included very detailed instructions for greasing the transfer of patentable knowledge to the private sector, but said nothing about reasonable pricing or ensuring access in the public interest. Bayh-Dole's "march-in" was the nearest tool it had to override the patent, but as its architects later admitted, it was not intended to actually work that way.

Days after Burroughs Wellcome's scandalous price announcement, Henry Waxman announced an investigation into the AZT patent by the House Subcommittee on Health and the Environment. The hearings showed the company's price justifications to be nonsense. They were based on "projected costs" (including "opportunity costs" incurred by taking on the project) that were dwarfed by expected profits upward of $100 million in the remaining months of 1987 alone. When pressed to explain the markup, company executives turned to a time-honored industry tactic for deflecting price questions: they talked instead about their company's "compassionate use" program. The strategy backfired, however, when the discount program touted by Thomas Kennedy, Burroughs Wellcome vice president for corporate affairs, was revealed to be limited to trial participants and less than fifty people dying of AIDS.

Kennedy maintained that his company bore no social responsibility for making AZT accessible. In one of the banner statements of the Bayh-Dole decade, he suggested it was the responsibility of governments to subsidize the purchase of the drug from Burroughs Wellcome. "Somewhere, society has a responsibility beyond Burroughs Wellcome to assist in the funding of care for AIDS patients," Kennedy told the committee. "Because even if we did everything we could do, we would bankrupt the company."

The hearings created pressure on the government to go through the motions of defending the public, but it was a pathetic sort of mimicry. When the NIH challenged Burroughs Welcome's six patents in the Federal Circuit Court, its lawyers let stand the company's assertion that the NIH had merely functioned as "a pair of hands" in the development of AZT. "The government was not prepared to defend its position. It did not want to," Broder later said. "The Justice Department seemed very unhappy with the whole litigation and did not put forward, in my view, a spirited defense, or sufficient energy and resources. The government, for whatever reason, did not choose to act as an equal in the litigation."

The AZT controversy revived fundamental questions posed by generations of patent reformers, inside and outside of government. These questions had been hotly debated during the 1979 Bayh-Dole hearings, yet the press reacted as if they were brand new issues, never before seen in Washington. During the Waxman hearings, *The Washington Post* asked readers to consider, about seven years too late: What is the public owed "when it supports, through the government, development of a highly profitable product? And how can the government assure, when it cooperates with private enterprise, protection of the public's need for life-saving drugs at reasonable costs?"

The answer to the second question is stated in the fine print of Bayh-Dole, requiring that all inventions arising from federally funded research be made available to the public on "reasonable terms," and provides that the government can "march in" on private patent claims to "protect the public against nonuse or unreasonable use of inventions." The government did not pull the Bayh-Dole "march-in" trigger in 1987, or in any year since. Among those who reinforced the misperception that marching in was not an option was Broder himself. "We didn't put strings on at the beginning, and we couldn't do it at the end," he said at the time. "The inability of many people to afford to pay for this drug makes me very sad."

Between the end of the Waxman hearings and summer, Burroughs Wellcome reported selling $25 million worth of AZT in a growing market with no competition in sight and seventeen years of market exclusivity. That December, succumbing to eight months of protests and public pressure, the company announced a reduction in the price of a hundred-capsule bottle of AZT from $188 to $150. Most AIDS patients continued to struggle to pay for the drug, as they would for the next second of government-developed HIV treatments.

In March 1989, a Bayh-Dole-style reasonable pricing clause was added to the Technology Transfer Act of 1986 that expanded Stevenson-Wydler. The text expressed the NIH's "concern that there be a reasonable relationship between the pricing of a licensed product, the public investment in that product, and the health and safety needs of the public. Accordingly, exclusive commercialization licenses granted for NIH intellectual property rights may require that this relationship be supported by reasonable evidence."

Like the Bayh-Dole "march-in" clause that served as its model, the NIH "reasonable relationship" clause was unused during its short lifespan. In 1996, NIH director Harold Varmus removed it from the bylaws of the agency's CRADA program. "Enforcement of a pricing clause," said Varmus in announcing the decision, "would divert NIH from its primary research mission and conflict with its statutory mission to transfer promising technologies to the private sector for commercialization."

In fact, there is no such statutory mission to "commercialize" anything, let alone on monopoly terms, under Bayh-Dole or NIH policy. The stated purpose of both is utilization—"practical application"—a goal that can be achieved through any number of licensing arrangements, including those based on the public ownership of patents.

By the time Varmus made this statement, NIH policy was no longer Broder's concern. He had moved into the private sector to become the medical director at Celera, the so-called Microsoft of biology known for its founder's quest to sequence, patent, and commercialize the human genome. Given Broder's role in the AZT scandal, he could not avoid being asked to answer for Varmus's decision. Shortly after he left the government to join Celera, an NIH historian pressed Broder for his thoughts on his former agency's decision to self-amputate the public-interest provision attached to Stevenson-Wydler.

"I think that it is perfectly fine," he replied. "It is simply an expression of the fact that you cannot please everybody. Now that I am in the private sector, I understand a little bit more about these things."

Eleven

THE WORLD TRADE ORGANIZATION

Drug Monopolies at the End of History

THE POST-ETHICAL DRUG INDUSTRY WAS DESTINED TO HAVE global ambitions. It consolidated within the sole industrial power to survive World War II intact. It flourished selling products for essentially bottomless markets at home and abroad. Not just any products, but "wonder drugs" like penicillin and streptomycin that seemed to fall from the robes of Jesus Christ himself, spoonful cures for tuberculosis and infections that once meant certain death. The biggest and most ambitious of the U.S. firms developed expansion plans to conquer a world newly populated by nations emerging from colonial rule. It didn't matter that U.S. patents had no legal standing in these countries. They would buy American drugs because they had to. And most had just enough wealth—concentrated in a middle or "creamy" class—to make it worth the trouble.

Then, in the late 1940s, the American Century took a troubling turn.

The United Nations and its do-gooder agencies began meddling in the health and development agendas of countries across Latin America, Africa, and Asia. This meddling focused on establishing public health systems, including public drug companies to provide cheap medicines for national and regional populations. More troubling still, these efforts enjoyed the backing of the U.S. government, now in a contest for the allegiance and affection of these same nations. Even before the postwar decolonization wave was complete, the countries shook off UN tutelage. The global south as a political identity was born in 1955 in Bandung, Indonesia, where 120 low- and middle-income countries established the Non-Aligned Movement. Together they would decide their own fates independent of Moscow and Washington. This movement's political and development agenda was fleshed out further at the first UN Conference on Trade and Development in 1964, where the poorest of these countries formed a negotiating bloc to call for full decolonization and south-south cooperation. They called themselves the Group of 77.

The global south was alert to the role of intellectual property in the rich countries, and within the U.S. pharmaceutical industry above all. They observed Pfizer's early efforts to enforce U.S. drug patents in Europe and left no uncertainty about their position: they considered intellectual property a purposeful fiction of the rich north—a neocolonial tool used to block north-south technology transfer and siphon wealth in the other direction. The demands of the G77 grew more strident into the 1970s, becoming a regular feature of UN conferences and assemblies. They were framed as matters of justice, not charity.

When these demands reached their crescendo in 1977, the drug industry had heard enough. Amid the calm of détente, the pioneers of corporate red-baiting decided their biggest threat was the global south's generic drug industry. This alternative system posed a risk to their global expansion plans, but also represented a provocation and challenge that might one day reach the lucrative and always vulnerable home market. Unless it was countered, soon and with force, there was no telling what troubles it might bring.

The south-based system that so worried the industry in the 1970s was led, as during the immediate postwar years, by Nehru's India. The small penicillin firm built by UN technicians in the early 1950s, Hindustan Antibiotics, had realized the vision of its architects and become the cornerstone for a prospering India-based generics industry that produced dozens of antibiotics and other essential medicines for the developing world. Just as the companies feared, its associated research center had expanded to a dozen facilities where Indian scientists provided the formulas that built India's global reputation as the "pharmacy of the poor."

One of the pivotal events in the rise of India's generics industry was a 1959 hearing convened by Estes Kefauver. In testimony delivered to his subcommittee, it was revealed that U.S. drug companies often reserved their highest markups for the small middle classes in developing countries, with India getting the worst of them. This was poorly received in India, and the resulting protests pushed Nehru to accelerate the timeline for his country's independence from Western drug makers.

At the same time, New Delhi initiated overdue plans to replace the Raj-era patent regime still on the books. This alarmed U.S. companies more than India's expanding public sector product line. Ignoring U.S. patents was bad, but drafting a law to formalize the temerity was worse. Again, it was the power of example that most alarmed the industry. An explicit refusal to recognize U.S. drug patents by Nehru's India would carry weight and influence throughout the developing world. A domino effect of such laws would remove the last legal strictures, however ceremonial, binding south-based drug companies to the patent regimes of northern countries. Legal rebuttals of monopoly medicine also threatened to undercut the permanent industry campaign to reinforce the official "drug story" in the American mind. The Kefauver hearings rattled executives by exposing shocking price differentials between branded drugs sold in the United States and generic versions sold abroad. The spread of alternative patent regimes likewise threatened troubling questions and comparisons back home.

In 1970, India's legislature, the Lok Sabha, passed the country's first patent reforms since independence. The Patents Act was not as radical as it might have been. Modeled on the systems of Western Europe, it banned drug patents but allowed room for temporary monopolies on methods related to their manufacture.[40]

The companies did not lie down, but proceeded to lobby the government in New Delhi as they would in Washington, D.C.

"The Western corporations aligned with conservative sections of the

---

40. Since India had world-class researchers adept at reverse engineering Western drugs, they usually came up with different and sometimes better methods in any case.

Indian government to bitterly oppose and obstruct the public drug sector and patent reforms," says Prabir Purkayastha, a veteran of the Indian People's Health Movement. "Nehru's vision represented an especially fearsome threat: A developing country with its own scientific institutions, cutting-edge capacity, no patent protection, and factory lines that could provide pharmaceuticals to its own huge internal market and other developing countries."

The U.S. pharmaceutical industry proved powerless to stop the Patents Act. Upon its passage, Merck CEO John Connor, who served under Vannevar Bush in the OSRD, announced the law "a victory for global communism." As Connor and his industry colleagues feared, the law indeed became a beacon and symbolic antipode to the capitalist model of monopoly medicine. G77 countries from Southeast Asia to the Andes used the Indian law as a model for their own patent systems, further dimming prospects for the U.S. pharmaceutical industry.

On May 1, 1974, the G77 passed a declaration in the UN General Assembly calling for a "New International Economic Order." The statement called upon member states to fulfill the UN charter by eliminating "the remaining vestiges of alien and colonial domination [and] neocolonialism in all its forms." The NIEO underscored patents and knowledge monopolies as among "the greatest obstacles to the full emancipation and progress of the developing countries." High on its list of founding principles was

> giving to the developing countries access to the achievements of modern science and technology, and promoting the transfer of technology and the creation of indigenous technology for the benefit of the developing countries in forms and in accordance with procedures which are suited to their economies.

The G77 took the NIEO agenda into the World Health Organization, where developing nations had the two-thirds majority needed to set policy. In 1973, the G77 agenda for patent-free north-south medical tech transfer gained a powerful ally with the appointment of Halfdan Mahler as WHO director general. A Danish doctor who had spent a decade as director of India's tuberculosis program, Mahler supported the G77 agenda and spent the mid-1970s working with its governments on a blueprint to achieve "health for all" by the year 2000. The plan was unveiled in September 1978 at a WHO-sponsored conference on primary health care held in the Soviet city of Alma-Ata, Kazakhstan. The resulting Declaration of Alma-Ata affirmed the agency's commitment to "health as a human right based on equity and social justice" and called for the creation of a WHO program to help G77 countries achieve self-sufficiency. A principal component of its plan to close the north-south health gap: UN assistance in building up domestic drug industries across the south. This was not health as a general concept, but involved concrete products still mostly manufactured in the north. Later that year, Mahler released the first WHO list of essential medicines, a shot across the bow of the companies and cartels profiting off their control of those drugs' production and pricing.

"The G77 was claiming the right to the kind of institutional capacity that would make it self-sufficient in a pandemic," says David Legge, an Australian co-founder of the international People's Health Movement, a global activist and academic network. "The calls for a New International Economic Order and the declaration at Alma-Ata were about scaling the model of the UN penicillin projects."

Of the dozen or so executives atop the biggest U.S. drug companies, Edmund T. Pratt Jr. was the most unsettled by these events. Since being named CEO of Pfizer in 1972, Pratt had made a close study of the rising south-based generics industry and G77 assertiveness. A military man who served as secretary of the army in the Kennedy administration, he brought to the job a strategic long view on global threats to his company's international expansion plans, especially for drugs and agricultural products in Asia. After years of musing on the shape of a possible counterassault, it was the scene at Alma-Ata—with its calls for UN-funded generics production, essential medicines as a human right, "health for all"—that finally forced Pratt into action. He had seen enough. In the winter of 1978, he gathered a few of his fellow CEOs for a meeting to hash out a plan.

✦

Pfizer was a natural choice to lead the industry's foray against the G77 and allied UN agencies. The company was legendary for launching kamikaze drug patent infringement suits around the world, just to spite foreign governments that refused to bow to the authority of the U.S. Patent Office. In 1961, it sued Britain after the country's National Health Service purchased Italian-made generic tetracycline, a Pfizer-patented antibiotic. Throughout Europe, where medicine patents were still nearly universally banned, the suit was a sobering introduction to the "post-ethical" U.S. drug industry. British and European editorials reminded readers that Pfizer owed its power to wartime contracts to produce fermented penicillin, based on the discoveries of British scientists who were directed by the government to place their work in the public domain. Pfizer lost its 1961 tetracycline suit against the British policy of "Royal use," then lost again when it sued the NHS for "infringing" on a different drug patent four years later.

Pratt's initial plan did not involve activating his company's fleet of patent lawyers. Rather, he sought to build support for stronger intellectual property protections within the UN system where the G77 was agitating for technology transfer. Given the majoritarian and consensus rules that govern most UN business, success was always unlikely. But in 1978, there were not a lot of options. The UN's World Intellectual Property Organization, or WIPO, was the only international forum for shaping intellectual property rules and settling disputes. The agency's main purview was the 1883 Paris Convention for the Protection of Industrial Property, a document limited to requiring signatories to treat foreign and domestic companies equally under their national patent laws. Pratt considered it a toothless convention, but also a possible toehold. Although WIPO and the Paris Treaty lacked enforcement mechanisms and did not legitimize patents outside of national borders, perhaps that could be changed from within.

Following the Alma-Ata conference, Pratt focused on toughening the U.S. position ahead of a scheduled 1980 conference on the first revisions to the Paris Treaty since 1967. He did not have to work hard to get the government's attention. In 1979, Carter named Pratt to the Advisory Committee for Trade Policy and

Negotiation, an elite board of a few dozen executives founded in 1974 to better align U.S. trade policy with the interests of leading U.S. companies.

In the end, none of it mattered—not the support of the Carter and Reagan administrations, not two years of planning and organizing. The U.S. delegation's proposals to even *discuss* strengthening patent protections ran smack into the fifty-five Paris Treaty signatories who also belonged to the G77. When Pratt's proposals met with stony stares from the south, the U.S. delegation noticed that its ostensible rich-nation allies were staring at their shoes. In the estimation of a legal adviser to the German delegation, patent lawyer Hans Peter Kunz-Hallstein, the U.S. delegation was "alone and almost isolated."

The G77 didn't shoot down the U.S. proposals in defense of the status quo. They arrived in Geneva seeking to revise the Paris Treaty in the opposite direction and advance the agenda of the New International Economic Order: preferential treatment, subsidized technology transfer, the right to circumvent patents in chains of production and trade.

The U.S. patent lobby was taken aback by the unity and strength of the G77 negotiating position. If France, Canada, and Japan were half as committed to globalizing Western drug patents by force, Washington might not have to do all the work. The mood inside the U.S. drug and patent lobbies was captured by a statement published at the 1981 gathering of the American Bar Association's Patent, Trademark, and Copyright division. The group called upon the newly arrived Reagan administration to withdraw from the Paris Treaty and denounce any amendments that allowed "special dispensations or privileges for developing countries" or imposed "special burdens on developed countries."

No formal statement announced a change in what was now the joint drug industry–White House position on global patent enforcement. But a break had occurred. Pratt believed the United States had tried to be reasonable— magnanimous, even. They had made a good-faith effort to open a dialogue with the developing world, on neutral UN ground, and negotiate. But they'd been insulted for their efforts, a victim of a UN system that gave equal weight to votes by Washington, Nairobi, and Mexico City.

Pratt and his inner circle returned to their drawing board. Only now they were cracking their knuckles. "The experience with WIPO was the last straw in our attempt to operate by persuasion," Pfizer's general counsel at the time, Lou Clemente, later told researchers Peter Drahos and John Braithwaite, authors of *Information Feudalism.*

Because the UN gave too much leverage to the G77 and its bureaucratic allies, a less democratic forum was needed. If such a forum did not exist, it would have to be created.

Pratt's stature in the industry rose following the Paris Treaty debacle in Geneva. In the winter of 1981, the White House appointed Pratt and John Opel of IBM as cochairs of the Advisory Committee for Trade Policy and Negotiation. As the Reagan administration intended, the executives focused the committee's work on the patent issue, establishing an intellectual property task force and stacking it with patent lawyers and executives from patent-based manufacturing associations. Most of them represented chemicals and pharmaceuticals, but the task force also featured new players in the budding high-tech information economy—entertainment, software, biotech, agriculture, semiconductors—who were learning to see the world through pharmaceutical eyes.

The patent-globalization train gained momentum during the Carter-Reagan transition year, but it still wasn't clear where it was going. This changed in 1982, when the industry-administration nexus overseen by Pratt and Opel settled on a destination: the Uruguayan resort town of Punta Del Este. It was there, on a peninsula overlooking the south Atlantic, that in September 1986 the next round of global trade negotiations would begin on the treaty known as GATT, or the General Agreement on Tariffs and Trade. Since 1947, the GATT had been the closest thing to a rule-setting global trade authority. But it was a strange, disembodied kind of authority. It had no institutional home, no enforcement power, no governing directors, no president. It was a floating set of policies and norms updated every decade or so in negotiating "rounds" named after the cities that hosted them.

For the United States—where no daylight existed between the administration and Pratt's patent coalition—the upcoming Uruguay Round of

GATT offered an appealing structure. Approved amendments were often sweeping, all-or-nothing deals, hammered out in a format that slanted the advantage to the richest countries. That advantage, however, was only useful when all sides agreed on the agenda and were within negotiating range. That was a long shot in 1982. One, the global south had made their unified position emphatically clear at the WIPO conference. The second problem was more fundamental. GATT was premised on the advancement of free trade. For three decades, its work focused on removing tariffs and other barriers to the flow of goods between nations. Patent monopolies, by definition, exist to restrain trade and limit competition. Moreover, intellectual property was understood as a form of protectionism within, not between, nations. Patents were dispensed and enforced according to national laws; their legitimacy ended at water's edge.

The patent-based industries weren't the first corporate alliance to attack this paradox. During the GATT Tokyo Round, Levi's and other companies associated with famous trademarks pushed the U.S. delegation to establish an anti-counterfeiting code. The attempt failed. Developing nations rebuffed the idea as out of place—WIPO was the proper forum—and hypocritical. GATT signatories from the global south were "unsympathetic to the plight of Western owners of luxury brands," write Drahos and Braithwaite. "For years, the Western multinationals that controlled the packaging and distribution of food had made extensive use of the territorial insignia of developing countries such as Darjeeling tea and basmati rice without much regard for whether the products they were distributing actually originated from these regions. No one in the West considered that a problem."

This discouraging precedent for the United States was a fresh memory. The Tokyo Round ended in 1979 without a counterfeiting code.[41] If the United States couldn't even get a vote on protecting its iconic blue jeans, what hope

---

41. One result of the Tokyo Round that proved useful to U.S. designs was a solidification of a novel trade concept: "linkage." By arguing that an issue was a "link" to legitimate trading issues such as tariffs and quotas, negotiators could more easily place it on the agenda. This was the strategy used to pass amendments related to customs procedures and invisible export subsidies.

existed for globalizing its monopolies on lifesaving medicines, a concept that was only recently and after much debate accepted by Washington's closest allies?

The political pieces, at least, were fully in place by 1982. Pratt and Opel's committee was working closely with the White House and trade officials. The most powerful patent- and copyright-based industries had been educated and enlisted, in the United States and in other wealthy countries. Some members of the U.S.-led coalition were considered weak links—notably Canada and Japan—but there was time to toughen them up in the four years remaining before Punta Del Este.

When it came to the broader business community and the public, there was still work to be done. Many small and medium-sized businesses saw patent monopolies the same way developing countries did: as weapons used by the strong against the weak. Small businesses had been central to the TNEC hearings on patents and were intentionally left out of postwar strategy sessions organized by the National Association of Manufacturers' Committee on Patents and Research. Public opinion still bore the marks of scandals unearthed in the Senate investigations of Kefauver, Nelson, and, more recently, Ted Kennedy.

The drug industry had struggled for decades to change public perceptions of patents. In the campaign around GATT, the old wine of "innovation" was paired with newer vintages labeled "competitiveness" and "national security." Similar to the way Howard Forman capitalized on public anxiety about economic decline to attack the Kennedy patent policy, the campaign marshaled by Pratt and Opel sought to rebrand the U.S. patent as a symbol of free enterprise and national primacy in the global economy. Nations that refused to recognize the authority of the U.S. Patent Office were rogue nations, *pirate* states, whose intellectual larceny threatened factory jobs in Detroit, rising high-tech industries in Silicon Valley, and the American Way.

To amplify and augment this message, Pfizer poured money into research projects at right-wing and centrist think tanks, including the Brookings Institution. Pratt personally took the message on the road, delivering rousing calls for action against piracy to business groups across the country.

The campaign leaned hard on the idea that intellectual property was the same as any other kind of property—sacred, rarely if ever inviolable, and one the U.S. government had a duty to protect at home and abroad.

The fact that this was not yet self-evident to the general public suggested that some things hadn't changed since the eighteenth-century campaign that birthed the phrase *intellectual property* in post-revolutionary France. In a 1950 essay, economists Fritz Machlup and Edith Penrose tell the story of how beleaguered patent advocates in the French Constitutional Assembly coined an apparent oxymoron to obscure the royal origins of monopoly and deflect attention from the true object of intellectual property claims, which is not knowledge but markets. Since markets don't fit easily into modern theories of rights and property, "those who started using the word property in connection with inventions had a very definite purpose in mind," write Machlup and Penrose:

> They wanted to substitute a word with a respectable connotation, "property," for a word that had an unpleasant ring, "privilege." [They] knew that there was no hope of saving the institution of patent privileges except under an acceptable theory . . . and in deliberate insincerity "construed the artificial theory of the property rights of the inventor" as a part of the rights of man.

A variation on this ruse was delivered under the byline of Barry MacTaggart, chairman of Pfizer International, in an op-ed that appeared in *The New York Times* on July 9, 1982, titled "Stealing from the Mind." MacTaggart informed readers that a "tense worldwide struggle for technological supremacy" was underway. The inventions of America's high-technology research-based industries "have been 'legally' taken in country after country by governments' violation of intellectual-property rights, especially patents." He exhorted all freedom-loving nations to get in line behind the "proper enforcement and honorable treatment" of intellectual property, singling out "computers, pharmaceuticals [and] telecommunications" as areas of knowledge being "stolen by the denial of patent rights."

MacTaggart pointed a finger at the UN, where the G77 was "trying to grab high-technology inventions for underdeveloped countries," an outrage that constituted an attack on "the principle underlying the international economic system."

In fact, no such principle underlay the international economic system. The deepest patent traditions were territorial. Drug patents, as the Pfizer executive well knew, had extremely shallow roots even in the richest countries of the north, where they cut against centuries of moral, ethical, legal, and scientific norms. It was not the "pirate nations" of the global south and Far East who were waging war on norms and principles. It was Pfizer.

Five years passed between MacTaggart's op-ed and the U.S. government's announcement of its intellectual property agenda at Uruguay. In a letter to the GATT secretariat dated October 19, 1987, U.S. Trade Representative Clayton Yeutter outlined a "basic framework" for the negotiations that amounted to what Drahos and Braithwaite call "a declaration of principles of property wanted by big business for the coming global information economy."

The G77 that faced this challenge was not the same G77 that called for a New International Economic Order and demanded health as a basic human right at Alma-Ata. By the mid-1980s, the global south was reeling from a debt crisis and tumult in the global political and economic order. Development funds and technology from the Soviet Union were disappearing, and the World Bank and International Monetary Fund were stepping into the void. This "upstreaming" of expertise and influence came at the expense of the UN Conference on Trade and Development (UNCTAD), the agency that during the 1960s and '70s had championed and assisted a G77 development agenda. UNCTAD no longer backed structural reforms to create a more just and democratic world system and retreated into a technocratic role focused on helping poor countries balance their checkbooks.

"We are now reduced to a shadow of what we were between 1964 and 1980," one agency official told researchers Quentin Deforge and Benjamin Lemoine. "There is a very strong opposition to the idea that UNCTAD continues to work on systemic factors, from the United States in particular, but also from [advanced] countries in general."

This environment created favorable conditions for the U.S. strategy being readied for Uruguay. With few other options or institutional allies, developing countries were increasingly focused on selling raw materials and textiles to the United States and other wealthy markets. More than one hundred countries had increased their trade with the United States since the 1976 establishment of the Generalized System of Preferences (GSP), a program designed to expand trade between the United States and the global south. Both sides benefited from the program, but the poor countries were not in a position to dictate terms as its expiration approached in 1984. The law that continued the GSP, the Trade and Tariff Act of 1984, added an intellectual property requirement to participating countries ahead of Uruguay.

Another amendment to the Trade Act passed that year created the stick to the GSP's carrot. It essentially weaponized a section of the 1974 Trade Act—section 301—by making lax intellectual property enforcement a tripwire for investigation, censure, and retaliation by the U.S. government. The stick was named after the section it refashioned: Special 301.

Washington's punishment-reward approach to softening up resisting nations made halting progress. In 1985 the United States rattled developing countries and its allies by brandishing the threat of Special 301 action against Brazil, Japan, and South Korea.[42] Clayton Yeutter, the U.S. trade representative, announced that Special 301 was the new "H-bomb of trade policy." His successor would praise it as a "crowbar." Between 1984 and 1994, the United States invoked Special 301 in a dozen confrontations with G77 leaders, including one with India and three with Brazil, resulting in tariffs and reduced access to U.S. markets.

When the Uruguay talks opened in September 1986, the United States had concerns on two fronts. One was a lack of zeal among its supposed allies. Canada, Japan, and European countries struggled to overcome attachment to non-monopoly drug traditions, including price controls and government support for generics. To help stiffen the spines of its allies and remind them what

---

42. That year, the Reagan administration cut U.S. support for the WHO over the anti-intellectual property implications of its Essential Medicines program.

they signed up for, Pratt and Opel organized a new lobby group that year called the Intellectual Property Committee. Top-heavy with drug majors, including Pfizer, Bristol Myers, Johnson & Johnson, and Merck, the group's lobbying efforts included the publication of a handy hundred-page pamphlet for negotiators to study called *Basic Framework of GATT Provisions on Intellectual Property: Statement of Views of the European, Japanese and United States Business Communities.*

The second, bigger problem was ongoing resistance to the "basic framework" by most of the global south. Though many countries had been persuaded to drop their opposition, a number of countries pledged to fight. That number was steadily reduced during the first two years of the talks. By 1989, it had been whittled down to a core Group of Ten, led by the generic drug powers India and Brazil. That year, the Cold War ended, dooming the India–Brazil axis. The crumbling of the Berlin Wall liberated the United States from the need to practice international restraint, and it entered a historically unique period of global dominance. Inside the GATT negotiating process, the U.S. negotiators invited resistant counterparts into side rooms for chats that became known as Black Room consultations.[43]

U.S. officials ratcheted up the application of Special 301, opening investigations into five of the ten "hard-liners" opposing the draft document known as Trade-Related Aspects of Intellectual Property Rights, or TRIPS. India and Brazil, the leaders of the group, got the worst of it. Brazil broke first, after the United States imposed crippling tariffs on its imports. India held out a little longer, but by 1990 had also succumbed to U.S. pressure. Under the terms of TRIPS, the country would have ten years from the date of signing to revise its 1970 Patents Act to fit a mold cast by Western drug giants. The Nehru-era patent act was more than an institution of national pride—it was the foundation for a generics industry known as the pharmacy to the poor, the source of affordable treatments for malaria,

---

43. This reflected a general post–Cold War impatience with going through the motions of compromise and negotiation. "The GATT is beginning to smell like the United Nations," huffed Harvey Bale of the Pharmaceutical Manufacturers Association to *Inside US Trade* in January 1992, two weeks after the official dissolution of the USSR.

cancer, and tuberculosis across the global south. When the news reached India, street protests against the government of Rajiv Gandhi broke out across the country.

With the countries in line, it was left to the newly arrived Clinton administration to oversee the details. Not long before, Bill Clinton seemed an unlikely candidate for the role. He had campaigned against the "unconscionable" greed of health and drug industries that he had described as pursuing "profits at the expense of our children." He identified the high price of drugs as "one example of why the health care system doesn't work." None of those concerns remained when he toasted the globalization of drug patents that the vast majority of countries still considered unconscionable and unlawful.

Clinton seemed genuinely happy at the ceremony in the Moroccan city of Marrakesh on April 15, 1994, when 124 states signed the Final Act of the Uruguay Round, bringing the World Trade Organization (WTO) into existence. According to the text of the treaty, the WTO heralded "a new era of global economic cooperation, reflecting the widespread desire to operate in a fairer and more open multilateral trading system for the benefit and welfare of their peoples." In return for enforcing Western patents on medicines and other technologies, G77 nations were promised access to rich northern markets and a conditional "freedom from fear" of finding themselves on the wrong end of a Special 301.

At the time of the signing ceremony, this trade-off was widely reported as fair and consensual. It was neither, but the consensual part seemed to stick. A dozen years later, as sophisticated a critic of the WTO as Joseph Stiglitz would write, "[A]s they signed TRIPS, the trade ministers were so pleased they had finally reached an agreement that they didn't notice they were signing a death warrant for thousands of people in the poorest countries in the world."

Except they did know. It's the reason they fought as long and as fiercely as they did. It's why some negotiators from G77 countries called each other in tears when Brazil cracked, and why future WTO ministerial meetings would be held amid shrouds of tear gas. A lot of people understood perfectly well in 1994 that TRIPS was a mass death sentence. Before the end of the decade, everybody else would, too.

✦

When the World Trade Organization came into force on January 1, 1995, the only approved AIDS therapy was AZT, the repurposed cancer drug developed by the NIH and sold under patent by Burroughs Wellcome for $10,000 and more. In 1996, AZT reappeared as an ingredient in one of the first AIDS combination therapies sold by Glaxo Wellcome (formerly Burroughs Wellcome, soon to become GlaxoSmithKline). As the news spread about the effectiveness of the new drug cocktails in interrupting the progression of the disease, the WTO was pressuring developing countries to speed up the process of reforming their patent systems in accordance with TRIPS. As with AZT, these antiretroviral therapies had been developed with heavy support from governments in the United States and Europe before their titles were transferred to the monopoly hands of Glaxo Wellcome, Bristol Myers Squibb, and Boehringer Ingelheim. Like AZT, they hit the market with prices of between $10,000 and $15,000 for a year's course. This priced out 99 percent of the world's 25 million AIDS patients. For many developing countries, the cost of providing the pills for every infected citizen would have exceeded the national GDP.

For those who could afford them, the drugs transformed HIV from a death sentence to a chronic condition. Almost all of these people lived in northern countries, representing around 10 percent of global cases. The coming collision—between rising AIDS numbers in the south and the new WTO-imposed patent regime—was visible even before the promise of the new drugs had been proven. At the 1996 World Health Assembly, the southern countries made a point of requesting that the WHO monitor the WTO's impacts on their access to new drugs and essential medicines.

According to the letter of WTO law, these impacts were still in the future. The 1994 agreement gave developing nations ten years to bring their patent laws into accordance with TRIPS. In theory, this was enough time to begin producing generic versions of the new combination therapies so urgently needed, especially in sub-Saharan Africa, where in some countries up to a fifth of the population was at risk of an agonizing illness and death.

But TRIPS had always been about the realities of power. "The reality is we do not spend a lot of time thinking about legal issues when we negotiate GATT," wrote Emory Simon, a U.S. TRIPS negotiator, in a 1989 law journal symposium about the negotiations. "The concerns that we have are with the commercial results . . . rather than with the legal niceties of it." In the late 1990s, the Clinton administration worked to ensure that the commercial results of TRIPS were protected drug monopolies and unfathomable amounts of needless human suffering.

When the clock started ticking on the ten-year TRIPS grace period, Washington began a pressure campaign on key countries to make their patent laws "TRIPS compliant" immediately, rather than waiting until 2005. In Brazil and Argentina, left-wing parties, unions, and civil society groups organized conferences to resist this pressure. All of them failed. Buckling under threats by the United States and European nations to raise tariffs on its exports and block access to northern markets, Brazil legalized drug patents in 1997, all but invalidating another law, passed the year before, guaranteeing antiretroviral therapy for its growing HIV population.

Argentina posed a special challenge. The country's generic drug industry was the largest in Latin America and had the power to kill any bill, especially one as unpopular as a patent reform that would hurt the economy and sacrifice a decade of affordable drugs to appease Washington and foreign drug companies. In 1994, President Carlos Menem threatened to circumvent the strong parliamentary opposition by executive order. Though the gambit had dubious legal standing under Argentina's post-junta constitution, it was pushed hard as the best solution by the Clinton administration. Al Gore was dispatched to Buenos Aires during a Senate debate over the bill to remind Menem of the benefits of accelerating the TRIPS reforms—and the potential costs of not doing so.

James Love, a central figure in that era's emergent global medicines-access movement, was also in Buenos Aires for the debate. "Argentina was under a military dictatorship a decade earlier, and the U.S. was pressuring them to circumvent the parliament to shave a decade off their rights under the WTO," says Love. "The U.S. was also leaning on them to eliminate their right to 'parallel trade,' meaning the right to buy and import drugs from another market. European countries in the Common Market do this every day, but the U.S. was pushing Argentina to give up the right, also by executive order. It was very heavy handed. I'd been fighting special interests my entire professional life, but Argentina was my introduction to the real face of U.S. policy on drug patents and TRIPS. Hyperinflation was causing extreme poverty across Argentina and Brazil, shanty towns of cardboard boxes, and the U.S. government is sticking it to them on drug prices."

In South Africa, the Mandela government passed a Medicines Act in December 1997 that gave the health ministry powers to produce, purchase, and import low-cost drugs. The industry backlash came fast. In February 1998, more than three dozen multinational drug companies and the South African Pharmaceutical Manufacturers Association filed a suit against Nelson Mandela and the government of South Africa, alleging violations of the country's constitution and its looming obligations under TRIPS.[44] The same Western leaders who continued to praise Mandela in public began chastising him in private meetings. In the summer of 1998, Al Gore put U.S. drug patents high on the agenda of that year's U.S.–South Africa Binational Commission. The U.S. Trade Representative, meanwhile, put the country on notice for retaliatory measures under Section 301. In his 2012 documentary about the generic AIDS drugs fight, *Fire in the Blood*, Dylan Mohan Gray observes that it took the U.S. government forty years to threaten apartheid South Africa with sanctions, but less than four to do so against the government of Nelson Mandela.

Though South Africa was not a major market for multinational drug companies—it barely registered—in the drug industry's version of Cold War "domino theory," the appearance of cheap drugs anywhere was a threat to monopoly-priced drugs everywhere. Allowing the poorest nations to "free ride" on U.S. science (as the biggest companies themselves did) and build parallel drug economies would eventually cause problems closer to home,

---

44. Muddying the legitimacy of the suit, the South African commitment to TRIPS had been signed by the apartheid government of P. W. Botha in the late 1980s.

where the industry spent billions keeping the lid on public discontent over drug prices. The companies suing Mandela had devised TRIPS as a long-term strategic response to the south-based generics industry that arose in the 1960s. They had come too far to be set back by the needs of Africans.

They couldn't say this out loud, so they paired old standby arguments about patents driving innovation with racist pseudo-science: U.S. officials and industry figures claimed that Africans, if allowed broad access to combination therapies, would prove unable to follow instructions and take the drugs on schedule, thereby giving rise to new and dangerous drug-resistant viral mutations. Among the media figures who parroted this line was the HIV-positive blogger Andrew Sullivan, who at the height of the controversy was revealed as a recipient of undisclosed funding from the drug industry trade association.[45]

Mandela's government held its ground under sustained pressure that some believe took forms associated with espionage against foreign enemies. In 1997, South Africa's health minister, the legendary activist Dr. Nkosazana Clarice Dlamini-Zuma, was summoned to Washington by Al Gore to meet with U.S. officials and drug company lawyers to discuss the Medicines Act. When Dlamini-Zuma met privately with two medicines-access representatives in her room at the Watergate Hotel, U.S. officials contacted her immediately after, naming those same individuals in a reminder that outside experts were not welcomed in the following day's meetings. Dlamini-Zuma and the South African government suspected that the room had been bugged.

The fifty-second General Health Assembly opened in May 1999 as the African AIDS crisis and related drug controversy matured as issues of global public concern. The WHO building in Geneva was riven by a north-south

---

45. After the drug industry payments were disclosed and he was forced to end the sponsorship, Sullivan remained defiant. "It behooves me to say I see absolutely no problems with [drug industry sponsorship]," he told a reporter. "In fact, I am extremely proud to get some support from a great industry that has saved my and countless other people's lives, despite a massive attempt to penalize them for their work."

fault line. On one side were the home countries of the Western drug companies; on the other, the G77 countries and a rising "third force" of civil society
groups. The immediate point of conflict was a resolution proposed by the
global south that the richest countries saw as a threat to the conquest of monopoly medicine achieved five years earlier with the founding of the WTO.
The resolution described a "Revised Drug Strategy" and called for WHO
member states

> (1) to reaffirm their commitment to developing, implementing,
> and monitoring national drug policies and to taking all necessary
> concrete measures in order to ensure equitable access to essential
> drugs; (2) to ensure that public health interests are paramount in
> pharmaceutical and health policies; (3) to explore and review their
> options under relevant international agreements, including trade
> agreements, to safeguard access to essential drugs.

As global public opinion and WHO member-state sentiment shifted further in favor of the resolution in the weeks leading up to the Assembly, the
companies and their allied embassies sought to turn the tide. Their angst is
captured in a series of leaked cables that George Moose, the U.S. ambassador
in Geneva, sent to Washington that April and May. In one, Moose expresses
alarm over the growing number of WHO delegations making

> STATEMENTS THAT PUBLIC HEALTH SHOULD HAVE PRI-
> MACY OVER COMMERCIAL INTERESTS UNDER WTO TRADE
> AGREEMENTS SUCH AS THE TRIPS (TRADE-RELATED AS-
> PECTS OF INTELLECTUAL PROPERTY RIGHTS) . . . THEREBY
> POTENTIALLY UNDERMINING INTELLECTUAL PROPERTY
> RIGHTS (IPR).

Moose worried that the drug companies were not helping their own cause
and seemed incapable of doing anything but parroting old talking points
about intellectual property as "the fuel of interest." The pharmaceutical industry, Moose cabled on the eve of the Assembly,

SHOULD BE CARRYING MORE OF ITS OWN WATER ON THIS ISSUE, ESPECIALLY IN DEVELOPING COUNTRIES, AND NOT SOLELY DEPEND ON THE ARGUMENT THAT IPR PROTECTS PROFITS THAT THEN ARE USED FOR DEVELOPMENT OF NEW DRUGS IN THE FUTURE. THE SOUTH AFRICANS AND OTHERS ARE MOSTLY CONCERNED ABOUT AVAILABILITY OF DRUGS NOW. PROBLEMS RELATED TO LOCAL AVAILABILITY AND PRICING OF DRUGS THAT ARE UNRELATED TO TRIPS WILL UNDOUBTABLY REQUIRE FURTHER DISCUSSION.

Over the course of weeks, a picture begins to emerge from Moose's accounts of the countermobilization against intellectual property rules written by U.S. drug company executives. It is the image of a pharmaceutical industry against the ropes, punch-drunk and out of ideas.

After walking into a buzz saw at the 1999 World Health Assembly, the industry would botch an attempt to negotiate lower prices on AIDS drugs, and tumble onto the doorstep of what *The Washington Post* called close-to-pariah status.

It was around ten o'clock on the morning of November 30, 1999, when an armored police vehicle blasted a canister of tear gas into the intersection of Sixth Avenue and Union Street. Whoever fired the weapon had decent aim. Landing in the dead center of the axis, the chemical bloom scattered hundreds of protesters sitting in the street. Most made dazed and staggering escapes, some screaming in pain. Others wrapped T-shirts around their faces and returned the fuming canisters to their source. Trade officials, in town from more than a hundred nations, were told to stay in their hotel rooms. The "Battle of Seattle" had begun.

The size and intensity of the protests against the World Trade Organization surprised even their organizers. Trade negotiations were supposed to be low-profile affairs conducted away from public notice in luxury hotel conference rooms. Five years after the creation of the WTO in Morocco, Seattle announced the end of the era of sleepy trade rounds passing unnoticed in the developed world. The accelerating U.S.-led process called globalization had produced consequences at odds with the decade's free-trade mantras. A global network of civil society groups emerged to challenge these mantras, but Seattle demonstrated the difficulty of synthesizing them into a coherent narrative. The diversity of causes and institutions seen on "anti-globalization" protest banners in Seattle—labor standards and development loans, free trade and sea turtles, genetically modified seeds and public health budgets—gave champions of the new economic order an opening to dismiss its mostly youthful challengers as, at best, romantic naïfs too ignorant to understand that the world of Washington-led free trade was the best of all possible worlds. Before the smoke had cleared, *New York Times* columnist Thomas Friedman described critics of this world as "a Noah's ark of flat-earth advocates, protectionist trade unions and yuppies looking for their 1960's fix."

The drugs at issue in Seattle were not the recreational kind suggested by Friedman's metaphor. Since the WTO signing ceremony in Morocco, the AIDS epidemic had worsened across the developing world. By 1999, the virus was the leading cause of death in Africa. Poor countries had put barriers to generic AIDS drugs on the list for discussion by the TRIPS Council in Seattle, which placed it at the bottom of an official agenda. At the top was a lengthier description of the problem of "geographical indications," concerning the scope of protections enjoyed by national products named after places such as "Champagne," "Tequila," and "Roquefort."

This north-south rift—French negotiators concerned about naming rights on cheese, their African counterparts pleading for the right to save millions of lives—was ultimately what doomed the Seattle talks, more than the police-protester melees on television. The talks ended in stalemate with no schedule to resume.

In March 2001, the South African government called the drug companies' bluff by allowing the case to go to court. An attempt to scare and intimidate South African officials had ended with the companies under the harsh lights of a growing international scandal, suing Nelson Mandela to maintain rules that were killing thousands of people every day.

The lawsuit wasn't the only driver of global attention to the issue. Weeks before the industry's lawyers delivered their opening argument to the Pretoria High Court, *The New York Times* published a bombshell by Donald McNeil Jr. titled "Indian Company Offers to Supply AIDS Drugs at Low Cost in Africa." An Indian drug company called Cipla was offering to make generic combination therapies and sell them to poor countries for less than a dollar a day. The company represented everything that TRIPS had been designed to snuff out. The company's founder, Khwaja Abdul Hamied, had been influential in shaping the Indian nationalist movement's view of scientific development as a state-level expression of Gandhian self-reliance. Mahatma Gandhi would sanction this relationship in a visit to Cipla's laboratory shortly before his assassination. Hamied's son Yusuf followed his father's political example and took pride in India's role as pharmacy to the world.

Following the *Times* report, the industry position, always weak, became untenable. The patent-based drug companies were now seen to be blocking a solution that required only that they get out of the way. The figure offered by Cipla—$350 per year—exposed Big Pharma's sticker prices as bloodstained shams, including its $4,000 "concessional" price.

Under the circumstances, the industry did the only thing it could do: In April 2001, it quietly dropped its suit against the Mandela government. Its attention turned to Doha, the antiseptic seaside capital of the Qatari monarchy, where the WTO was scheduled to meet in November 2001 for the first time since Seattle. The contrast in cities was symbolic of the profound changes that had taken place in the intervening two years. A global medicines-access movement had come of age and shamed the drug-producing countries into allowing a global trade in generic combination therapies. Now the same forces were pushing to institutionalize that permission. The naming rights on French cheese would not top the TRIPS agenda in Doha.

The September 11 attacks on New York and Washington, meanwhile, had downshifted drug patents as a matter of Western diplomatic concern. Just two weeks before the Doha talks began, the world was treated to the related spectacle of the Bush administration threatening to infringe on the patent of a U.S. drug company, Bayer, over the price of its branded anthrax medicine, Cipro. The Department of Health and Human Services told Bayer it was prepared to contract with a generic drug maker, Barr Industries, unless it reduced its offer price of $1.83 per tablet. When Bayer agreed to sell the drug for under $1, Washington's five-year campaign to protect 1,000 percent monopoly markups on AIDS drugs was fresh in the memory of the developing world, and here it was invoking its sovereign right to disregard patents over ninety cents, all in preparation for a far-fetched threat to the health and safety of a hypothetical American city.[46]

The Doha talks ended with the first revisions to the TRIPS regime established in 1994. Language was added that recognized the right to prioritize people over patents as a matter of policy, not just during public health emergencies: "The TRIPS agreement does not and should not prevent members from taking measures to protect public health." The right to issue compulsory licenses was expanded and clarified. Developing nations praised the changes, as did Médecins Sans Frontières, now the leading international voice of the medicines-access movement.

But the Doha TRIPS reforms had a hole at their center. The power to issue compulsory licenses and manufacture generics for domestic use is meaningless if a country lacks a native medicine manufacturing base. It would take another two years to enshrine the right of third-party nations like India to fill orders and ship generics under TRIPS protection.

As with Bayh-Dole critics in the U.S. context, developing countries soon came to suspect that the escape clauses in the TRIPS Agreement were never intended to function. The "flexibilities" written into TRIPS between 2001 and 2003 are only as valuable as the freedom countries enjoy to use them. In practice, that freedom has been constrained by politics, especially the continued pressure exerted by the Western countries.

"As soon as countries began to use the flexibilities, there was a pushback,"

---

46. Canada, another member of the U.S.-led patent "quad," also threatened infringement if Bayer did not lower its price.

says K. M. Gopakumar, a legal adviser on intellectual property issues at the Third World Network, an international think tank focused on issues affecting developing countries.

He continued, "You can go down the list, from Thailand to Colombia, countries that seek to issue compulsory licenses face political pressure from the EU and the U.S., the legal wrath of the drug companies, and joint pressure demanding they ratchet up the TRIPS standards. It's a human rights violation that's all about defending the high prices on these patented drugs. For many countries, the Doha flexibilities only exist on paper."

Twelve

COVID-19 AND THE BATTLE OVER BUSINESS AS USUAL

OVID-19 BEGAN ITS PUBLIC LIFE AS A HOLIDAY NEWS DUMP. While much of the world prepared to celebrate the new year on December 31, 2019, officials in Wuhan, China, quietly confirmed rumors that had been swirling for weeks about a strange pneumonia spreading through the city. An unsettling pause in further information followed the announcement. Public health and infectious diseases experts knew the first days and weeks were crucial; they worried China would suppress needed information as the virus spread to other countries.

The moment of collective relief arrived on January 11, when researchers at Shanghai's Public Health Clinical Center uploaded the virus's rough genetic sequence to open-access websites, including GenBank, maintained by the U.S. NIH as part of an international consortium of open databases, and virological.org. The news was announced to the English-speaking world by Edward Holmes, a virologist at the University of Sydney whose team had been working with the Shanghai clinic. Within hours of Holmes's tweeting out the links, scientists around the world had sketched a family tree that identified the virus as a close relative of SARS, a fatal zoonotic coronavirus that caused outbreaks in mainland China, Hong Kong, and Canada in 2003.

Later that same day, China reported the new virus's first fatality: a sixty-one-year-old Wuhan man had recently perished at a local hospital. This news did not disturb the general public. Another two months passed before the WHO declared the virus a pandemic, crashing global markets and triggering runs on basic supplies like toilet paper. The public health and research communities, however, did not have the luxury of waiting or trusting Donald Trump's January 20 promise that "it's going to be just fine." With the confirmation of the new virus's close resemblance to SARS, experts understood the window for containment had almost certainly closed. They were operating on a code-red basis weeks before the agency announced a "global health emergency" on January 30, and months before "war footing" became a pandemic cliché that spring.

What does it mean to approach a microbe with a war mentality? Who is fighting whom, exactly? In science fiction films depicting alien invasions of Earth, nations unite against the extraterrestrial enemy. If this scenario had a chance of coming to pass in the fight against COVID-19, our microbial Martian invader, its nearest inspiration was the global scientific community leading the defense, which maintains an internationalist ethos and code that has not been fully extinguished by the pressures of politics and commerce. During the winter of 2019–2020, this ethos illuminated a collaborative and globally unified path forward, beginning with the Shanghai-Sydney genome collaboration.

This path was always going to be fraught. In late February 2020, the Shanghai institute that provided the virus's genetic sequence without state approval was shut down by Chinese authorities. But by then, enough data existed to provide the basis for a much broader collaborative program led by the Center for Structural Genomics of Infectious Diseases, a global consortium of research institutions that included the world's handful of particle accelerators that were capable of producing atomic scale maps of the virus's proteins and enzymes. At sites in North America, Europe, and China, teams pooled their findings to produce, in record time, a detailed picture of the virus and how it attacks cells and reproduces. Like the Shanghai-Sydney collaboration, the teams posted their findings to open-access online repositories. This data formed a starting line in the effort to treat and contain the virus. "Work that needed two months for SARS in 2003, this time took just one week," observed the editors of *Nature*. "[Further] work that would normally have taken months—or possibly even years—has been completed in weeks."

If the frame of this viral scientific puzzle was built in record time, it was logical to stay on the path of cooperation and continue condensing the timeframe for the development and testing of treatments and vaccines, which would in turn increase the time available to build out the infrastructure required to produce vaccines for billions of people. This was the working assumption at a two-day conference convened by the WHO at its Geneva headquarters on February 11, 2020. Burdened by a sense of borrowed time, the attendees—leaders in public health policy and infectious disease research—sketched a crash "R&D Blueprint" for a world upended by the virus and disease that they officially named SARS-CoV-2 and COVID-19.

The meeting unfolded in the open-science spirit of the January collaborations. Specialists compiled a comprehensive summary of coronavirus research and proposed ways to accelerate the development, testing, and production of diagnostic kits, treatments, and vaccines. The WHO conference produced a document premised on the assumption that researchers would work together, maintaining open communication channels and common stores of knowledge. Pooling resources and findings would minimize duplication and accelerate discovery. They expected this to hold true at every stage, from basic research to the WHO-run global comparative trials that attendees prepared as the best way to assess the merits of eventual candidate treatments and vaccines.

One topic not raised in the WHO expert planning document: intellectual property. If the worst came to pass, the experts operated on the premise that a model of cooperation would triumph. It did not occur to them that proprietary barriers would be permitted to obstruct research development or the manufacture of products on the scale that would be needed.

They were naïve to think this way, but they weren't alone. Even the most cynical veterans of the medicines-access and open-science movements felt that this time, in this pandemic, the obvious benefits of collaboration and sharing would override the dominant paradigm of proprietary science and monopoly medicine. The tantalizing glimpses of this alternative paradigm lingered as February turned to March. It found support from unexpected quarters. Anxious governments spoke of shared interests and global public goods; drug companies pledged "precompetitive" and "no-profit" approaches to development and pricing.

In cases where actions belied these words, the industry looked oddly weak and devoid of its fighting spirit. When Gilead Sciences quietly tried to extend its monopoly on remdesivir in mid-March, after the drug developed with federal funds showed promise as a treatment for severe COVID-19, public pressure forced the company to rescind the application. Two days after Gilead's retreat, on March 25, the Swiss drug giant Roche announced a similar surrender to public outrage in the Netherlands, where it had initially refused an emergency request by the Dutch government to share its proprietary ingredients and specifications for a COVID-19 test. When Israel announced plans to order generic versions of an AbbVie Inc. HIV drug that showed promise in treating severe COVID-19, despite ongoing patent protections that limit its noncommercial distribution in that country, there was no talk of lawsuits or "Special 301." AbbVie simply dropped its protest. Other cracks in the TRIPS regime appeared in Germany, Costa Rica, Canada, and Ecuador—each proclaiming the right to override patents to facilitate research and produce affordable treatments.

When the *Financial Times* editorialized on March 27 that "the world has an overwhelming interest in ensuring [COVID-19 drugs and vaccines] will be universally and cheaply available," the paper expressed what felt like a hardening conventional wisdom. This sense of possibility emboldened the forces working to extend the cooperative model. Grounding their efforts were plans, beginning in early March 2020, to remove intellectual property walls from the equation and create a model for public and private actors to collect science and associated intellectual property in a shared knowledge fund until the pandemic was over. The idea became real in late May with the launch of the WHO COVID-19 Technology Access Pool, or C-TAP, hereafter the Pool.

✦

The idea of open science is as old as science itself: knowledge is published to be built upon by others, who in turn publish refinements and additions to the benefit of yet others. This endless process is the giant whose shoulders Newton references in his famous line about what allowed him "to see further." According to ancient and Enlightenment ideals, this process is for the benefit of mankind. It provided fame and glory, but never ownership.

As a formal movement, open science dates to the first international science journals in the seventeenth century, which posed a challenge to those who would keep their discoveries secret or stored in a royal patent repository. As a philosophy defined in opposition to proprietary and otherwise walled-off knowledge, open science acknowledges the fundamentally transpersonal nature of knowledge: as understood by everyone from Heraclitus to Ben Franklin to Francis Crick, every discovery is built from prior discoveries, each of them "parts of the great mental whole of society." Every "invention" resists the notion of a solitary origin or creator. The folly of trying to assign one is compounded by assigning fictive creators the powers of ownership and control. In the context of a pandemic, this folly rises to a crime not just against science but humanity.

Only one thing could deliver on the rhetoric about COVID-19 research as a "global public good": a mechanism for pooling research, shearing it of intellectual property claims, and assisting poor nations with the technology required to apply that research to production. This was the vision of the Pool visible behind scaffolding inside the WHO in early March 2020. Its supporters understood the stakes, because behind the rhetoric about the world "being in this together," the outlines of "vaccine apartheid" in utero were already visible. Wealthy countries had begun signing the first bulk purchase preorders for vaccines in development. These contracts, like the state research subsidies that enabled them, contained no stipulations on pooling or tech transfer to the rest of the world.

The Pool was the last best chance to arrest this worrying drift. Costa Rican president Carlos Alvarado Quesada took the lead in rallying support for the initiative. In his direct appeal to WHO member states, Quesada emphasized the Pool was a temporary emergency measure. Participation would be voluntary. Companies and countries would place their research and related IP in an open-access innovation hub coordinated by the WHO, and modeled on an existing HIV/AIDS medicines patent pool overseen by the UN. The WHO would ensure that the aggregated intellectual property was licensed broadly to qualified actors of all sizes to maximize production and ensure access. Even within this alternate paradigm, patent holders would be due royalties on their products. The arrangement would end with the pandemic, with all titles reverting to their owners.

On May 15, 2020, two weeks before the Pool was activated at a formal announcement in Geneva, Donald Trump held a press conference in the White House garden to announce Operation Warp Speed, a federal program to coordinate and subsidize private-sector COVID-19 research and development, with a focus on vaccines. After his opening remarks, Trump introduced the man who would oversee the operation, a bullet-headed Moroccan-born scientist and pharmaceutical executive named Moncef Slaoui.

A scientist and drug industry executive, Slaoui has spent most of his career at the multinational pharma giant GlaxoSmithKline. Before accepting the invitation to manage Warp Speed, he was on the board at Moderna, the Cambridge, Massachusetts, biotech company that would receive more than $2 billion of the operation's total budget of $20 billion dispersed by the NIH and the Pentagon's Biomedical Advanced Research and Development Authority. As a condition of taking the job, Slaoui unburdened himself of $12 million of Moderna stock. (Three days later, his former colleagues would make headlines for selling millions' worth of Moderna shares at a much higher price, following a press release designed to juice the company's valuation.)

The program's details and Slaoui's selection were bad omens for the Pool. It institutionalized a law of the jungle that Trump first signaled in March by seeking to purchase the German biotech CureVac and acquire its rumored vaccine candidate as U.S. property. Operation Warp Speed extended that impulse and pressed a template for the coming wave of corporate vaccine nationalism. It was a model for rich countries to lock down redundant levels of domestic supply by lavishing chosen drug companies with subsidies and preorders without asking anything in return: no requirements to share technology or license widely, no transparency on production or pricing.

On the eve of Trump's announcement, 140 political and civil society leaders published an open letter urging other nations to choose a different path. Instead of funding proprietary vaccines—a Moderna or AstraZeneca vaccine—they called for the development of a "people's vaccine." This would be a vaccine defined not by the technology used or the company that owned the rights, but its status as a public good, manufactured transparently, as widely as possible, and sold at cost, nonexclusive to any government or corporation.

"Action must start urgently to massively build capacity worldwide to manufacture billions of vaccine doses," wrote the signatories, top-signed by the South African president and serving chair of the African Union, Cyril Ramaphosa. "Now is *not* the time . . . to leave this massive and moral task to market forces . . . We cannot afford for monopolies, crude competition and near-sighted nationalism to stand in the way . . . Only a people's vaccine— with equality and solidarity at its core—can protect all of humanity and get our societies safely running again."

This letter was addressed to the health ministers scheduled to gather virtually later that week for the 2020 World Health Assembly. It did not mention the Pool to be announced at the end of the month, but proposed a more radical measure: a mandatory knowledge pool administered by the WHO, where technologies could be gathered and licensed, whether their owners consented or not.

The letter's undertone of bitterness reflected the scars of what it called the "painful lessons from a history of unequal access." This was a not-so-subtle reference to the last time the pharmaceutical industry was allowed to control publicly funded medicines during a pandemic, when it chose to let millions of people die as a symbolic statement about the lengths it will go to protect its patent monopolies.

✦

The chance that the drug companies and their governments might yet embrace the vision behind a people's vaccine, if only out of self-interest, receded further during the writing of the consensus statement that opened the World Health Assembly on May 18, 2020.

The convening resolution set the tone and guided the agenda of the two-day conference. The drafting of the first pandemic statement found health ministers split along a familiar north-south divide. The developing countries wrote a draft anchored by the call for an open-licensing regime and a condemnation of monopoly medicine that was also a call for global justice. All of it was stripped out on objections by the United States, England, and Switzerland. The gummy compromise text merely acknowledged the Doha reforms to TRIPS and tersely noted the existence of the voluntary UNAIDS patent pool. It ended with a perfunctory statement of support for "universal, timely and equitable access to" COVID-19 technologies.

This was too much for the leader of the U.S. delegation, Health and Human Services secretary Alex Azar. The former president of Eli Lilly declined to sign the final resolution and instead delivered a video statement blaming the WHO for the pandemic and touting the recently announced Operation Warp Speed. For good measure, Azar posted a letter on HHS letterhead expressing his concern that the resolution contained implications that "may negatively affect countries' abilities to incentivize new drug development." Azar encouraged developing countries and their handful of rich-country allies to dispense with any fanciful ideas about pooling and "engage with innovators to find mutually-acceptable solutions that achieve increased access to affordable, safe, effective, and high-quality COVID-19 health products."

Despite the theater of U.S. objections, the resolution contained the seed of a possible north-south pooling coalition. The call for "universal, equitable access" was endorsed by every country of the Africa Group and the European Union. Perhaps these countries would give meaning to the words by coming together in the Pool that was about to open for business. Or perhaps another document in the news on May 18 would prove a more accurate omen for a vaccine "race" taking on a shape that looked all too familiar.

✦

It was lunchtime in Geneva on the opening day of the Assembly when the good news arrived. With global deaths from COVID-19 approaching half a million, Moderna had posted a press release offering an anxious world a spring bud of hope: among dozens of healthy subjects injected with the company's vaccine candidate, mRNA-1273, eight randomly selected volunteers all showed neutralizing COVID-19 antibodies. The statement did not clear even the lowest scientific bar—the data set was small, preliminary, and partial— but at a time when good news was a precious commodity, this was good news. It also bode well, perhaps, for the trials of other vaccines, notably Moderna's German-U.S. mRNA rival, Pfizer-BioNTech.

As Moderna basked in glowing press that afternoon, the company's science officer delivered a virtual presentation to the UBS Global Healthcare Conference, a major investor event. The talk was followed by a second press release announcing a $1.25 billion public offering of Moderna common stock. Morgan Stanley was running the book and ready for orders. As it had that morning, the company's second announcement touted mRNA-1273, but this time left out any mention of its senior partner, the National Institute of Allergy and Infectious Diseases, the NIH body leading the trial.

The first stories detailing scientific concerns over the skimpy Moderna trial data appeared a day later, after the company's share price spiked nearly 30 percent.[47] Catching the pump near the top were the company's chief financial and medical officers, who between them dumped shares worth $30 million. It wasn't the first or the last time drug company executives benefited from a well-designed and timed press release. It did, however, unmask the forces beneath the rhetoric that would determine the rollout of the first vaccines. This illuminating flash drew mild rebukes from those who

---

47. Moderna announced publication of its full Phase 1 interim report in the *New England Journal of Medicine* on July 14, hours after announcing its imminent listing on the elite NASDAQ 100 stock index, reserved for the most capitalized non-financial firms in the U.S. economy.

understood the importance of keeping the grubby reality at least partially obscured by rhetoric of global unity. "In this volatile time, please practice good corporate hygiene," Securities and Exchange Commission chair Jay Clayton politely reminded Moderna and other recipients of Operation Warp Speed funds.

On the scale of corporate misdeeds, the Moderna sell-offs were small-time. But during a pandemic they served as a reminder that the private interests positioned to dominate the first wave of vaccine production were hardwired to maximize market control and profits, and not to inoculate the world with the most effective vaccines as quickly as possible.

On May 29, the floating alternative paradigm of pooling COVID-19 technologies became real with the launch of the C-TAP. The WHO's Ethiopian director, Dr. Tedros Ghebreyesus, opened the ceremony with a "Solidarity Call to Action" that invited the world's drug companies and their home governments to join the effort.

"This is a time when people must take priority," said Ghebreyesus. "Science is giving us solutions, but to make them work for everyone, we need solidarity. COVID-19 has highlighted the inequalities of our world, but it is also offering us an opportunity to build a fairer world, in which health is not a privilege for the few, but a common good."

Of the 130 nations that pledged commitment to "universal access" at the World Health Assembly on May 18, only thirty-four signed on to the Pool. Only three—Norway, Luxembourg, and the Netherlands—were high-income countries.[48] Brazil was on the list, but not India, its old ally against monopoly medicine. It was a small and fractured alliance. Not a single drug company was present.

---

48. In July, the European Parliament adopted a resolution paving the way for the creation of two new EU-wide public health agencies that contained strong language in support of compulsory licensing and the WHO C-TAP, among other positions not reflected in the EU's actions internationally.

The Pool did have a small handful of individual supporters on the industry side. Speaking to a panel discussion following the WHO announcement, Gregg Alton, former executive vice president at Gilead Sciences, described the Pool as a moral imperative as well as an opportunity to measure the benefits of open-science models of innovation. This was also the view of longtime pharmaceutical executive Paul Fehlner, the CEO of reVision Therapeutics who served nine years as head of global intellectual property for the Swiss pharma Novartis. Fehlner emerged early in the pandemic as a rare industry voice for pooling. Privately, he waged a futile campaign to change the minds of his fellow executives.

"There is a suspicion by many in the industry that C-TAP is just a ruse by civil society to undermine intellectual property," said Fehlner. "But that's not a useful frame in a crisis of this magnitude, where governments are the major investors and the goal is to aid rapid innovation and development. My belief that transparency and sharing speed development is based on thirty years' experience helping companies *prevent* sharing and maintain intellectual property barriers. Patents, trade secrets, knowhow—they're designed to slow down competitors. If you reverse this approach to facilitate sharing, it will have the opposite effect—the one you want during crises on this scale. This won't be the last viral pandemic."

To illustrate the advantages of pooling and cross-fertilization, Fehlner pointed to the vaccine "race" between Moderna and Pfizer-BioNTech to develop the first mRNA vaccine. "The Pfizer-BioNTech shot is based on similar mRNA technology as Moderna's vaccine, but they ended up with much more demanding storage and temperature requirements," he said. "Framing the vaccine projects as a 'race' was a mistake, because once you start a process, you can't deviate from it, any more than you can stop running a marathon to change clothes. Pfizer couldn't stop and rewind the work that led to the vaccine requiring sub-freezing storage. Perhaps if they had access to Moderna's data, we'd have two mRNA vaccines that could be stored in a normal freezer."

Some prominent critics of the intellectual property regime thought the Pool too weak—a reflection of the neutered state of the WHO under the sponsorship of private actors like Bill Gates. Proposing a voluntary and temporary suspension of intellectual property, in this view, only affirmed the legitimacy of an illegitimate system. This was championed by the South Centre, a research organization led by Argentinian economist Carlos Correa, who rose to prominence during the TRIPS negotiations in Uruguay. Low- and medium-income countries should not settle for being "mere recipients of vaccines," according to a South Centre paper, but must become "partners in their production." This will require an agency willing to back up its words with actions, including non-voluntary pooling mechanisms that can "ensure that the required technologies and data are made available [and] manufactured on a large scale, distributed rapidly, equitably and affordably in all countries."

The Centre paper concluded, "The crisis is also an opportunity for WHO member countries to reinvent the Organization, making it a stronger and more independent international public agency with the capacity [and] instruments to implement its resolutions and initiatives."

This vision for the WHO harkens back to the mid-1970s surge of the G77 as a political project. It was in response to these ambitions that the drug companies initiated the building of TRIPS as a seawall. When the pandemic hit a quarter century later, the industry had full confidence the wall would hold, but was not quite so confident that it could completely ignore the challenge posed by the Pool. On the evening before the Pool's launch, the industry held an event to announce it had everything under control, and that the world created by TRIPS was still the best of all possible worlds.

On the night of May 28, the International Federation of Pharmaceutical Manufacturers and Associations (IFPMA) preempted the Pool launch scheduled for the following morning by livestreaming a panel Q&A from a black box studio in its Geneva headquarters. To maximize press interest, the event featured an unusually high-level panel of five senior executives, including the CEOs of AstraZeneca, GlaxoSmithKline, and Pfizer. Joining the moderator live in the studio was Thomas Cueni, the IFPMA's director and permanent representative in Geneva.

Many of the hundred-plus questions submitted by journalists concerned the Pool. This was expected. Allowing the executives to share their views on why pooling was unnecessary was the entire point of the event. Four of the five executives began with feigned ignorance and surprise about the Pool's existence. Only Pfizer CEO Albert Bourla, impatient with the act, broke ranks to dismiss the idea of pooling intellectual property as "dangerous nonsense." In any event, Bourla argued, it was not necessary. Echoing previous statements by his colleagues, he pointed to specific evidence of his industry's commitment to ensuring "access and equity."

The evidence provided by the executives was something called the ACT Accelerator. This initiative, they said, featured the partnership sought by the Pool, bringing together industry, governments, and major foundations, notably the Bill and Melinda Gates Foundation and its subsidiaries, Gavi, the Vaccine Alliance, and the Coalition for Epidemic Preparedness Innovations. Each executive in turn invoked support for the Accelerator as proof of their humanity and dedication to ending the pandemic as quickly as possible. The Accelerator's existence, stated Cueni, obviated the need for additional efforts and initiatives. "The Gates Foundation plays a crucial role here," he said. "We already have platforms, the industry is already doing all the right things."

As the seventy-five-minute event progressed, the industry's shared Accelerator script began to sound less like a series of talking points than a violent and uncontrollable tic. Responding to a second question about intellectual property barriers, GlaxoSmithKline CEO Emma Walmsley emitted a stream of undigested Gatesian word salad: "We are absolutely committed to this question of access, and deeply welcome the formation of ACT, a multilateral organization . . . With multiple stakeholders . . . organizations like the Gates Foundation and Gavi and others . . . where we actually look at these principles of, uh, access and so clearly, we're engaged in that as well."

If the Accelerator had not provided a go-to answer for every question concerning access, equity, and intellectual property, the stammering would have been much worse. Again, it was Pfizer CEO Albert Bourla who brought a refreshing honesty to the proceedings. During one of his odes to the

Accelerator, he interrupted himself to offer gratitude directly to the event's invisible sixth speaker.

"I want to take the opportunity to emphasize the role that Bill Gates is playing," said Bourla. "This man is an inspiration for all."

Thirteen

PHARMA'S BEST FRIEND

Bill Gates and COVID-19

I N LATE SEPTEMBER 2019, A FEW WEEKS BEFORE THE FIRST UN-reported human-to-human transmission of SARS-CoV-2 in Wuhan, the streaming service Netflix released a docuseries about Bill Gates called *Inside Bill's Brain*. The film's authorized celebration of Gates is calibrated in the manner of a thousand other profiles from the last twenty years: once a brash, restless, and perhaps overly ambitious genius, Gates has become philanthropist-philosopher touched by humility, heroically channeling his genius and wealth into repairing a world in crisis. The series shows Gates crunching the numbers and studying the angles with darting eyes that feed the mighty processor of his visionary mind. If we are to survive climate change, the energy transition, and infectious disease, Gates concludes, "It's important that we start deploying solutions unnaturally fast."

A few months after the release of *Inside Bill's Brain*, Gates received an opportunity to demonstrate his commitment to historically speedy solutions.

As described in the last chapter, COVID-19 triggered urgent planning sessions and international debates about the most effective strategies to defeat the first airborne pandemic virus in a century. At the WHO, public health experts met in February to sketch a plan to cooperatively research, develop, test, manufacture, and deploy treatments and vaccines. Producing and distributing billions of shots was a daunting task, but also an urgent one given the opportunistic nature of viruses to adapt and mutate. This conversation was informed by the hard-earned lessons of the AIDS, Ebola, and avian flu crises—each a showcase for how intellectual property and profit concerns contribute to artificial scarcities and inequities.

No individual was better positioned in early 2020 to advance an "unnaturally fast" scale-up of research production than Bill Gates. Next to the Trump White House spectacle of antiscience incompetence, he arrived in the costume of de facto czar of global public health policy, a title purchased with billions of dollars dispensed by his eponymous foundation since stepping down as Microsoft CEO in 2000. Gates's influence over global public health policy is unique in its scope and ability to take different forms at different levels of power—from directing the budget choices of cash-strapped African governments to setting long-term agendas at international health and development agencies. He brought authority and sway with him into the offices of publishers, prime ministers, nonprofits, and pharmaceutical executives.

Gates did not use this authority to support or even engage with experts and leaders from the global south who warned about the dangers of leaving COVID-19 science in the hands of intellectual property-hoarding corporations. Instead, he threw his weight on the other side, working to ensure the pandemic response remained in line with the deep ideological commitment to knowledge monopolies that is a running feature of every stage and endeavor of Gates's life.

In private meetings with drug company executives, government officials, and international health agency brass, Gates and his deputies affirmed their support for proprietary control and attempted to head off any discussion of pooling intellectual property or suspending the TRIPS regime. Instead, they teased a plan for pooling procurement orders. Alongside Gates at the front of this effort was Richard Wilder, a former head of intellectual property at Microsoft who serves as general counsel and director of business development at Gates's flagship infectious disease research initiative, the Coalition for Epidemic Preparedness Innovations (CEPI). A public-private initiative launched with Gates seed funding at the 2017 World Economic Forum in Davos, CEPI embodies the intellectual property–friendly philanthropic model that his organization would replicate in his attempt to orchestrate the global response to COVID-19.

"Early on, when governments and the companies were using a rhetoric of global public goods, there was space for Gates to have a major impact in favor of open models, like pooling," says Manuel Martin, a policy adviser to Médecins Sans Frontières. "He could have stepped up and said, 'We're going to hold you to that, because we have a moral obligation to turn a race into a collaboration where everyone exchanges information across platforms and subject areas.' The Gates people dampened enthusiasm early by saying intellectual property is not an access barrier in vaccines. That's just demonstratively false. It's not the only access barrier, but nobody ever said it was."

The impact of Gates's actions rippled throughout the radius of his influence in the world of public health, which is to say it left nothing untouched.

"He has immense power," says James Love of Knowledge Ecology International. "He can get you fired from a UN job. He knows that if you want to work in global public health, you'd better not make an enemy of the Gates Foundation by questioning its positions on intellectual property and monopolies."

On March 10, 2020, the Bill and Melinda Gates Foundation announced a partnership with the Wellcome Trust and Mastercard. The three were combining forces to seed a new mechanism called the Therapeutics Accelerator, to identify potential treatments for the novel coronavirus that would be pronounced a pandemic the following day.

An initiative that performed double duty as a social branding exercise for a financial services company chimed with Gates's signature management-consulting approach to corporate philanthropy, an early signal he would approach the looming global crisis with the same old toolkit. Those close to the debates taking place over how to organize the global research effort—debates that were beginning to unnerve industry—say Gates's timing was not a coincidence.

"Gates wanted exclusive rights maintained, and he acted faster than the WHO by announcing the Accelerator and signaling business-as-usual rules on intellectual property," says James Love. "Things could have gone either way at the time. Gates used his influence to stop the push for sharing the knowledge needed to make the products—the know-how, the data, the cell lines, the tech transfer. The C-TAP [Pool] would have included all of that. Gates's contracts [with industry through the Accelerator] asked little in return and required none of the transparency that is critically important in about twenty different dimensions. Since the late 1990s, Gates has been telling everyone they can go to heaven by paying lip service to discounts to poor countries, but still be selfish."

Gates launched a larger version of the Accelerator on April 24. The Access to COVID-19 Tools Accelerator (ACT-A) was introduced as a full-service solution to what many were predicting would be a dual crisis of supply and access. It consisted of four "pillars," covering health systems, diagnostics, treatments, and vaccines. The vaccine pillar, COVAX, was always the centerpiece. Officially launched in June by Gavi, the Vaccine Alliance, a public-private Gates organization focused on childhood vaccination in the global south, COVAX was conceived as a procurement pool and transaction hub for vaccines serving rich and poor countries alike. The plan called for CEPI to identify and invest in enough promising vaccine candidates to result in a portfolio of working vaccines. Gavi would then organize procurement and distribution through a finance mechanism called the Advance Market Commitment—essentially a buyers' club that would subsidize vaccines to cover what the WHO calls the priority fifths, or the most vulnerable 20 percent, of the world's ninety-two poorest countries. To cover the remaining fifty percent needed to achieve herd immunity, the countries would be left to compete on the global market.

Launched to great fanfare by industry and Gavi's media relations department, COVAX was based on a faith that the market could be nudged and guided into balance between global public health and safety needs, and the profit motives of monopoly-wielding companies in possession of the first WHO-approved vaccines. It also depended on rich governments—"self-financing countries" in the COVAX lingo—not racing against each other to close bilateral deals with manufacturers, and thus leave everyone else staring at empty shelves. Both premises proved to be catastrophically incorrect.

"The Gates model assumed that production will follow demand, and had no answer to the supply issue that the companies had no interest in solving," said James Krellenstein, director of the advocacy group PrEP4All. "It was a

dangerously incompetent plan that guaranteed the emergence of more vari-
ants as the virus spread."

Within the first few months of COVAX's launch, the U.S. government
signed seven bilateral preorders for close to a billion doses; the U.K. inked
five deals, giving it access to 270 million doses, more than enough for twice its
population. The other G7 countries accounted for most of the rest.

If the Gates organization had merely failed to anticipate the supply crisis, or blundered in a good faith attempt to deploy a technical fix to a fundamentally political problem, COVAX would amount to an epic miscarriage of
power by someone who knew better. But the project must be judged on the
basis of things far worse than a mere failure of planning and imagination.
Gates personally sought to sabotage the efforts of those who predicted the
scope and source of the supply crisis, and he did so while using every form of
leverage at his disposal—including direct ownership of rights—to actively
restrict licensing and production outside the monopoly model.

When the director of Oxford's Jenner Institute announced his desire to
place the rights to its CEPI-supported vaccine candidate in the public domain, Gates intervened. As reported by Kaiser Health News, "A few weeks
later, Oxford—urged on by the Bill & Melinda Gates Foundation—reversed
course [and] signed an exclusive vaccine deal with AstraZeneca that gave the
pharmaceutical giant sole rights and no guarantee of low prices." In the case
of CureVac, a company that received more than $20 million from CEPI to
develop an mRNA vaccine, the "access obligation" was removed from the
contract without explanation. "It's baffling," Public Citizen's Zain Rizvi told
The Nation. "CEPI helped jumpstart CureVac's work on the vaccine, but then
seemingly waived away its own leverage to expand production around the
world."

The CureVac deletion was reminiscent of the fate suffered by the access obligation written into CEPI's original contract with participating drug
companies. At the CEPI launch at Davos in 2017, much was made about the
initiative's pricing pledge to hold partner companies accountable to the social
values and mission of the initiative. After the media spotlight went dark, the
companies decided the language went too far. CEPI dutifully watered the
language down to a see-through gruel.

Gates's use of contractual Potemkin villages to obscure his commitment to monopoly raises the question of whose interests are being served, and how. Industry understands well that the details and outcomes of these access pledges get less attention than the fact they exist at all. As long as they and the organizations touting them exist, they serve to run effective interference for an industry that would otherwise be mute in the face of calls for more radical reforms to address the systemic failure that make access pledges necessary in the first place.

This aspect of Gates's philanthropic endeavors was on display at the ACT Accelerator launch ceremony in April 2020, which featured a number of "founding partners" from industry. Thomas Cueni, director general of the International Federation of Pharmaceutical Manufacturers & Associations, praised the initiative as a "landmark global partnership," one that—as he would say many times over the next weeks and months—also happened to make unnecessary the consideration of other frameworks. It was the only thing that allowed Pfizer CEO Albert Bourla to wave so many questions about intellectual property away at the IFPMA media event, and say, "The industry is already doing all the right things. We already have platforms."

If Gates had used his influence to back the calls for pooling, suspending rights, and organizing global tech transfer, it would have snapped decades of dedication to knowledge monopolies dating to his vengeful teenage crusade against the open-source computer programming culture of the 1970s. In the 1980s and '90s, it was a novel use of intellectual property—copyright applied to computer code—that made Gates the richest man in the world for most of two decades beginning in 1995. That was the year TRIPS went into effect, following an expensive lobbying campaign by an industry coalition that included Microsoft. Four years later, Gates would arrive on the public health scene, checkbook in hand, just as his beleaguered partners in the TRIPS coalition were flailing in response to the global campaign to break their death grip on lifesaving AIDS drugs.

In May 1999, Gates was transitioning. Though focused on defending Microsoft from antitrust suits on two continents, he was in his final months as the company's CEO. As his business reputation suffered high-profile beatings from U.S. and European regulators, he began the process of moving on to his second act. In 2000, he would merge two smaller foundations into the Bill and Melinda Gates Foundation and commence an unlikely rise to the commanding heights of global development and public health.

Gates debuted in this world during the May 1999 World Health Assembly. Big Pharma was richer than ever, but its lawsuit against the Mandela government had left it more hated than ever, and more exposed. Despite a billion-dollar public affairs machine and a fully functioning echo chamber, it was bleeding legitimacy and appeared incapable of producing a mask resembling a credible human face. By every nonfinancial measure, it was an industry in distress. To borrow a title from a future Bill Gates production, you could say it was waiting for its Superman.[49]

As the U.S. ambassador in Geneva rang the alarm over the future of TRIPS in the spring of 1999, Gates was preparing to launch Gavi, the Vaccine Alliance, with a seed grant of $750 million. His billionaire profile didn't count for much at the raucous WHO Assembly, and it was a source of consternation when officers from Gates's charity—still known as the William H. Gates Foundation—began distributing a glossy brochure touting the role of intellectual property in driving pharmaceutical innovation. James Love remembers seeing the Gates staffers joined in the distribution effort by Harvey Bale, a former U.S. trade official serving as director of the International Federation of Pharmaceutical Manufacturers & Associations.

"It was this nice full-color pamphlet about why patents don't present an access problem, with the Gates Foundation logo at the bottom," says Love. "It was a little strange. I thought, 'OK, I guess this is what he's doing now.' Looking back, that's when the pharma-Gates consortium set the markers down on intellectual property. It pretty aggressively transformed the dynamics and perception of the civil society side of the debate. Instead of 'Pharma versus Médecins Sans Frontières,' it became 'Gates versus Médecins Sans

---

49. In 2010, the Gates Foundation would bankroll a documentary advocating the privatization of U.S. public education, titled *Waiting for Superman*.

Frontières.' He's been sticking his nose into every intellectual property debate since."

Following the 1999 World Health Assembly, the AIDS debate entered a new stage. Industry attempted to defuse the opposition and salvage its reputation by offering discounts to African countries. The compromise prices it offered were still obscenely high, but even this insulting peace offering to critics was too much for Pfizer, who stormed out of the industry coalition in protest. As during the first months of the COVID-19 pandemic, the more opinion swung against the drug companies, and the better the stakes were understood, the more it seemed possible that momentum was building toward an overdue system-level break with the status quo.

"The movement was successfully building pressure for structural, more decisive solutions into the aughts," says Asia Russell, a veteran HIV-AIDS activist and director of Health GAP, an advocacy group. "It was very focused, and just when it started to have effect, here's this new version of the industry narrative emerging from Gates and Pharma. It was still about how anything that interferes with industry profits will undermine research and development, but with a new dynamic. The same op-eds and talking points weren't coming just from industry, but also from philanthropy in the form of the Gates Foundation."

The rise of the Gates Foundation and Gavi, the Vaccine Alliance, quickly changed the perception of the conflict and its possible solutions, says Martin, the Médecins Sans Frontières policy adviser. "When drug companies could just give money to Gates's institutions, it diffused the real issue of decolonizing global health," he says.

The appearance of space between the industry and Gates as a third force was always an illusion. After the companies backed down from their lawsuit against Mandela and South Africa, Gates remained unhappy when a voluntary AIDS patent pool was set up inside the UN. Brook Baker, a law professor at Northeastern University and senior policy analyst for Health GAP, recalls Gates's coolness toward the Unitaid Medicines Patent Pool, a pioneering voluntary pool seen by many as a successful working model for the WHO COVID-19 Pool proposed in May 2020. "Initially, Gates was unsupportive and even hostile toward the AIDS Medicines Patent Pool. He brought that same hostility to relaxing industry's iron-fist control over its technologies into the pandemic response, backed by his enormous influence," says Baker.

It was a somber reunion of sorts when South Africa and India introduced a motion in the TRIPS Council on October 16, 2020, calling for the suspension of all IP barriers to COVID-19 technologies, including vaccines. A bloc of the richest countries rebuffed the request with the same ploy used by the drug companies—by pointing to Gates's COVAX. In response, South Africa demanded the partial contribution of COVAX be measured, not against a world without COVAX, but one without the IP regime that made COVAX necessary in the first place. In a statement circulated at the TRIPS Council in late February 2021, South Africa spoke for the waiver bloc and asked those delegations opposed to the waiver to recognize that

> [a] rather large gap exists between what COVAX can deliver and what is required in developing and least developed countries. Irrespective of the amount of money any of the donor countries may throw at the problem, the model of donation and philanthropic expediency cannot solve the fundamental disconnect between the monopolistic model it underwrites and the very real desire of developing and least developed countries to produce for themselves. Philanthropy cannot buy equality. The artificial shortage of vaccines is primarily caused by the inappropriate use of intellectual property rights; this cannot be allowed to continue.

When South Africa delivered this statement in February 2021, 75 percent of all existing vaccines had been administered in *just ten countries*. On the other side of these 130 million doses, close to 130 countries containing 2.5 billion people had yet to administer a single shot. The sporadic donations to COVAX turned out to be paltry. In some cases, they amounted to boxes containing just a dozen vials, enough to cover the occupants of a single presidential palace. The 20 percent goal set by COVAX, never sufficient, seemed remote. Prime ministers and executives continued to express rhetorical support for COVAX in the morning, only to continue signing bilateral deals in the afternoon. The European Commission had bypassed COVAX to enter into a regional procurement pool administered by the EU.

Not even Gates's mighty media operation could stop the spread of growing public interest in the waiver debate and intellectual property more broadly. This interest led quickly back to Gates himself, who came to be on the receiving end of questions that drew out the old Microsoft monopolist, who now took the form of a vaccine monopolist cloaked in the expensive costume of a humanitarian visionary.

The pandemic revealed the mythmaking at the heart of Gates's multi-billion-dollar reputation-laundering operation. His interventions to manage the COVID-19 response not only failed, they revealed the hollowness of his stated commitment to "access and equity" in medicines and vaccines. When confronted with the contradictions between his organizations' stated goals and ideological commitment to inviolate private knowledge monopolies, he lashed out like a boy emperor. This version of Gates was distantly familiar to anyone who remembered Gates's first career.

In interview after interview, Gates dismissed his critics on the issue—who now represented the majority of the global population in the poor south—as spoiled children demanding ice cream before dinner. "It's the classic situation in global health, where the advocates all of a sudden want [the vaccine] for zero dollars and right away," he told Reuters in late January 2021. When a *Fast Company* reporter raised the growing concerns over intellectual property barriers in February, she described Gates "raising his voice slightly and laughing in frustration" before snapping, "It's irritating that this issue comes up here. This isn't about IP." Sometimes Gates larded his dismissals with comments equating state-protected and publicly funded monopolies with the "free market." After a *New York Times* journalist brought up the issue, Gates replied, "North Korea doesn't have that many vaccines, as far as we can tell." The *Times* journalist might have pointed out that North Korea doesn't spend much on vaccine research, but the countries that do have produced most of the world's vaccines within public and nonprofit research environments.

The more Gates was pressed on the issue, the more imperious grew his reactions, revealing his vaunted mastery of public health issues to be not just a mirage, but one manipulated to purpose. When asked by a Sky News reporter in April 2021 if he thought lifting intellectual property restrictions on vaccines "would be helpful," Gates bristled. "No," he said. "There's only so many vaccine factories in the world and people are very serious about the safety of vaccines." Both halves of the response were specious. From Canada to Bangladesh, owners of idle factories had tried and failed to sign licensing deals with vaccine companies, and further spare capacity existed, or could have been built up, in a number of countries. Many of these countries were already producing the vaccines that Gates insinuated were above the pay grade of developing countries to safely produce. Aside from the extreme condescension of this judgment, it conflicts with the fact—one that Gates knows well—that close to half of the 161 vaccines approved by the WHO, amounting to 70 percent of the world's vaccine supply, are manufactured in developing countries such as India, Brazil, Cuba, Thailand, Senegal, and Indonesia, according to the Global Vaccine Market Report. The difference between those vaccines and the COVID-19 shots has nothing to do with the quality of those countries' production lines, and everything to do with patents, trade secrets, and proprietary knowhow.

In May 2021, the stalemate inside the TRIPS Council was shaken up by the Biden administration's announcement that it would support an emergency waiver of some sort. Amid the political repositioning that followed, the Bill and Melinda Gates Foundation posted a short announcement by CEO Mark Suzman that stated, "No barriers should stand in the way of equitable access to vaccines, including intellectual property, which is why we are supportive of a narrow waiver during the pandemic."

As discussed in the next chapter, a "narrow" waiver would not accomplish much, and could be worse than nothing to the extent that it undermines calls for a broad waiver encompassing trade secrets and test data, matched with a mandatory tech-transfer mechanism. That it took the organization so long to admit intellectual property constitutes a "barrier" at all cast a shadow over Suzman's reminder that the foundation had "been working urgently since January 2020" on organizing the manufacture and flow of global vaccine supplies.

Before that statement, the closest Gates ever came to conceding a relationship between IP and the supply crisis was during a January interview with South Africa's *Mail & Guardian*. When asked about the growing intellectual property debate at the WTO, he responded, "At this point, changing the rules wouldn't make any additional vaccines available."

Gates's use of the phrase *at this point* suggests he lacked the power to influence the debate when it mattered, as if he'd been living on an atoll in the South Pacific in the winter and spring of 2020. If Gates was counting on readers not to know anything about his machinations early into the pandemic, it was a safe bet. Most of the general public had more pressing matters at the time than following obscure debates about intellectual property. Of those that were aware of these debates, most probably thought themselves unqualified to have an opinion. Who were they to question the man they'd been told for years was the smartest guy in the room?

Gates's refusal to entertain the possibility of a supply crisis, and his rejection of those who anticipated it in full, has not aged well. If any voices appear prophetic, they belong to the 140 political and public health leaders who first called for a "people's vaccine."

"Those who do not remember the past are doomed to repeat it," reads the group letter published in May 2020. "Applying these lessons, we call for a global agreement that ensures mandatory worldwide sharing of all COVID-19 related knowledge, data and technologies with a pool of COVID-19 licenses freely available to all countries [and] establishes a global and equitable rapid manufacturing and distribution plan . . . Action must start urgently to massively build capacity worldwide to manufacture billions of vaccine doses and to recruit and train the millions of paid and protected health workers needed to deliver them."

This was the plan that Gates did his best to deprive of oxygen in the critical early months of the pandemic. When the failure of his plan became impossible to ignore, and public attention turned in Gates's direction, what people saw was not the quirky genius of *Inside Bill's Brain*, carrying the world on his narrow shoulders. They saw the entitled know-it-all monopolist of the Microsoft antitrust hearings. Turns out he was right here, working the same beat in plain view, all this time.

Fourteen

CROWN JEWELS IN A BLACK BOX

Trade Secrets and Lies

IN THE FINAL DAYS OF SEPTEMBER 2020, GLOBAL DEATHS FROM COVID-19 hit 1 million. This ghastly statistical milestone was sobering but ultimately hollow, a string of zeros unable to measure the forsakenness and agony of dying alone from an untreatable disease. The casualties endured final days alone, intubated in chaotic and overcrowded hospitals or gasping for air in makeshift isolation wards. Whatever the details, it was misery.

The specter of the next million deaths shadowed a scramble among the wealthiest nations to lock up vaccine supplies. As the pandemic's second winter loomed, rich countries placed massive preorders at market rates running as high as $30 per dose for Moderna. When the U.K. and Canada secured enough vaccines for their populations, they kept going, padding their overstocks.

Meanwhile, the promise that COVAX would come to everyone else's rescue was not aging well. Its stated goal of providing subsidized vaccines for 20 percent of the poorest populations was pushed back a year, maybe two—nobody could say. But even as COVAX failed to meet its limited targets, it succeeded in providing vaccine companies and their sponsoring governments a way to deflect growing calls for removing from monopoly control the technology and science needed to make the most effective vaccines. COVAX and

Gates first ran interference for industry following the establishment of the C-TAP. On October 2, 2020, they became foils used against a proposal inside the TRIPS Council to waive intellectual property rights around COVID-19 products for the duration of the pandemic.

The waiver motion had the virtue of simplicity. Rather than seek technology-specific uses of the council's byzantine compulsory licensing rules, it called for what amounted to a blanket waiver that would release all nations from legal obligations "to implement, apply or enforce most categories of intellectual property" on products related to the "prevention, containment and treatment" of COVID-19. It covered all forms of intellectual property—patents, trade secrets, copyright, data—until "widespread vaccination is in place globally, and the majority of the world's population has developed immunity."

The proposal sparked life into the stalled debate over intellectual property with a powerful historical charge that linked COVID-19 to the African AIDS crisis. In the late 1990s, South Africa and India faced down the G7-backed pharmaceutical industry and brought cheap off-patent combination therapies to sub-Saharan Africa and other poor regions of the world. In its opening statement to the TRIPS Council, South Africa made sure the symbolism was not lost on its fellow delegations.

"We have seen this before," said South Africa's ambassador, Xolelwa Mlumbi-Peter. "At the height of the HIV crisis, prices set for [combination therapies] to treat HIV were simply too high and out of reach for many developing countries. As death rates due to AIDS plunged in rich countries, infected people across the developing world were left to die. Our leaders vowed that this would never happen again."

Opposition to the waiver split along a north-south axis that suggested the lessons of the 1990s had not been learned equally.[50] The United States,

---

50. The original cosponsors included sixty-two developing countries, made up of the Council's Africa Group, the Least Developed Country Group, Bolivia, Fiji, Indonesia, Pakistan, Mongolia, Vanuatu, and Venezuela. The support would grow by another hundred countries by the summer of 2021.

the United Kingdom, Canada, Japan, and the nations of the European Union objected on grounds that current global voluntary mechanisms were sufficient (bilateral licensing, COVAX). Where these mechanisms fell short, the rich countries cited the "flexibilities" adopted at Doha as an available backup plan that already existed within the bounds of the treaty.

The waiver countries were not surprised by the resistance and responded to each objection in a series of detailed counter-statements. Into the spring of 2021, the two sides went through the Kabuki theater of explaining to each other what both already understood perfectly well: the compulsory licensing reforms adopted at Doha were not designed to address a highly complex vaccine shortage during a pandemic. Similar to the public-interest triggers in U.S. law, they were designed to placate the critics and be admired in theory, but only rarely if ever deployed.

The centerpiece "flexibility" adopted at Doha in 2001—the right to issue a compulsory license—allows countries to manufacture, or contract out the manufacture, of drugs otherwise subject to intellectual property claims in the event of public health and national security emergencies. The first version of the reform, known as Article 31, featured a giant hole in its middle: it protected only the country that issued the compulsory license. Since most countries lack the capacity to produce drugs, and need to outsource the job, another section was added to Article 31 indemnifying the third party under contract. It was named 31*bis*.

Developing countries at first celebrated the adoption of 31*bis* in 2003. If not quite a full release from the straightjacket of TRIPS, it seemed to recover some ground following "the first significant push back to the relentless march to strengthen private intellectual property rights without regard for societal consequences in poor countries," in the words of Ellen 't Hoen, an activist and scholar of the global medicines-access movement.

The reforms allowing compulsory export licenses, however, have been used just once in nineteen years. In 2007, Rwanda invoked Article 31 and 31*bis* and contracted with a Canadian company to export a patented combination

AIDS therapy called TriAvir. The generic drug company, Apotex, produced the pills quickly at a cost of nineteen cents each. Two shipments spent a year each collecting dust in a Toronto warehouse while the TRIPS Council worked out the legal details.

The explanation for these delays, and for why compulsory export licenses are never used, begins with the text. Article 31 and 31*bis* are loaded with requirements, exceptions, and asterisks that form a legal and procedural maze, greatly complicating an act already fraught with political and economic risk. "The nineteen sections and hundred sub-clauses that set conditions on importing and exporting generics make the 'flexibility' so impractical as to be meaningless," says K. M. Gopakumar, a legal adviser to the Third World Network, a research group focused on trade and development. "For countries without the capacity to produce the medicine at scale domestically, it's often not necessary to exert pressure against them."

When pressure is required to stop a country from breaking patents on drugs priced beyond the reach of sick and dying people, it is applied without mercy in off-the-books diplomatic black sites known as TRIPS Plus. This is where the Doha flexibilities are exposed to real-world conditions, far from the castle grounds of the WTO headquarters, and shown not to be so flexible after all.

TRIPS was always conceived as a floor. It is, in WTO parlance, a "minimum standards" treaty that sets a floor for intellectual property enforcement, such as the recognition of the standard twenty-year drug patent term. Beyond these foundations, it is a treaty al fresco, whose possibilities are limited to the imaginations and bullying powers of the countries seeking to enforce them. The details of TRIPS Plus vary according to the situation and countries involved, but are usually determined in side rooms during regional and bilateral trade agreements, in the running conversations of general diplomacy, and in negotiations with international agencies and development institutions. It is the informal reality of TRIPS Plus, not the legalese of TRIPS itself, that has doomed the Doha flexibilities to decorative status. "When Thailand and other countries started to invoke the public health clauses in the Doha flexibilities in the 2000s, they faced strong and immediate pushback from Washington and Brussels," says Gopakumar. "The drug companies and their governments have always used political pressure, threats, and legal tools to ensure that the flexibilities exist only on paper."

This pressure to adhere to TRIPS Plus is not secret, even if the details aren't often reported or made public. A typical case occurred in 2016 when Colombia threatened to issue a compulsory license on a Novartis-patented leukemia drug. The Swiss company and its local embassy responded by first threatening retaliation through the WTO. It then activated TRIPS Plus by enlisting the U.S. embassy in Bogota to warn Colombia's health minister that stepping on Novartis's patent—though justified under Article 31— would jeopardize Washington's support for upcoming negotiations with the Marxist rebel group FARC.

The Office of the U.S. Trade Representative (USTR) publishes an annual *Special 301 Report* (like the EU's annual copycat version), which is used to keep countries locked into a TRIPS Plus mindset by publishing a tiered, naughty-or-nice "watch list." Under the statute that created the 301 review process, USTR must prepare punitive "action plans" for countries that appear on the "priority" list two years running. The 2021 *Special 301 Report* editions listed thirty-two countries of concern.[51]

The reports also serve as windows into how Washington and Brussels understand the dimensions and trendlines of TRIPS Plus. In recent years, the reports put out by both capitals have focused on trade secrets and proprietary data, two forms of intellectual property at the heart of the debate over the WTO waiver. But the place to begin understanding these categories and why they matter isn't in Geneva, although the waiver proposal mentions them by name. It's the curious announcement made six days later by a newly

---

51. Nations on the list included Argentina, Chile, China, India, Indonesia, Russia, Saudi Arabia, Ukraine, and Venezuela. Those of lesser but growing concern included Algeria, Barbados, Bolivia, Brazil, Canada, Colombia, Dominican Republic, Ecuador, Egypt, Guatemala, Kuwait, Lebanon, Mexico, Pakistan, Paraguay, Peru, Romania, Thailand, Trinidad and Tobago, Turkey, Turkmenistan, Uzbekistan, and Vietnam.

famous vaccine company based out of the cobblestoned biotech hub of Cambridge, Massachusetts.

On October 8, 2020, Moderna popped back into the news. Without mentioning the waiver proposed by South Africa and India the week before, the company announced it was temporarily suspending the patents around the vaccine candidate it developed in partnership with the U.S. government. "We feel," the company stated, "a special obligation under the current circumstances."

The tone suggested Moderna was just happy to help during a difficult time; an example of regal magnanimity of a piece with the industry's coordinated message of "We're all in this together." As the company hoped, the result was praise for what seemed an act of social conscience. Never mind that many of the patents never fully belonged to the company in the first place—the U.S. government owns, shares, or has legal claims on most of them—the media allowed it to stand as a credible display of noblesse oblige. Moderna's patent pledge would, as Reuters put it, allow "other drugmakers to develop shots using the company's technology."

The company knew the public would draw a false conclusion—that Moderna was facilitating vaccine production at the expense of its own profits—because it knew that the public and the media have an outdated understanding of intellectual property. A pledge singling out "patents" on mRNA technology only sounds meaningful if you don't understand that patents are a *form* of intellectual property, not a synonym. In the context of mRNA vaccines, using "patents" as a stand-in for knowledge monopolies is a throwback reference that obscures far more than it explains, like calling the supercomputer in your pocket a telephone.

For centuries, the "patent" symbolized a limited-term social contract by containing the information society received in return for the privilege of a limited-term monopoly. By containing the details of the invention, it served as a note of collateral. When the monopoly expired, the state would diffuse the knowledge by lifting restrictions on its use. Not a part of it, or a piece of it, but all of it as contained in the patent.

As technological inventions grew more complex, patents required more detailed assembly instructions. Until 1880, the U.S. Patent and Trademark Office required that patent applications include miniature, three-dimensional models of the invention, along with detailed instructions, blueprints, and diagrams to ensure the government possessed everything that someone "skilled in the art" would need to reproduce the invention.

In 2022, this is all as quaint as the miniature riverboat buoyancy device a young Abraham Lincoln submitted for patent consideration in 1849.

It did not become quaint from age alone. The patent and the social contract it once symbolized are anachronistic because it benefited some to tear up the constitutional tracks that required knowledge diffusion for social benefit. They were intentionally replaced with tracks built to *deter* the application of knowledge—for as long as possible, even and especially by someone "skilled in the art." The intent behind this change is clear in the world of pharmaceuticals, where new medicines are often barricaded indefinitely behind a broad category of intellectual property called undisclosed information, home to the subcategories of know-how, trade secrets, and data.

As opposed to information disclosed in public patent filings, knowledge claimed as "undisclosed information" remains private under a right to secrecy protected by law; few levers short of a federal police raid can force companies to cough it up. The waiver debate and what follows will turn not on patents but on this black box of intellectual property.

The patent remained the primary container of information related to inventions into the 1970s. A reappraisal took place as U.S. knowledge-based industries developed a vision for the 1980s and beyond: rolling back the G77, locking the world into a global intellectual property regime, updating Cold War scripts with horror stories of foreign "pirate" states. Drug companies were at the center of the project begun at Chicago to construct new intellectual property narratives and legal paradigms. At drug industry–funded think tanks and legal clinics, the idea of elevating and protecting trade secrets as a form of intellectual property received infusions of money and brainpower. The resulting literature was folded into the lobbying scripts already in use in support of Bayh-Dole and the early push for a TRIPS-like treaty at Uruguay: intellectual thieving by U.S. rivals in Europe and Asia, some of them "pirate" states, demanded urgent revisions to laws and norms concerning intellectual property to protect the country's "competitiveness."

The Uniform Trade Secrets Act of 1979 was established as a national standard to displace the varying state-level common-law traditions. Previous to the law, many states had defined trade secrets as information in "continuous use in the operation of the business." The UTSA broadened the legal definition of trade secrets to any information in the claimant's possession, regardless of its history of use. This could mean "a formula, pattern, compilation, program device, method, technique, or process, that: (i) derives independent economic value, actual or potential, from not being generally known . . . and (ii) is the subject of efforts that are reasonable under the circumstances to maintain its secrecy."

In other words, anything. In a medical context, this made all research acquired in a buyout a trade secret. Every folder and data point from every study ever conducted with a government grant—trade secrets. The knowledge of how to best manufacture a patented drug—now a trade secret on par with Coca-Cola's venerable secret formula.

In 1985, a series of amendments tightened up the law and increased the scope for damages and criminal prosecution. The Economic Espionage Act of 1996 extended the logic by making the theft or "misuse" of trade secrets, formerly a civil matter, a federal crime. Despite the name's reference to the original Espionage Act of 1917, the law was not limited to actions benefiting foreign governments. It raised the domestic theft of commercial information (including those related to medicines) to a level previously reserved for classified national defense information, allowing for fines up to $5 million and up to ten years' imprisonment. A year after the law went into effect, U.S. attorneys indicted a Taiwanese national, James Hsu, for attempting to illegally acquire proprietary information related to producing Taxol, an anti-cancer drug, by bribing a Bristol Myers Squibb employee. Indicted on multiple counts of conspiracy and attempted theft of trade secrets, Hsu pled guilty to the conspiracy charge and was sentenced to two years' probation and a fine.[52]

The Economic Espionage Act placed razor wire around a new intellectual property paradigm. Trade secrets had become "the crown jewels of corporations" and patents merely "the tips of icebergs in an ocean of trade secrets," in the words of one of this paradigm's architects, Karl F. Jorda. The longtime chief intellectual property counsel for Ciba-Geigy, a Swiss firm that merged with Sandoz to form Novartis in 1996, Jorda was a hinge figure who connected the age of mid-century cigar-chomping patent lawyers to their information-age descendants who identify less as lawyers than as "competitive intelligence" professionals working as white hats in a double-game of industrial espionage. Their job is not to secure twenty-year patents, but to achieve what Jorda calls the "synergistic integration of patents and trade secrets to secure invulnerable exclusivity."[53] In the 1990s, after a quarter century

---

52. The first criminal prosecution for intellectual property theft in the United States preceded the 1996 law by six years. The case involved an undergraduate chemistry student at the University of South Florida named Petr Táborský. A citizen of what was then Czechoslovakia, Táborský was working as a research assistant in a joint project of the public university and a local power firm, Florida Progress Corporation. After the project ended in failure—the goal was a method to remove ammonia from wastewater, to be patented and licensed in the manufacture of cat litter—Táborský retreated to his private lab and continued working on the problem as part of his thesis subject. When he made a breakthrough, the university administration and Florida Progress claimed ownership. When Táborský refused to hand his research over, the university charged him with theft of trade secrets and a Florida court sentenced him to a year of house arrest and fifteen years' probation. When Táborský was granted a patent on the invention by the U.S. Patent Office, the university filed *another* slate of criminal charges. These landed the exchange student on a chain-gang at the waste-management plant of a maximum-security prison. Over two years, the university spent $330,000 pursuing the case, or ten times the cost of the federal grant that underwrote the partnership with Florida Progress.

53. The emcee of the ceremony marking his 2007 induction into the global Intellectual Property Hall of Fame praised Jorda for his "outstanding contribution to the development of intellectual property law and practice, thereby helping to establish intellectual property as one of the key business assets of the 21st century."

at Ciba-Geigy, Jorda directed the Center for the Law of Innovation and En-
trepreneurship at the Franklin Pierce Law Center, now the University of
New Hampshire Franklin Pierce School of Law, an industry-funded incuba-
tor clinic for new theories of intellectual property strategy and management
in the age of "undisclosed information."

When Jorda says "invulnerable exclusivity," he means infinite. Unlike
patents, claims on "undisclosed information" have no term limit. This voids
the original patent bargain not once, but twice. It keeps knowledge central to
the invention from entering the public domain, and in doing so unnaturally
extends its control of the market. Instead of providing society with meaningful collateral in exchange for a temporary monopoly, companies hand off
partial maps to technologies they have no intention of revealing in full—
fragments intended to frustrate, obfuscate, and occlude, providing knowledge that's necessary but not sufficient to actually make the thing.

By the time Bill Clinton signed the Economic Espionage Act, this betrayal wasn't just a U.S. problem. Like so much else in the mid-1990s, the
trade secret regime was about to go global.

In 1993, the United States inserted domestic trade secret law into the intellectual property section of the North American Free Trade Agreement. The
following year, it appeared more or less intact in the Marrakesh Agreement
establishing the World Trade Organization. TRIPS Article 39, Section 7
ensures the protection of "undisclosed knowledge," defined as anything "not
generally known" and that "has commercial value because it is secret."

There is no public health or national emergency carve-out enumerated
for the compulsory disclosure of such information. The Doha flexibilities in
Article 31 do not extend to Article 39.

COVID-19 has summoned the mystery created by the gap between the two
Articles: What constellation of power would be required for the compulsory
disclosure of trade secrets to produce vaccines in the context of TRIPS? Given
the history of compulsory licensing, it is difficult to even imagine any scenario
where the attempt did not make the booby-trapped maze of horrors that is
Article 31 look like a Sunday afternoon singalong of "Kumbaya." A waiver that

included undisclosed information would move the ongoing north-south debate over technology transfer and intellectual property into unknown territory.

In the U.S. context, precedents for such action are few. The Federal Trade Commission and the Pentagon have both commandeered trade secrets, but never for the purpose of providing them to foreign firms in a public health emergency. Against any form of authority short of a federal raid, pharmaceutical firms would almost certainly sue the government and perform the corporate equivalent of resisting arrest by going limp. This would effectively undermine any waiver strong enough to help countries produce complex new medicines like mRNA vaccines. Under the cover of trade secrets, drug and biotech companies can shield technical designs and specs, process and quality control procedures, best production methods, instruction manuals, and trial data. Robert Sherwood, an intellectual property theorist and consultant for the Fortune 500, calls trade secrets the "workhorse of technology transfer." Without them, you might as well make paper airplanes from the actual product patents.

All of this explains why, a week after the Biden White House announced it would back a waiver, Moderna CEO Stéphane Bancel told Wall Street analysts he "didn't lose a minute of sleep over the news."[54] It also explains why, six months earlier, Bancel had been willing to trade some patent enforcement for a good news cycle. The crown jewels were safely secured elsewhere under a level of legal protection approaching that accorded the secrets of the country's nuclear weapons program.

The industry was not completely sanguine about the turn of events, of course. Biden's announcement pushed its stock prices down, and the industry has never abandoned its traditional red line around intellectual property. Precedents are dangerous. They can have unpredictable consequences. So, too, can the conversations around them, and the ones that follow them. During the first quarter of 2021, the Pharmaceutical Research and Manufacturers of America spent more than $8.5 million on federal lobbying, putting

---

54. The company reported revenues of close to $2 billion in the first quarter of 2021, almost all from sales of its COVID-19 vaccine developed in partnership with the NIH.

it on track to beat its record lobbying spend of $30 million in 2019. Its media budget is likewise running on every one of its many cylinders. In the weeks leading up to and after Biden's waiver announcement, the trade group spent more than $245,000 on digital ad campaigns targeting the D.C. area that warned that "Biden's Damaging IP Stance" risked the health of Americans while doing nothing to address vaccine inequality.

Thomas Cueni, the director of the industry's global trade association, delivered a similar message at the media event held on the eve of the launch of the C-TAP in May 2020. When asked about the possibility that countries might issue compulsory licenses on COVID-19 vaccines, he smirked.

"The focus on [patents] in vaccines shows a lack of understanding, because with vaccines, it's all about know-how," he said. "In the history of IP, there's never been a compulsory license for vaccines. Not for nothing. It really doesn't solve the problem."

He's not wrong. This was the very argument advanced by those supporting pooling early in the pandemic. Effectively ramping up vaccine manufacture would require planning ahead to build tech-transfer mechanisms that allow for conveying know-how that includes trade secrets. To appreciate the inadequacy of a simple TRIPS waiver to accomplish this, it's helpful to walk through a hypothetical case of a country invoking its rights under Article 31 during COVID-19 and future pandemics.

Compulsory licensing has been deployed most successfully as a threat. When a government has all the information it needs to begin generic production of a drug, or knows another nation that does, it can, in theory, force the patent owner to join them at the negotiating table. In the first year of the pandemic, India used this power to attain licenses for the local production of generic remdesivir. Most famously, this threat was the fulcrum that, together with a historic activist campaign, delivered AIDS combination therapies to developing countries.

For the threat to work, however, it has to be credible. If the drug company knows its patent is padlocked by trade secrets and know-how, the threat of a compulsory license can be safely ignored; or, in the case of Thomas Cueni, dismissed with a subtly taunting reminder that some locks cannot be picked.

Imagine that a country seeks to manufacture or contract out a generic vaccine during a public health crisis. Say, Chile, one of the countries on the 2021 *Special 301 Report* "priority watch list." After gathering the political will and courage to challenge the combined weight of the industry and its allied embassies, the government in Santiago presents the monopoly-controlling drug company with a choice. It can attempt to block the compulsory generic order with legal challenges and private threats; it can offer to negotiate a voluntary compromise solution; or, if the product in question is protected by "undisclosed information," it can place its thumb on its nose and wiggle its fingers.

If the company chooses the third path, the Chilean scientists (or their contractors) must try to make the off-patent version with whatever information is publicly available. If they manage to produce a working recipe for the product, they must do the same for every component and active ingredient, which may themselves be under padlocks—a matryoshka doll of trade secrets.

The scientists next face the hurdle of producing a functioning manufacturing design without access to hundreds and possibly thousands of trade secrets and pieces of technical know-how. Before the rise of trade secrets, patents were required to include all information related to the product's "best production method." Now, patentees are allowed to meet a much lower standard for production methods; they can keep the details of the best method undisclosed until the end of time.

If the Chilean government manages to overcome all of this and produce an exact molecular replica of the original medicine, they must then confront the big boss of pharmaceutical IP—the monopoly system's last fail-safe against generic competition.

He will usually be found with his feet up, sitting behind a desk at the country's own regulatory agency. His name is Data.

✦

The right to exclusive data is just what it sounds like: a right to maintain secrecy around all data amassed during the researching, developing, and testing of a medicine or vaccine. Data rights are multipurpose from the perspective of the monopolist. During the early stages of a "vaccine race," they allow for the suppression of knowledge around research failures and dead ends that, if public, might save competing researchers time. Early in the pandemic, advocates of open science supported the creation of open data pools for precisely this reason: they would deepen collaboration and knowledge exchange rather than impede it, and accelerate progress by allowing teams to benefit from the lessons of others.

The benefit of pooled and transparent data seemed most self-evident with regard to large-scale human vaccine trials. But the global comparative trials planned by the World Health Organization never happened, because in pharma and biotech, the diamonds of data are the trial results submitted to regulators containing proof of a drug's safety and efficacy. When all else fails to protect a monopoly, proprietary trial data can act as a final defense— the safe room of "undisclosed information."

"If the originator company has trial data exclusivity, you will have to repeat everything and reinvent the wheel," says K. M. Gopakumar, the legal adviser to the Third World Network. "Even if you copy the original invention perfectly, and there is no patent on the other product, the claim on protected data turns the regulatory agencies into enforcers of trade secrets."

The pharmaceutical industry is built on lies about the cost of developing new drugs, but it is being honest when it says clinical trials are expensive. They're so expensive that often only the largest drug companies can afford to run them. If generic competitors can prove their product is nearly identical to the original drug, regulators can approve the generic based on the name-brand trial data. Unless, that is, the name-brand company hides this data under an "undisclosed information" claim.

The windows on data exclusivity vary between countries, but their expansion is a regular subject of TRIPS Plus political pressure applied during bilateral and regional trade negotiations, such as the recently negotiated United States–Mexico–Canada Agreement. "In the 1990s, patents were considered the primary puzzle for access-to-medicines advocates to solve," says Christopher Morten, a patent lawyer who used to represent the pharmaceutical industry and now teaches at New York University. "Today, it's proprietary clinical trial data, regulatory exclusivities, and other forms of non-patent exclusivity."

Of all the forms of "undisclosed information" that have downgraded the patent, data is a tool of unique flexibility and stealth, able to retroactively create monopolies even where no product patent exists.

This strange phenomenon was seen following the 2016 signing of the EU-Ukraine Deep and Comprehensive Free Trade Area agreement. As part of the deal, Ukraine was forced to adopt the EU policy of granting drug companies eight years' data exclusivity. When it signed the deal, Ukraine was importing a generic version of Gilead's pricey hepatitis C treatment from Egypt. Despite having no patent on its name-brand drug in Ukraine, Gilead sued the Ukrainian government for infringing on its trial data, which Kyiv had used as the basis for granting a license to the (chemically identical) Egyptian generic. Under the terms of the EU trade pact, Ukraine was forced to revoke the Egyptian company's license. Under Gilead's zombie monopoly, the price of not dying from hepatitis C increased to several hundred dollars per pill.

Nothing in the 2021 edition of the *Special 301 Report* suggests the U.S. government is about to push for compulsory disclosure of trade secrets, data, or any other subset of "undisclosed information." As a signal of U.S. intent, the document is a giant neon arrow pointing in the exact opposite direction. Like the latest EU report, it emphasizes trade secret protection as an area of growing concern in U.S. trade policy. It delivers a sharp warning to dozens of developing countries that use undisclosed data as the basis for approving generic drugs and agrochemical products. The *Special 301 Report* highlights "the growing need for trading partners to provide effective protection and enforcement of trade secrets" in the interests of "pharmaceutical and medical device innovation." More than just core business assets, it describes these as issues of national security requiring the assistance of the National Counterintelligence and Security Center.

From the perspective of the USTR, blocking north-south medical tech transfer is not an unfortunate by-product of protecting trade secrets; it is an integral part of national security and industrial strategy. In a section of the *Special 301 Report* called "Forced Technology Transfer, Indigenous Innovation, and Preferences for Indigenous IP," the government highlights its displeasure with technology-transfer requirements deceptively "styled as means to incentivize domestic 'indigenous innovation,'" but which "put valuable trade secrets at risk of exposure." As an example, the report cites cases of Indonesia and India conditioning foreign companies' right to market pharmaceuticals "upon the transfer of technology to Indonesian entities or upon partial manufacture in Indonesia." This is the same rap the drug companies used seventy years ago in denouncing the terms of Jawaharlal Nehru's tender for a penicillin factory. The report urges these countries to reassess and "take account of the importance of voluntary and mutually agreed commercial partnerships or arrangements."

The coronavirus pandemic is a chance to interrogate the meaning of "voluntary and mutual" in a monopoly system. The countries that imposed TRIPS on the world and maintain TRIPS Plus define these words differently than their weaker counterparts in "commercial partnerships or arrangements." The COVID-19 vaccine economy also serves as a reminder that often there is no partnership or arrangement to begin with, because one side cannot afford the monopoly price or because the monopolist does not consider some markets as worth their time, effort, and proprietary technology. "We did not develop this product for the Indian market, let's be honest," said Bayer CEO Marijn Dekkers when asked by a Bloomberg reporter why his company didn't license production of its cancer drug Nexavar in India. "We developed this product for Western patients who can afford this product."

COVID-19 has pushed the issues around monopoly, intellectual property, and technology transfer beyond Special 301 reports and the industry's "drug story," and moved them closer to their rightful place as burning public questions of global security, health, and justice. It's understandable that the drug companies feel aggrieved by this. Decades after the industry's self-incrimination in the South African AIDS suit, putting monopoly medicine on trial during COVID-19 amounts to double jeopardy. By the standards of any civilization that views its medicines as crowning achievements, the regime that prices them beyond reach and restricts the knowledge to make them must be, and has been, ruled a failure. The task remains to enforce the judgment.

NOTES ON SELECTED SOURCES

OUT OF THE MISTS

The history of medicine runs deeper than we can see. Beyond the first faded mentions of plant elixirs on ancient chips of stone and papyri, the record goes blank but for the occasional unearthing of fossilized cannabis, opium's rival for the title of first remedy. Any account of the monopolies wielded by Gilead Sciences, Inc. begins in the mists shrouding the biblical balm of Gilead. In our species' five-thousand-year medical records, intellectual property is not just a pushy outsider, it is an extreme latecomer. Before the patent attached itself to the face of medicine around the time of the first radio transmission, humanity's everlasting struggle against death and disease was many things, but it was not a business and finance story.

A large and inviting literature is devoted to the eras of medicine before the first hedge fund bought its first drug company. Paul Devereux excavates the shamanistic origins of medicine in *The Long Trip: A Prehistory of Psychedelia* (2007). In *One River: Explorations and Discoveries in the Amazon Rainforest* (1996), Wade Davis masterfully reconstructs Richard Evans Schultes's investigative adventures with indigenous medical plants and traditions during the 1930s and '40s. Alexander the Great's conquest of Egypt was a momentous event in the deep history of pharmaceuticals, resulting in the seeding of Pharaonic embalming chemistry and the religion of Ra with Arab science and Greek biology and philosophy. The consequences of this civilizational blending for modern medicine are teased out in John Read's *From Alchemy to Chemistry* (1961). Nicholas Everett curates the formative work of the late Bronze Age Greek physician Galen in his annotated translation, *The Alphabet of Galen: Pharmacy from Antiquity to the Middle Ages* (2012). Gary B. Ferngren charts Christianity's displacement of pagan ideas as the dominant framework for understanding suffering and treating disease in *Medicine and Religion: A Historical Introduction* (2014). On the turn from alchemic to rational science, and the birth of pharmacy as a guild and profession, see Stuart Anderson, *Making Medicines: A Brief History of Pharmacy and Pharmaceuticals* (2005).

EARLY PATENT LAW

Histories of medicine don't mention patents much before the twentieth century, because for centuries they had little to no impact on the business and practice of medicine. For the same reason, scholars of early patent systems don't say much about medicine. (Accounts of the fury aroused by food monopolies are another story.) On the purpose and politics of patents in Renaissance Italy and medieval England, see Chris Dent, "'Generally Inconvenient': The 1624 Statute of Monopolies as Political Compromise" (2010). Three good studies of the transplantation of English common law to the American colonies, and the ambivalence of early Americans toward the awarding of limited market monopolies to new inventions, are Oren Bracha, *Owning Ideas: The Intellectual Origins of American Intellectual Property, 1790–1909* (2016); Craig Allen Nard, "Constitutionalizing Patents: From Venice to Philadelphia" (2006); and Randolph J. May and Seth L. Cooper, "The 'Reason and Nature' of Intellectual Property: Copyright and Patent in *The Federalist Papers*" (2014).

In *Common as Air: Revolution, Art, and Ownership* (2012), Lewis Hyde revisits Article I, Section 8 of the Constitution through the skeptical contemporary eyes of Jefferson and Franklin, products of a transatlantic Enlightenment that held views of ancient lineage about knowledge as the common store of humanity, and that saw each discovery as an addition to a cumulative, multigenerational project that had no place for the idea of the "sole inventor." These ideas dovetailed with the democratic ethos of an early American republic that rejected private claims smacking of royal privilege. The historically unique fierceness of this rejection and its origins are the subject of Gordon S. Wood's classic study, *The Radicalism of the American Revolution* (1991). For a critical look at how Congress and the courts have used the Progress Clause as constitutional cover for constitutionally questionable acts, from trade to foreign policy, see Jeanne C. Fromer, "The Intellectual Property Clause's External Limitations" (2012).

The Jacksonian refashioning of the patent as an instrumental and increasingly industrial property right—private, exclusive, transferrable, and drained of social obligations—is examined in Herbert J. Hovenkamp's *Enterprise and American Law, 1836–1937* (1991) and, with a tighter focus on patents, "The Emergence of Classical American Patent Law" (2016). The use and abuse of the post-Jackson patent system did much to spark the rural radicalism of the Grange and the Populists. For two excellent accounts of these movements and the social and economic changes they reflected, see Richard R. John, *Ruling Passions: Political Economy in Nineteenth-Century America* (2010) and Lawrence Goodwyn, *The Populist Moment: A Short History of the Agrarian Revolt in America* (1978).

The courts became an increasingly important player in shaping intellectual property laws and norms in the second half of the nineteenth century. Major decisions legitimized the patent-as-property-right by upholding innovation-retarding industrial patent strategies and exempting patent-based monopolies and cartels from the Sherman Antitrust Act. The point of intersection between patents and a modernizing drug industry was fast approaching, but the idea of monopolizing a medical innovation would have been laughed out of court during the first of the Singer sewing machine patent trials in the 1850s. On the Singer case and the role of the Supreme Court in shaping post-Sherman patent law, see George E. Frost, "The Supreme Court and Patent Abuse" (1965) and Adam Mossoff, "A Stitch in Time: The Rise and Fall of the Sewing Machine Patent Thicket" (2011). Later in the century, the legal challenge to Alexander Graham Bell's claim to "inventing" the telephone would revive older debates about the nature of progress and discovery and prefigure arguments that would later appear in the patent skepticism and antitrust politics of the New Deal. See Christopher Beauchamp, *Invented by Law: Alexander Graham Bell and the Patent That Changed America* (2015).

As Americans followed the Singer and Bell cases on the front pages of the late editions, the nations of Europe were debating whether or not to recognize any patents at all. On the widespread and dogged resistance to the notion of intellectual property in Europe, see Fritz Machlup and Edith Penrose, "The Patent Controversy in the Nineteenth Century" (1950).

THE HOUSE OF "ETHICAL" MEDICINE DIVIDED

Into the twentieth century, the medical community and much of the public associated the patenting of medicines with literal and figurative fraud—indicative of both a scheme and a betrayal of the deep traditions that made medicine a humane and noble calling. The knavery of the patent-medicine peddler takes human form in a number of the century's novels, notably Herman Melville's *The Confidence-Man: His Masquerade* (1857) and Mark Twain's *The Gilded Age* (1873). On Twain's long and complicated personal relationship with patent medicines, see K. Patrick Ober, *Mark Twain and Medicine: "Any Mummery Will Cure"* (2003). For a visceral understanding of why so many nineteenth-century Americans preferred nostrums to trained physicians, see Wyndham Miles's "Benjamin Rush, Chemist" (1953).

For the definitive account of how the nineteenth-century medical and pharmaceutical establishments developed identities around the concept of "ethical medicine," and how those identities were based on a loud and steadfast rejection of medical patenting, see Joseph M. Gabriel, *Medical Monopoly: Intellectual Property Rights and the Origins of the Modern Pharmaceutical Industry* (2014). The irony and limits of using *ethical* as a descriptor for nineteenth-century medicine are illustrated to powerful effect in Harriet Washington's *Medical Apartheid: The Dark History of Medical Experimentation on Black Americans from Colonial Times to the Present* (2006). Jill A. Fisher adds to this history with a focus on recent decades in *Adverse Events: Race, Inequality, and the Testing of New Pharmaceuticals* (2020).

The first challenger to the Hippocratic status of the patent taboo came from within the house of "ethical" medicine: the Detroit drug company Parke-Davis. A thorough account based on personal and company archives from the period is Joseph M. Gabriel's "A Thing Patented Is a Thing Divulged: Francis E. Stewart, George S. Davis, and the Legitimization of Intellectual Property Rights in Pharmaceutical Manufacturing, 1879–1911" (2009). How the German chemical combines inflicted deeper cracks in the patent taboo is explored in Jonathan Liebenau's *Medical Science and Medical Industry: The Formation of the American Pharmaceutical Industry* (1987) and Thomas Martin Reimer's "Bayer & Company in the United States: German Dyes, Drugs, and Cartels in the Progressive Era" (1996). A window into the lives and professional concerns of the corner-store druggists who led the resistance to the German patents is opened by the era's archives of *The Druggists Circular: A Practical Journal of Pharmacy and General Business Organ for Druggists* (2018).

The broader transformation in the industry brought about by the rise of "scientific medicine" is well told in Graham Dutfield, *That High Design of Purest Gold: A Critical History of the Pharmaceutical Industry, 1880–2020* (2020). Jonathan Liebenau makes a case study of "ethical" medicine's capital in *Medical Science and Medical Industry, 1890–1929: A Study of Pharmaceutical Manufacturing in Philadelphia* (1981). Alfred D. Chandler Jr. offers a business school view on the rise of the post-ethical drug industry in *Shaping the Industrial Century: The Remarkable Story of the Evolution of the Modern Chemical and Pharmaceutical Industries* (2005). On the little-remembered prewar court decision that cleared the way for a spree of postwar patent claims, see Christopher Beauchamp, "The Pure Thoughts of Judge Hand: A Historical Note on the Patenting of Nature" (2012).

After World War I, the debate over the ethics of medical patents settled over the university, where administrations were experimenting with patenting inventions made with public funds and outsourcing the management of royalties to third parties. For the story of Steenbock's vitamin D patents and the birth of the Wisconsin Alumni Research Foundation, see Rima D. Apple, "Patenting University Research: Harry Steenbock and the Wisconsin Alumni Research Foundation" (1989). On the groundbreaking "ethical patenting" of insulin by the University of Toronto, see Michael Bliss, *The Discovery of Insulin* (1982). Nicholas Rasmussen makes an incisive study of the identity crisis suffered by the academic research world at the dawn of university patenting in "The Moral Economy of the Drug Company: Medical Scientist Collaboration in Interwar America" (2004).

The closest thing to the voice of God within organized medicine in the first half of the twentieth century belonged to Morris Fishbein, editor of the

AMA *Journal*. Fishbein's published speeches and editorials throughout the 1930s reflect the anguish, uncertainty, and internal conflict that accompanied the death throes of the "ethical" order. In the AMA *Journal*, see "Medical Patents" (1937) and, in the *Journal of the Patent Office*, "Are Patents on Medicinal Discoveries and on Foods in the Public Interest?" (1937). Robert K. Merton considers the breakdown of the patent taboo in relation to the personal and professional motivations of scientists in *The Sociology of Science: Theoretical and Empirical Investigations* (1973).

LEVIATHAN AND WORLD WAR II

The most comprehensive historical overview of U.S. science policy is Michael S. Lubell's *Navigating the Maze: How Science and Technology Policies Shape America and the World* (2019). A good account of how ineffective and haphazard the government's public health spending was before World War II is Stephen P. Strickland's *Politics, Science, and Dread Disease: A Short History of United States Medical Research Policy* (1972).

The Allies' wartime penicillin collaboration is a scientific adventure story with a complicated legacy. Eric Lax tells it well in *The Mold in Dr. Florey's Coat: The Story of the Penicillin Miracle* (2004). Three essays that assess the program in light of subsequent debates about government patent policy are Robert Bud, "Upheaval in the Moral Economy of Science? Patenting, Teamwork, and the World War II Experience of Penicillin" (2008); Peter Neushul, "Science, Government, and the Mass Production of Penicillin" (1993); and Roswell Quinn, "Rethinking Antibiotic Research and Development: World War II and the Penicillin Collaborative" (2013).

The postwar battle to steer the direction of science and patent policy revolved around Vannevar Bush and Harley Kilgore. For a judicious and comprehensive biography of Bush and the worlds he straddled as a giant during the middle decades of the century, see G. Pascal Zachary's *Endless Frontier: Vannevar Bush, Engineer of the American Century* (2018). For another portrait of Bush's milieus in Boston and Washington, see Jennet Conant's *Man of the Hour: James B. Conant, Warrior Scientist* (2017). The political and corporate influences that shaped the debate and the Republican bill that replaced Kilgore's proposed legislation for the National Science Foundation is covered in Daniel Lee Kleinman, "Layers of Interests, Layers of Influence: Business and the Genesis of the National Science Foundation" (1994); Daniel J. Kevles, "The National Science Foundation and the Debate over Postwar Research Policy, 1942–1945: A Political Interpretation of *Science—The Endless Frontier*" (1977); and R. F. Maddox, "The Politics of World War II Science: Senator Harley M. Kilgore and the Legislative Origins of the National Science Foundation" (1979). On the deep cultural resonance that Bush tapped in the title of *Science—The Endless Frontier*, see Greg Grandin, *The End of the Myth: From the Frontier to the Border Wall in the Mind of America* (2020).

The classic New Deal statement on public-minded science and patent policy remains the 508-page Justice Department report prepared by David Lloyd Kreeger, a special assistant to Thurman Arnold from 1941 to 1946 who went on to become the CEO of GEICO Insurance. Gathering highlights of wartime testimony submitted to Kilgore's committee, the collective statement was published in 1947 as *Investigation of Government Patent Practices and Policies: Report and Recommendations of the Attorney General to the President*. Kreeger also published a more personal law review essay on the findings and conclusion of the Department of Justice report, "The Control of Patent Rights Resulting from Federal Research" (1947). The article lifted the curtain on an era where "a golden stream of patentable inventions pours from the scientific research and development conducted or financed by the Federal Government."

NEW DEAL, ANTITRUST, AND CHICAGO

The neoliberal project that brought the drug companies into a strategic partnership with the law and economics departments at the University of Chicago began in Republican Party–wide loathing and fear of Roosevelt in 1932. See Eric Rauchway, *Winter War: Hoover, Roosevelt, and the First Clash Over the New Deal* (2018). How this curdled into various extreme forms is the subject of Frank Mintz's *The Liberty Lobby and the American Right* (1975), Kim Phillips-Fein's *Invisible Hands: The Making of the Conservative Movement from the New Deal to Reagan* (2009), Rick Perlstein's *Before the Storm: Barry Gold-water and the Unmaking of the American Consensus* (2001), and Nancy Ma-cLean's *Democracy in Chains: The Deep History of the Radical Right's Stealth Plan for America* (2017). See also Smedley Butler, *War Is a Racket* (1935) and the front-page, above-the-fold story in the November 21, 1934, edition of *The New York Times*, "GEN. BUTLER BARES A 'FASCIST PLOT.'"

Roosevelt's enemies in industry were most fearful that he would begin to vigorously apply the country's antitrust laws and more generally lead a government revival of the country's forgotten anti-monopoly traditions, re-shaping entire industries and rewinding the civic clock on patents. A pri-mary source for New Deal thinking on patents and competition is the book Thurman Arnold wrote before becoming attorney general, *The Folklore of Capitalism* (1938). Also see Alfred Kahn, "Deficiencies of American Patent Law" (1940). The legal, historical, political, and economic bases of the New Deal position on patents are carefully presented in the TNEC report by Walton Hamilton, *Investigation of Concentration of Economic Power, Mono-graph No. 31: Patents and Free Enterprise* (1941).

Thurman's impact and legacy are critically assessed by Alan Brinkley in "The Antimonopoly Ideal and the Liberal State: The Case of Thurman Arnold" (1993) and *The End of Reform: New Deal Liberalism in Recession and War* (1996). Arnold's relationship with the TNEC and his investigation of the AMA receive special attention in Spencer Weber Waller, "The Anti-trust Legacy of Thurman Arnold" (2004). Barry C. Lynn situates Arnold and the New Deal within the broader sweep of American anti-monopoly traditions in *Cornered: The New Monopoly Capitalism and the Economics of Destruction* (2011).

Matt Stoller tells the story of the New Deal antitrust project in a pan-oramic study that encompasses the Republican policies that preceded it, and extends to the final victory of the neoliberal project that overturned its leg-acy, in *Goliath: The 100-Year War Between Monopoly Power and Democracy* (2020). On the patent and monopoly revisionism that made neoliberalism a novel and ultimately heretical form of "classical economics," see Robert Van Horn, "Chicago's Shifting Attitude Toward Concentrations of Busi-ness Power, 1934–1962" (2011) and Robert Van Horn and Matthias Klaes,

"Chicago Neoliberalism versus Cowles Planning: Perspectives on Patents and Public Goods in Cold War Economic Thought" (2011).

For the origins of the drug industry's longtime working relationship with Chicago economist George Stigler, see Edward Nik-Khah, "Neoliberal Pharmaceutical Science and the Chicago School of Economics" (2014). Neoliberal arguments about drug patents and regulation were trial ballooned during the first decade of *The Journal of Law and Economics* (1958–1968). A good article on the ideology's enduring impact on access to medicines is Amy Kapczynski, "The Right to Medicines in an Age of Neoliberalism" (2019). The legacy of the Chicago School's focus on patents and antitrust revisionism is assessed in two volumes of essays: Dieter Plehwe, Quinn Slobodian, and Philip Mirowski, *Nine Lives of Neoliberalism* (2020), and Robert Pitofsky, *How the Chicago School Overshot the Mark: The Effect of Conservative Economic Analysis on U.S. Antitrust* (2008).

THE MAKING OF A MONSTER

The prescription drug boom of the 1950s in many ways created the drug industry we know today—its marketing techniques, its symbiotic financial relationship with physicians and medical journals, its reactionary alliance with organized medicine. These threads are exhumed and woven in a groundbreaking work by Dominique A. Tobbell, *Pills, Power, and Policy: The Struggle for Drug Reform in Cold War America and Its Consequences* (2012). On the long and consequential partnership between the AMA and the drug companies, cemented in opposition to the expansion of government regulatory and social welfare programs, see Paul Starr's monumental work, *The Social Transformation of American Medicine: The Rise of a Sovereign Profession and the Making of a Vast Industry* (1982). The decline of antitrust during this time is reflected in Richard Hofstadter's subtly bemused appraisal of the demise of anti-monopoly in public debate, "What Happened to the Antitrust Movement?" (1965).

The rise of blockbuster prescription drugs is chronicled in two excellent case studies: Andrea Tone, *The Age of Anxiety: A History of America's Turbulent Affair with Tranquilizers* (2008), and Nicolas Rasmussen, *On Speed: The*

Many Lives of Amphetamine (2008). See also Tone's edited collection, with Elizabeth Siegel Watkins, *Medicating Modern America: Prescription Drugs in History* (2007). Steven Wilf reviews the shifting legal backdrop of the first postwar decades, "The Making of the Post-War Paradigm in American Intellectual Property Law" (2008).

The Salk polio vaccine remains the most celebrated counterpoint fable to the postwar rise of the profit-driven, post-ethical drug industry. See Charlotte Jacobs, *Jonas Salk: A Life* (2015), and Jeffrey Kluger, *Splendid Solution: Jonas Salk and the Conquest of Polio* (2006). For an investigative near-contemporary account, see John Rowan Wilson, *Margin of Safety: The Fight Against Polio* (1963).

The FTC's reports on price-fixing in the antibiotics industry during the 1950s are available online, as are the Kefauver hearings that they inspired. When Kefauver died while writing a book on those hearings, the manuscript was taken over by his former staff economist, Irene Till, who published it as *In a Few Hands* (1965). See also Daniel Scroop, "A Faded Passion? Estes Kefauver and the Senate Subcommittee on Antitrust and Monopoly" (2002) and Joseph Bruce Gorman, *Kefauver: A Political Biography* (1971).

KENNEDY, CARTER, AND BAYH-DOLE

The only detailed study of Kennedy's 1963 patent memorandum, and the industry boycott it sparked, is the four-volume "Harbridge Report" commissioned by the Senate, *Government Patent Policy Study* (1968). For a clear statement of industry opposition to the Kennedy policy, written by the Commerce official who oversaw its reversal as a primary architect of Bayh-Dole, see Howard Forman, "How the Chemical-Pharmaceutical Industry Views the Government's Patent Policy" (1970).

The first stop for anyone researching the saga of Bayh-Dole is the Bayh-Dole archive maintained by the IP Mall at the University of New Hampshire Law School. Most of the documents, including the personal papers of the principals, are online. The second stop is the archive of articles about Bayh-Dole at Gerald Barnett's blog, *Research Enterprise*. For critical perspectives on Bayh-Dole's impact on the culture of academic research, see Rebecca

Eisenberg, "Universities: The Fallen Angels of Bayh-Dole?" (2018); David Dickson, *The New Politics of Science* (1988); Daniel S. Greenberg, *Science, Money, and Politics: Political Triumph and Ethical Erosion* (2001); and Philip Mirowski, *Science-Mart: Privatizing American Science* (2011). Clifford M. Gross and Joseph P. Allen's *Technology Transfer for Entrepreneurs: A Guide to Commercializing Federal Laboratory Innovations* (2003) provides a more honest picture of Bayh-Dole than any academic work ever could.

THE G77, THE WHO, AND THE WTO

For good general overviews of the UN's founding and early years, and the sharpening of a north-south divide, see Paul Kennedy, *The Parliament of Man: The Past, Present, and Future of the United Nations* (2006); and Mark Mazower, *Governing the World: The History of an Idea* (2012). On the importance and function of the UN Conference on Trade and Development in the formation of the global south's political program, see Diego Cordovez, "The Making of UNCTAD: Institutional Background and Legislative History" (1967). John Toye takes stock of the legacies of UNCTAD and the New International Economic Order in "Assessing the G77: 50 Years After UNCTAD and 40 Years After the NIEO" (2014). Nasir Tyabji examines Jawaharlal Nehru's ideas about industrialization and self-sufficiency in "Gaining Technical Know-How in an Unequal World: Penicillin Manufacture in Nehru's India" (2004). Peter Drahos and John Braithwaite's *Information Feudalism: Who Owns the Knowledge Economy?* (2002) remains the best study of the Uruguay Round of GATT leading to the founding of the World Trade Organization. For wide-ranging critical examinations of the TRIPS regime from global south perspectives, see *Political Journeys in Health: Essays by and for Amit Sengupta* (2020) and Carlos Correa, *Trends in Drug Patenting: Case Studies* (2001) and "Bilateralism in Intellectual Property: Defeating the WTO System for Access to Medicines" (2004).

On the birth and uses of Special 301, see Judith H. Bello, "Section 301: The United States' Response to Latin American Trade Barriers Involving Intellectual Property" (1989). Johanna von Braun writes on the strong-arm tactics of the U.S. negotiators inside and outside the WTO framework in

The Domestic Politics of Negotiating International Trade: Intellectual Property Rights in US-Colombia and US-Peru Free Trade Agreements (2012). Two detailed studies of the TRIPS regime in theory and practice are Ellen 't Hoen, *Private Patents and Public Health: Changing Intellectual Property Rules for Access to Medicines* (2016) and *Practical Applications of the Flexibilities of TRIPS: Lessons Beyond HIV for Access to New Essential Medicines* (2018).

Books documenting the pharmaceutical industry's failure to match investments and innovation with global public health needs are unfortunately plentiful. See Peter J. Hotez and Soledad O'Brien, *Forgotten People, Forgotten Diseases: The Neglected Tropical Diseases and Their Impact on Global Health and Development* (2020); Susan Craddock, *Compound Solutions: Pharmaceutical Alternatives for Global Health* (2017); and Paul Farmer's searing argument and portrayal of global health as a human rights issue, with Amartya Sen, *Pathologies of Power: Health, Human Rights, and the New War on the Poor* (2005).

COVID-19, VACCINES, AND TRADE SECRETS

The industry's steady disinvestment in vaccine research since World War II is documented in Kendall Hoyt, *Long Shot: Vaccines for National Defense* (2012). The industry's failure to innovate solutions to the AIDS crisis, and then its patenting of government-funded science for sale at monopoly prices, is a story told in the running contemporary accounts published by *The Washington Post* and *The New York Times*, and in the oral history archives of the National Institutes of Health. See the transcript of the Institute of Medicine's "Roundtable for the Development of Drugs and Vaccines Against AIDS," edited by Leslie M. Hardy (1994).

On the misalignment of drug industry research incentives and pandemic threats, and the lessons of pre-COVID-19 near-miss pandemics, see Mike Davis, *The Monster Enters: COVID-19 and the Plagues of Capitalism* (2020). On the role of Bill Gates and the larger political questions raised by corporate megaphilanthropy, see Linsey McGoey, *No Such Thing as a Free Gift: The Gates Foundation and the Price of Philanthropy* (2015), Michael Barker's *The*

Givers That Take (2022), and Tim Schwab's *Nation* magazine investigations into the Gates Foundation.

On the WTO waiver debate and practical issues related to the obstacles posed by intellectual property, see the original proposals submitted by South Africa, India et. al., "Waiver from Certain Provisions of the TRIPS Agreement" (2020). A running account of the debate, from the politics to the technical, can be found in the online archives of papers and policy briefs published by the South Centre, Knowledge Ecology International, the Third World Network, and the People's Health Movement. See also Nirmalya Syam, Mirza Alas, Vitor Ido, "The 73rd World Health Assembly and Resolution on COVID-19: Quest for Global Solidarity for Equitable Access to Health Products" (2020), and Krishna Ravi Srinivas, "Intellectual Property Rights and Innovation in the Times of Corona Virus" (2020). A knowledgeable and concise survey of the critical issues is David G. Legge, Sun Kim, "Equitable Access to COVID Vaccines: Cooperation Around Research and Production Capacity is Critical" (2020). On the legal and political aspects of undisclosed information and trade secrets, see Medicines Law & Policy, "Data Exclusivity in the EU: Briefing Document" (2020); K. M. Gopakumar et al., "Trade Secrets Protection and Vaccines: The Role of Medicine Regulatory Agencies" (2021); Tar Nealey et al., "Trade Secrets in Life Sciences and Pharmaceutical Companies" (2015); and Allison Durkin et al., "Addressing the Risks That Trade Secret Protections Pose for Health and Rights" (2021).

A number of organizations and researchers have put forward practical pathways to increase vaccine production in the absence of intellectual property barriers. See the "Call to Solidarity" issued at the launch of the WHO COVID-19 Technology Access Pool, as well as the online archives of the People's Vaccine Alliance, Médecins Sans Frontières, Oxfam, PrEP4all, Knowledge Ecology International, I-MAK, Health GAP, and Medicines Law & Policy. These groups and many more have proposed workable non-monopoly models for incentivizing and rewarding medical innovation, not just during the pandemic, but as a permanent arrangement. Read about Thomas Pogge's proposed alternative at HealthImpactFund.org and one by James Love at Delinkage.org.

ACKNOWLEDGMENTS

There's an old Borscht Belt joke—stop me if you know it—about a man who prays to God that he should win the lottery. "My wife is sick, the children need clothes, I've been virtuous and dutiful—just this once, I need your help," he says. After weeks pass, he turns to the sky, "What happened to 'Ask and it will be given, knock and it will be opened?' Every day I pray, and still I haven't won the lottery!" A booming voice from above responds, "You've got to meet me halfway, bubbelah. Buy a ticket!"

After months thinking about this project, buying the ticket turned out to be emailing Kate Garrick, as shrewd and wonderful an agent as one could ask for. She helped me turn an inchoate idea into a functioning proposal, then find it a welcoming home at Counterpoint under the editorial stewardship of Dan Smetanka. Dan's patience, direction, and use of the clock was a master class in manuscript and writer management. I am also grateful to Counterpoint's owl-eyed quartet of Dan López, Katherine Kiger, Laura Berry, and Wah-Ming Chang. The enthusiasm of Lena Moses-Schmitt on the publicity side was a much-needed shot in the arm down the home stretch.

Historians of medicine and the pharmaceutical industry form intimate guilds, and I had no good reason to expect a friendly reception as a nonacademic interloper. I am humbled that many of the field's most accomplished scholars proved generous with their time and knowledge. Some offered thoughts and criticisms on pages specific to their research and expertise; others read multiple chapters in draft. Another group straddling the worlds of science and activism contributed valuable insights and criticisms. Thanks to Lewis Hyde, Shamiso Zinzombe, Graham Dutfield, Sun Kim, David Legge, Joseph Gabriel, Dominique Tobbell, Prabir Purkayastha, J. M. Liebenau, Andrea Tone, Christopher Morten, Brook Baker, Edward Nik-Kah, James Love, Ellen 't Hoen, Mohga Kamal-Yanni, Quinn Slobodian,

Satyajit Rath, Thomas Pogge, Alfred Engelberg, Nicholas Rasmussen, Thiru Balasubramaniam, Gerald Barnett, and Rohit Malpani.

Early versions of several chapters were published online and benefitted from the notes of Chris Lehmann and Ryu Spaeth at *The New Republic*, as well as *TNR* researcher-reporters Jensen Davies, Noah Flora, and Parker Richards; Ryan Grim, Betsy Reed, Maia Hibbett, and Max Ufberg at *The Intercept*; and Connor Kilpatrick and Bhaskar Sunkara at *Jacobin*. Thanks also to John Strausbaugh, David Harding, Scott Malec, Naomi Baumgard, Brentin Mock, Ben Aleshire, Jeff Koyen, Adam Bulger, Chris Ketcham, KC Hoye, Josh Fox, Kadri Koop, Yarden Katz, Mike Manville, Cedric Howe, Alex Lawson, and Mark Zaitchik. All mistakes and shortcomings are nobody's fault but mine.

INDEX

ALEXANDER ZAITCHIK is a freelance journalist. His writing has appeared in *The Nation, The New Republic, The Intercept, The Guardian, Rolling Stone, Foreign Policy, VICE,* and *The Baffler,* among many other publications. This is his third book. He lives in New Orleans.